STANLEY KUBRICK

STANLEY KUBRICK

Adapting the Sublime

Elisa Pezzotta

University Press of Mississippi / Jackson

www.upress.state.ms.us

The University Press of Mississippi is a member
of the Association of American University Presses.

Copyright © 2013 by University Press of Mississippi
All rights reserved
Manufactured in the United States of America

First printing 2013

∞

Library of Congress Cataloging-in-Publication Data

Pezzotta, Elisa.
Stanley Kubrick : adapting the sublime / Elisa Pezzotta.
pages cm
Includes bibliographical references and index.
ISBN 978-1-61703-893-8 (cloth : alk. paper) — ISBN 978-1-61703-894-5 (ebook)
1. Kubrick, Stanley—Criticism and interpretation. 2. Literature—Adaptations—
History and criticism. 3. Film adaptations—History and criticism. I. Title.
PN1998.3.K83P49 2013
791.4302′33092—dc23   2013005444

British Library Cataloging-in-Publication Data available

To my daughters, Anna and Linda

CONTENTS

ix   Acknowledgments

3   Introduction

15   **CHAPTER ONE**
        A History of Kubrick Adaptations

34   **CHAPTER TWO**
        Plot Construction: Ellipses and Enigmas of Unrelated Scenes

56   **CHAPTER THREE**
        Plot Construction: A Chaotic Geometry

85   **CHAPTER FOUR**
        Music, Dance, and Dialogue

115   **CHAPTER FIVE**
        Dreamy Worlds

142   **CHAPTER SIX**
        Artificiality, Modernism, and the Sublime

183   Conclusion

187   Appendix

199   Notes

205   Bibliography

213   Filmography

219   Index

ACKNOWLEDGMENTS

Researching and writing are more gratifying and exciting if you have the luck to exchange ideas with enthusiastic and clever scholars, such as Dr. Stacey Abbott and Dr. Caroline Bainbridge (Roehampton University), and if you find yourself in a stimulating environment. Thus, first and foremost, I would like to express my gratitude to Stacey and Caroline for their precious suggestions to structure my manuscript, and their useful biographical references to develop my arguments. They also always encouraged and supported me during my work. It was a pleasure and an honor for me to listen to their suggestions; without their assistance and guidance this work would not have been possible. I would also like to thank Dr. Ian Hunter (De Montfort University) and Dr. Catherine Lupton (Roehampton University) for their valuable advice to improve my manuscript.

Deepest gratitude is also due to the scholars who held interesting and stimulating seminars, events, workshops, and conferences organized by the Graduate School and the School of Arts of Roehampton University. Furthermore, the Association of Literature on Screen Studies and the organizers of the conference Cultures of Translation: Adaptation in Film and Performance (held in Cardiff, June 2008) gave me the opportunity to take part in their conferences, allowing me to fruitfully compare my ideas with those of several scholars. An earlier version of Chapter IV appeared as an article, "The Metaphor of Dance in Stanley Kubrick's *2001: A Space Odyssey*, *A Clockwork Orange* and *Full Metal Jacket*," in the *Journal of Adaptation in Film & Performance* (vol. 5, no. 1, pp. 51–64), reprinted here with the kind permission of editors Prof. Richard Hand and Dr. Katja Krebs.

I would also like to convey thanks to the University Press of Mississippi for having given me the opportunity of publishing my manuscript and, in particular, to Valerie Jones and Leila Salisbury for their assistance and patience, to the anonymous readers for their precious suggestions, and to Peter Tonguette, copyeditor, for his invaluable help.

Finally, I would like to show my greatest appreciation to Prof. Stefano Ghislotti (Bergamo University), who first taught me how to analyze films during my MA, who encouraged me to attend a PhD course, and with whom I can always enthusiastically discuss my ideas. And I would like to thank other professors at Bergamo University, especially Prof. Giovanni Bottiroli and Prof. Richard Davies, for their stimulating, unforgettable lessons.

Most of all, an honorable mention goes to my family for their understanding and love. I hope they will appreciate my efforts and enjoy my work.

STANLEY KUBRICK

INTRODUCTION

Discussing Stanley Kubrick's adaptations could seem to be a challenge because, although the director adapted novels and short stories, his films are among the furthest from the written medium. In particular, since *2001: A Space Odyssey* (USA and UK, 1968), his films (i.e., *A Clockwork Orange* [USA and UK, 1971], *Barry Lyndon* [USA and UK, 1975], *The Shining* [USA and UK, 1980], *Full Metal Jacket* [USA and UK, 1987], and *Eyes Wide Shut* [USA and UK, 1999]) seem to definitively exploit all cinematic techniques, embodying a compelling visual and aural experience. But it is for these reasons that his cinema becomes the example *par excellence* of the fruitful encounter between two arts and, simultaneously, of their independence. Just remember the sentences chosen by Anthony Burgess in *A Clockwork Orange* to describe the episode in which his protagonist, Alex, fights against Billyboy, the rival gang's leader: "It was stinking fatty Billyboy I wanted now, and there I was dancing about." "And, my brother, it was real satisfaction to me to waltz—left two three, right two three—and carve left cheeky and right cheeky" (Burgess, 2000a: 14–15). Then visualize the corresponding sequence adapted in Kubrick's dystopian film, in which each member of the gangs is filmed hitting a boy of the opponent group, while the montage follows the rhythm of *The Thieving Magpie* (by Gioachino Rossini). The metaphor of dance, rendered in the book by the words "dancing" and "to waltz," and suggested by the repetition of "two three," "cheeky," "left," and "right," is present in the film thanks to the acting, the editing, and the music. Metaphors and repetition of words are adapted through the very techniques of the cinematic medium.

Furthermore, although the studies about the director and his films are numerous,[1] there are only a few discussions of his body of work from the point of view of adaptation studies.[2] And there exists only one text entirely devoted to an analysis of some of his films from this perspective: Greg Jenkins's *Stanley Kubrick and the Art of Adaptation: Three Novels, Three Films* (1997).[3] This scholar, before discussing *Lolita* (USA and UK, 1962), *The Shining*, and *Full Metal Jacket*, summarizes his method, claiming that his main concern is the comparison between the story of the novel and of the film: "Generally, my concern will go to changes in the story, and to the effects these changes bring about; where it seems appropriate, I will also

3

comment on what does not change" (1999: 29). Through this approach, which is almost entirely focused on stories, Jenkins draws conclusions so general about Kubrick's films that they could be applied to almost all adaptations. For example, he observes that usually a novel story is compressed to fit the length of the cinematic medium, and that dialogue is cut to speed up the story and to explain visually more than aurally. What is more, the moments with moderate to high drama are more numerous. He argues also that narrative complexity is reduced through characters' simplification and a depiction of a more conventional morality (1999: 149–161). The scholar, through the study of one director only, instead of highlighting Kubrick's peculiarities of adapting novels, underscores his similarities with other filmmakers. He himself claims: "So from this standpoint, one is brought not just to acknowledge the trends that emerge within Kubrick's work, but to realize that they seem loosely to prevail across the wide expanse of commercial adaptation. As an adapter, Kubrick must be viewed as part of a rhetorical community" (1999: 160). Moreover, Jenkins's statements reported above seem to corroborate the claims of the critics who, praising the faithfulness of an adaptation to its source novel, suggest the superiority of the written medium over the cinematic one.

✦ ✦ ✦

One of the implicit aims of this book is to challenge the tendency in adaptation studies to depend too much on literary studies. In the literature on cinematic adaptations three main approaches seem to shape discussions: "fidelity," "narratology," and "intertextuality." As regards the first method, film adaptations are often judged according to their faithfulness to source books. The inevitable corollary is that cinematic adaptations become a subset of novels. A lot of scholars strive to compare the narrative techniques of novels, such as literary tropes, the use of verbal tenses, characters' descriptions, and mental states, with the narrative features of films. Unable to find adequate renditions of literary narrative techniques in cinema, these critics demonstrate involuntarily and, in the majority of cases, voluntarily, the apparent superiority of the written medium over the cinematic one. The advantages and pitfalls of such a method are not difficult to identify. Firstly, adaptation studies have been developed mostly by literary scholars and, consequently, film adaptations have been studied and taught in academic institutions as subsidiary works to novels. Secondly, "fearful of seeing literature's narrative role usurped by the movies, and under the sway of New Criticism's religious reverence for serious art, these critics typically used adaptation study to shore up literature's crumbling walls" (Ray, 2000: 46). The main theoretical inadequacy of this approach is that the comparisons between novels and their adaptations are always discussed from the point of view of the former. The narrative features of books, their stylistic and thematic peculiarities, and their authors' aims and choices are sought in their adaptations.[4]

"The cinema, however, also produces a completely new kind of adaptation that claims that the source material is being faithfully translated into a new medium. It is important to stress that this relation between source and adaptation is effectively unknown to previous cultural eras" (MacCabe, Murray, and Warner, 2011: 5). If a director's artistic and/or economic goal is adapting, as faithfully as possible, a novel, a critic cannot ignore her purposes. But, once more, a comparison between a particular cinematic adaptation and its source book should not lead to general conclusions about the narrative techniques of cinema and the art of adapting texts to the big screen.

The theorists who follow a narratological method distinguish themselves from those who follow a fidelity approach because their position regarding the cinematic medium apparently seems less partisan. Their goal does not seem to demonstrate the superiority of one medium over another, but to compare, from a neutral position, the two media and their techniques. Instead of listing the narrative features of novels that cannot be adapted to the screen, they highlight what can be translated and, thus, the rigor of this reasoning provides an insight into the narrative features common to both media.[5] But the limits of the fidelity and the narratological method are one and the same. On the one hand, moving only in one direction, from novel to film and never vice versa, they cannot appreciate the peculiarities of the cinematic medium, of a personal adaptation, and of a director's style. On the other hand, they discard the context of the adaptation: the sociocultural period in which it is produced, the convention of its genre, the influences of the studio, of the cast and crew, and of censorship.

A lot of critics, understanding the limits of their approach, try to consider other variants and enrich their analyses with them. For example, some define different types of adaptation according to the different degrees of fidelity that a film shows towards its source book.[6] Some other scholars suggest substituting the term "adaptation." William Kittredge and Steven M. Krauzer, Michael Klein and Gillian Parker, and Robert Stam propose "translation" because adapting a novel to screen is like translating from one language, from one set of conventions into another (Kittregde and Krauzer, 1979: 7; Klein and Parker, 1981: 3; Stam, 2000: 62). Finally, other theorists, moving towards intertextuality, enrich their approach based upon the faithfulness of an adaptation to its source novel with considerations regarding the context of the production of the film, which is to say, its sociocultural period, the convention of its genre, the influences of the studio, of the cast and crew, of censorship, etc.[7]

Aragay Mireia underlines the importance and centrality of adaptation studies: they "may well turn out to be central to any history of culture—any discussion, that is, of the transformation and transmission of texts and meanings in and across cultures" (2005: 30). The immense possibilities of an intertextual approach to adaptations are summarized in the claim above. A cinematic adaptation is not the only child of its two parents, which is to say, its director and its source novel, but also of its mode and context of production and of the cinematic tradition that precedes it. In a perennial exchange among the filmmakers' style, the cinematic conventions and genres, fluctuating meanings and stories about our world and imaginary ones are continually re-actualized in different sociocultural contexts, subjected to different audiences' demands, industry's and censorship's regulations, and technological discoveries. Thus, according to the critics who adopt these concepts in adaptation studies,[8] adaptations should be analyzed according to their dialogical, dynamic relationships with their sources. A synchronic, ahistoric comparison between a book and its adaptation should be substituted by a diachronic, historic discussion of the dialogical exchange among different media and different texts of the same medium.

The difficulty of concretely applying an intertextual method is evident. A scholar cannot deal with so many variants and is impelled to choose some of them, discarding all of the others. For example, Stam, beginning with an analysis of a novel and discussing it according to its literary tradition, tries to find in its adaptation the elements that characterize it, but he does not discard either its director's style or the context of the adaptation, which is to say, the historical moment and geographical area of its production with its conventions, trends, censorship regulations, and sociocultural tendencies. In his analysis of the two adaptations of Vladimir Nabokov's *Lolita* (Kubrick; Adrian Lyne, USA, 1997), he tries to find the features that characterize the book such as its first-person, changing, unreliable narrator (2005: 223–243). In particular, he praises the way in which Lyne shows the protagonist's voyeurism because he adopts, unlike Kubrick, point of view shots. Indeed, in Lyne's version, we look with Humbert (Jeremy Irons) at Lolita (Dominique Swain), we quickly peep at her through half-open doors or from the unexpected, uncomfortable positions in which the protagonist finds himself. Therefore, we experience with him the dangerous, but inevitable impulse of gazing. Kubrick, instead, represents Humbert's (James Mason) voyeurism in a more impersonal manner. He often shoots the protagonist, Charlotte (Shelley Winters), and Lolita (Sue Lyon) in the same frame, with Charlotte noting Humbert gazing at Lolita. Thus, spectators catch Humbert's secret as Charlotte does, but they do not identify either with the protagonist's gaze or his wife's. Stam comments: "I am not suggesting that it is impossible to relay unreliable first-person narration in the cinema, but only that it would require relentless subjectification on various cinematic registers ... The Adrian Lyne version of *Lolita* ... takes a few, tiny steps in that direction" (2005: 232). The scholar implicitly argues that the more successful an adaptation, the better it is at adapting those features of the novel that the literary tradition praises as peculiar and original regarding the previous literary works of art. Thus, in his intertextual method, he moves from novels to films and not vice versa.

I adopt a narratological approach enriched with an intertextual one. The narratological method follows two directions: first from books to films and then vice versa. Through the first movement, from the written medium to the cinematic one, I compare the stories and plots of novels and films and their relationships.[9] The concrete result of this approach is the close comparison among the functions proper, the informants, and the tense of books, and those of the corresponding adaptations.

As regards functions proper and informants, Roland Barthes claims that to study a narrative the analyst should divide it into the smallest units that still conserve a meaning. These minimal signifying units are called functions. He distinguishes between functions proper and indices. The former are "distributional functions"—they refer to a complementary and consequential act, to a functionality of doing, and they move the story further on. The latter are "integrational functions"—they refer to a functionality of being, to a signified, and they concern the characters, their identities, feelings, and thoughts, they evoke atmospheres and philosophies, and they move the story to a higher level. Functions proper can be divided into: cardinal functions or nuclei, which are the real hinge points of the narrative and are consecutive and consequential units; and catalyzers, which are only consecutive units and fill in the narrative space separating cardinal functions. Indices can be divided into: indices proper, which refer to the identities, feelings, and thoughts of the characters, to the atmospheres and philosophies, and have implicit signifieds; and informants, which have immediate signification, and are used to set in time and space a situation (Barthes, 1977). Brian McFarlane (1996) and Jackob Lothe (2000) claim that cardinal functions, which constitute the real hinge points of narrative, should be respected during an adaptation if the director wants to maintain the narrative structure of a novel; while catalyzers, which fill in the narrative space separating cardinal functions, do not necessarily have to be adapted by the filmmaker, even if he wants to preserve the narrative structure of a book. Unlike functions proper and informants, indices proper cannot be directly translated because they concern the connotation, a second signified, which different readers can interpret in different ways.

I do not only analyze functions proper and informants, but I also compare the tense of the episodes in the films and in the adapted books,[10] paying attention to their duration. Firstly, I divide the films into main episodes and identify each of them through a brief title. Then, I divide the novels into main sections, following mostly the subdivision of the corresponding adaptations into main episodes. Secondly, for each main episode of a film I indicate how many seconds it lasts, and for each main section of a novel I report how many lines it occupies. Finally, I calculate the percentage that these episodes occupy in the entire duration of the films and books. In the case of adaptations, the percentage is calculated in the following way: (duration of a main episode in seconds · 100) / duration of the whole film in seconds. In the case of books, the percentage is the result of: (duration of a main section in lines · 100) / duration of the whole novel in lines. These durations can be visualized through some histograms that are reported in the Appendix. For each pair of film and source book there are one or two histograms, depending on the correspondences between their stories. If too many sections of the novel are not adapted or utterly changed, and if the corresponding film presents too many episodes that do not appear in its source book, then it is impossible to construct one graphic only. In these cases (i.e., *Barry Lyndon, The Shining,* and *Full Metal Jacket*) there are two histograms: one for the adaptation and one for the novel. In any case, all of the histograms are created following the same criteria: along the x-axis are all of the episodes of the books and/or films identified through brief titles, and on the y-axis are their percentages.

The final aim of this narratological approach, which follows a movement from novels to films, is the possibility of comparing and analyzing the *fabula* and the *syuzhet* of films and books, and of understanding whether there are constants in the way in which Kubrick adapts written stories and plots. Through a narratological approach that follows the opposite direction, from films to novels, first, I observe what is peculiar about a film and, then, I try to understand whether what distinguishes the film is present in the corresponding book, too.

As the narratological method that moves from films to novels tends to privilege the cinematic medium over the written one, the intertextual approach that is adopted in this book is focused more on films than on novels. Indeed, through Kubrick and his collaborators' statements, I try to understand how far the main features of his adaptations have been inspired by previous texts and films, and by the sociocultural context of their production. What is more, I try to discuss whether and how the director's choices have been guided by censorship and cinematic conventions, such as those pertaining to genre, or by technological innovations.

This method should implicitly discard the idea of the superiority of the written medium over the cinematic one. Moreover, this approach should highlight the main aesthetic and stylistic characteristics of Kubrick's last six adaptations, and compare them with their corresponding adapted novels, with the sociocultural context of their production, and with other works that directly or indirectly have inspired them. Therefore, this method, even if it mixes a narratological approach with an intertextual one, is basically different from the approach adopted by Stam because it is centered on the cinematic medium and not on the written one. Adaptation studies are still a hybrid field, intersecting both literary criticism and film studies, but they should be more centered on film studies for two reasons. Firstly, because up until now they have been discussed more from a literary perspective and, thus, a cinematic one could add new results that could enrich the old ones. Secondly, because when style and meaning leave a medium to shape another one, they are usually discussed from the point of view of the new medium. For example, when a subject taken from the Bible becomes a pictorial representation, the painting is usually studied more from the perspective of art history than from a theological one. Theology is adopted to explain some of the sacred symbols and meanings of the painting, but the painting is discussed mainly through its style, techniques, and sociocultural context.

✦ ✦ ✦

As already mentioned above, the main aim of this book is to find the stylistic devices that characterize Kubrick's last six films, and understand whether they are present in the adapted novels, too. To individuate them, first of all, I have adopted an inductive method, analyzing each pair of cinematic adaptation and source book separately and, finally, I have compared the results obtained and dedicated one chapter to each of the patterns that I have found.

In Chapter II, I discuss how the plots of Kubrick's adaptations are often constituted by *tableaux vivants* and/or unrelated episodes, which is to say, by sequences that are separated by ellipses and are not linked by a cause and effect chain. At a "more superficial" level, plots are full of gaps and mysteries that remain unexplained. At a "deeper" level, the features of classical Hollywood narrative, as described by David Bordwell and Kristin Thompson (1990), are implicitly sacrificed in the name of the *auteur*'s style: the scenes are linked through stylistic choices that create an aesthetically superb diegetic world. In Chapter III, I discuss how these unrelated sequences are, on the one hand, inserted in symmetrical *syuzhet* structures, in which the end mirrors the beginning, and/or in plots strongly ordered into parts. The geometry of the plot construction is often emphasized by sequences that evoke one another and by superbly composed images. But this order is usually disrupted by a play of cross-references among sequences and images through the *mise-en-scène* and the montage. This subterranean aesthetic play of cross-references, which seems to disrupt the symmetrical, ordered superstructure, is symbolized by the image of the maze, as in *The Shining*, and by sequences shot with a handheld camera or a Steadicam that follow the characters' sinuous and/or syncopated movements.

As in Chapters II and III, I discuss how Kubrick implicitly undermines the characteristics of classical Hollywood narrative in Chapter IV. I argue that he subverts the use of music in classical narrative sound films, as analyzed by Claudia Gorbman (1987). In the director's adaptations, music is often foregrounded, and images seem to emanate from it. Dialogue and voice-over seem to be used, in the majority of cases, as music is: they are adopted for their rhythm, for their signifier, and not for their signified. Everything seems to be subordinated to music, and language becomes one of the instruments in the filmmaker's orchestra. Furthermore, music contributes to the creation of a spectacle that unfolds in front of protagonists who, often, instead of taking part in it, remain motionless and inarticulate in front of it.

Thus, music, dialogue, and voice-over emphasize the characters' passivity that, as I discuss in Chapter V, is one of the features that help to create the dreamy atmosphere that envelops *A Clockwork Orange*, *Barry Lyndon*, *The Shining*, and *Eyes Wide Shut*. Kubrick's protagonists are often passive wanderers in their diegetic worlds. They remain entrapped in a dreamy world, governed by the director's aesthetic rules, in which the extradiegetic world is often cited.

Indeed, as I argue in Chapter VI, the films deliberately exhibit their awareness of being works of art in several ways. For example, the diegetic world is evoked in the diegesis itself through the presence of scenes that recall previous sequences or foretell subsequent scenes, often parodying them. Or the extradiegetic world is evoked in the diegesis both indirectly and directly. In the former case, the extradiegesis is recalled through the evocation of the making of the film and, in the latter, through the citation of the cinematic medium in the medium itself.

As discussed in each chapter, these features are present in some of the source novels, but not in all of them. What is more, they are almost always emphasized in Kubrick adaptations. Therefore, even if the director adapted books pertaining to different sociocultural periods, genres, and styles, he translated them through those aesthetic and structural patterns that seem to be the very essence of his style. For this reason, and because he always maintained a relative independence from major studios,[11] and controlled every phase of his work, supervising every decision,[12] I consider him an *auteur*. Furthermore, he is cited as an *auteur* by Peter Wollen in *Signs and Meaning in the Cinema* (1972: 112). And Thomas Leitch claims that Kubrick "earned his *auteur* status the old-fashioned way: by taking on authors directly in open warfare" (2005: 111). What is more, Norman Kagan (2000) and James Naremore (2007) explicitly claim that they consider the director an *auteur* and, consequently, interpret his body of work through thematics, following the tradition of the Young Turks. And the majority of the books cited above, which include analyses of the filmmaker's body of work, try to interpret his films through thematic and stylistic consistencies, often through oppositions and dichotomies that manifest themselves through particular stylistic choices (e.g., Michel Ciment [2003], Paul Duncan [2003], Mario Falsetto [1994], Luis M. Garcia Mainar [1999], Thomas Allen Nelson [2000], Randy Rasmussen [2001], Jason Sperb [2006], and Alexander Walker [2000]). These texts often include Kubrick's own statements about his films and information about his process of filmmaking to justify film analysis. Finally, when *A Clockwork Orange* was first released, Kubrick wanted his name above the title and, from that moment, the titles of his films were always preceded by his name. He was also chosen to be interviewed for Joseph Gelmis's *The Film Director as Superstar*, becoming, in the cinemagoers' imagination, a superstar director (LoBrutto, 1998: 354).

Jack Boozer discusses the centrality of screenplays in adaptation studies, lamenting the fact that scholars often ignore them. Scripts are the evidence of the screenwriter's role and importance in the process of adaptation and, consequently, of their authorship that, together with the director's *auteurism*, shapes the final work (2008: 1–24). In his discussion of *Eyes Wide Shut*, Boozer stresses the importance of co-screenwriter Frederic Raphael in the updating of the source novella: "It is hard to imagine that Kubrick could have developed the depth of story that this film became without the exhaustive efforts of Freddie Raphael, whose authorship remains central to its characterization and plot" (2008: 103). In this book, I underline what are the constants in the filmmaker's way of adapting novels and short stories. Thus, although I stress the importance of the scripts and of the director's collaboration with his co-screenwriters, I deal more with Kubrick's *auteurism* than with the screenwriter's authorship. Moreover, I do not privilege the role of the screenwriters in comparison with that, for example, of the actors, whom the filmmaker often allowed to develop the dialogue and interpret the mood of the scenes. What Colin MacCabe claims about Neil Jordan can be adopted to discuss Kubrick, too: "If then every film must have, at least during shooting, an authority, and if a director like Jordan also has the final say during script and preproduction as well as during editing and release, then it is clear that it is his authority that creates the film" (2011: 21–22). In this book, the stylistic consistencies of Kubrick's way of adapting novels are underlined, and the unique way in which the director exploited all the potentialities of the cinematic medium to adapt stories is emphasized. During the analysis of his adaptations, the filmmaker is not considered as an ahistorical individual, totally independent from his collaborators, but, on the contrary, as an artist who always tried to grasp as much information as possible about his subject matter and the way in which he could have filmed it. To gather these notions, he read, watched films, questioned experts in every field, and, during shooting, listened to his cast and crew's suggestions. Therefore, the analysis of his adaptations should underline his unique style and aesthetic as a result of the combination of his art and of his historical, sociological, and artistic context. Kubrick is here considered as a great architect who has to please his customers, to respect the planning permits, and who is influenced by his collaborators, by the sociocultural context in which he creates, and by the history of art.

Finally, in the last chapter, all of the features of the filmmaker's adaptations allow me to link his films: on the one hand, to the New Hollywood, and to art-cinema narration as discussed by Bordwell in *Narration in the Fiction Film* (1985) and, in particular, to the modernist avant-garde of the 1920s as defined by Wollen in "The Two Avant-Gardes" (1982); and, on the other hand, to the experience of the sublime in cinema. Indeed, whereas the director can be put in the tradition of the modernist avant-garde of the 1920s, his adaptations are not only centered on the ontology of the medium. At a "deeper" level, there is a critique of classical Hollywood films, at a "more superficial" level there is a sublime experience. And these levels are intertwined: the cinematic techniques and the narrative structures that break the narrative fluidity both implicitly criticize mainstream cinema and explicitly involve the audience in a sublime event. Furthermore, thanks to the introduction of the concept of the sublime in adaptation studies, adaptations can be rethought as a recreation of the sublime experiences lived by the director while reading the source novels, listening to the music that he adapted and, in general, contemplating, appreciating, and experiencing other artists' works. Thus, adaptations can be reinterpreted as an everlasting dialogue among artists and epochs.

Chapter One

A HISTORY OF KUBRICK ADAPTATIONS

KUBRICK: I don't like scripts that just give you dialogue and stage directions, stage directions and dialogue. I need to know more about the whole . . . what's going on. I even want to know what people smell like, you know? Anything you can think of that . . . might be relevant. Or irrelevant, but . . . know what I mean? You're a novelist. Make it like a novel, not like a Hollywood script.

RAPHAEL: If that's what you want. But it may get pretty long. They don't like that.

KUBRICK: Who's they? There is no they. There is me and there's you, and that's it.

—(Raphael, 1999: 80)

The first Kubrick documentary short, *Day of the Fight* (USA, 1951), is based on a director's pictorial that was published on January 18, 1949, in *Look* magazine, about a day in the life of boxer Walter Cartier. The screenplay is by Robert Rein (Phillips and Hill, 2002: 74). The other two documentary shorts, *Flying Padre* (USA, 1952) and *The Seafarers* (USA, 1953), are based on original material, and Will Chasen has writing credits for the latter short (Phillips and Hill, 2002: 116–117, 316–317). Similarly, the director's first two feature-length films, *Fear and Desire* (USA, 1953) and *Killer's Kiss* (USA, 1955), are based on original material. Kubrick and Howard Sackler, a playwright and a friend of the filmmaker from high school, collaborated on the scripts of both films, although Sackler does not share writing credits with the director for *Killer's Kiss* (Phillips and Hill, 2002: 111, 181). All other Kubrick films are adaptations of novels.

✦ ✦ ✦

Although at the beginning of this chapter I briefly mention *The Killing* (USA, 1956), *Paths of Glory* (USA, 1957), *Spartacus* (USA, 1960), *Lolita*, and *Dr. Strangelove, or: How I Learned to Stop Worrying and Love the Bomb* (UK, 1964), I do not discuss them in this book for stylistic and historical reasons. First of all, these films do not share all of the features that characterize Kubrick's last six adaptations, analyzed in the following chapters. For example, their plots are usually not constituted by *tableaux vivants* and/or unrelated episodes, which is to say, by scenes that are not linked by a causal chain and that are strongly divided by ellipses. *The Killing* is a perfect example of a film in which every sequence and flashback is causally and temporally linked to the other scenes, and in which almost all of the ellipses are filled in and/or are determined (which is to say, their presence is signaled by the text and the time of the story not narrated remains implicit [Genette, 1972: 135–161]).[1] The same happens in *Dr. Strangelove*, where events that take place in different spaces at the same time constitute an ensemble of causes that leads to an inevitable end of the world. Similarly, in *Paths of Glory* and *Spartacus* the sequences are usually causally linked to let the spectators follow the heroes' deeds. And the protagonists of these films are not passive wanderers in dreamy diegetic worlds: the characters who organize the robbery in *The Killing* are resolute, and also determined are Colonel Dax (Kirk Douglas) in *Paths of Glory* and Spartacus. The characters in *Dr. Strangelove* are certainly not heroes and do not succeed in stopping a nuclear war, but more than passive dreamers, they are caricatures of military and political men in a black comedy. Moreover, *The Killing*, *Paths of Glory*, *Spartacus*, and *Dr. Strangelove* do not present plots divided into different, recognizable parts, as for example in *2001: A Space Odyssey*, and they do not have symmetrical plot structures in which the end mirrors the beginning, as in *Eyes Wide Shut*. *Lolita* opens and closes with Quilty's (Peter Sellers) murder by Humbert. Cause and effect chains are looser than in the previous films because the plot follows a man's obsession for his young stepdaughter, an impossible relationship that often leads him to act and behave in an impulsive, irrational way. He can be depicted as a passive wanderer, at least when he drives hopelessly away with the object of his desire, in the dreamy world of his car, towards a dreamy future that exists in his mind only. But in *Lolita*, as in the other films mentioned above, music is not foregrounded, characters and objects' movements do not follow the rhythm of music and, consequently, there is no a visual and aural spectacle, a ballet of bodies, a dance of the montage. Words are still adopted for their meaning and not for their sound. Characters do not remain in contemplation of a cinematic spectacle created by the director. It is since *2001: A Space Odyssey* that Kubrick definitively creates cinematic sublime experiences. As is discussed in this chapter, this science-fiction film cannot be considered a "classical" adaptation. Perhaps the filmmaker, thanks to this experience, further from the written medium than in his previous films, had the chance to better exploit all of the potentialities of the cinematic medium, and to develop the structural and stylistic features that characterize his last films. What is more, *2001: A Space Odyssey* was first released in 1968 and, as is discussed in the last chapter, the director can be considered an exponent of the New Hollywood, which developed in the late 1960s. This Hollywood Renaissance was influenced by the European art cinema, and the links between the director and art cinema, especially the European avant-garde of the 1920s, are highlighted in this book.

✦ ✦ ✦

Knowing how Kubrick made choices about what novels and short stories to adapt, how he wrote scripts and worked with co-screenwriters and/or the authors of novels and actors, offers invaluable insights in understanding how the process of adaptation was, for the director, of the utmost importance for the realization of his films. He not only took great care in choosing a book to adapt, but he also spent a long time moving from the written to the cinematic medium and he continuously revised his scripts during shooting. The process of adaptation lasted for years during the pre-production and production periods, and it was often the cause of the long spans of time that passed between the release of one film and the beginning of the next project, and of the huge delays during the making of a film.

When asked about how he chose novels to adapt, Kubrick answered, "I read. I order books from the States. I literally go into bookstores, close my eyes, and take things off the shelf. If I don't like the book after a bit, I don't finish it. But I like to be surprised" (Cahill, 1987: 195). The director used to choose the stories that he found interesting, stimulating, and that he thought could be adapted without losing their originality. Those impressions that he felt while reading books for the first time guided his pre-production and production periods, animated his scripts and the making of his films, becoming his major source of inspiration and the principle of his films' coherence.

> What I like about not writing original material—which I'm not even certain I could do—is that you have this tremendous advantage of reading something for the first time. You never have this experience again with the story. You have a reaction to it: it's a kind of falling-in-love reaction. That's the first thing. Then it becomes almost a matter of code breaking, of breaking the work down into a structure that is truthful, that doesn't lose the ideas or the content or the feeling of the book. And fitting it all into the much more limited frame of a movie. And as long as you possibly can, you retain your emotional attitude, whatever it was that made you fall in love in the first place. (Cahill, 1987: 196)

A brief discussion of how Kubrick came to know about the novels and short stories he adapted (and about the stories and successes of these books before they were adapted) shows that the director did not look for a particularly successful text, but, rather, for a story that would surprise him and arouse those enduring, strong feelings that would keep him inspired during the entire process of filmmaking.

The Killing is adapted from *Clean Break* (1955) by Lionel White, a police reporter, newspaper editor, and crime novelist. It was Jim Harris who found this novel in a bookstore and asked Kubrick to read it (Hughes, 2000: 37). The director collaborated with another crime novelist, Jim Thompson, who is credited with additional dialogue, to adapt the novel. After *The Killing*, which was Thompson's first screenplay, the writer worked again with Kubrick at the adaptation of Humphrey Cobb's *Paths of Glory* (1935) (Phillips and Hill, 2002: 368–369). In this case, the filmmaker had read the book during high school and, years later, happened to find a copy in his father's studio (Hughes, 2000: 52). Calder Willingham, a novelist and screenwriter, and Cobb himself share writing credits with Thompson and the director (Phillips and Hill, 2002: 398). If White is a famous crime novelist, who is credited in Quentin Tarantino's *Reservoir Dogs* (USA, 1992) as a source of inspiration, and his *Clean Break* can be considered a classic heist novel, *Paths of Glory* is the only book published by Cobb. Although this novel was a Book-of-the-Month-Club selection, was praised by Elizabeth Bowen and other critics, and was adapted for the stage by Sidney Howard, it did not have great popular success (Phillips and Hill, 2002: 286).

After *Paths of Glory*, Kubrick, as mentioned in the Introduction, was asked by Kirk Douglas, executive producer and star of *Spartacus*, to direct this film after shooting had already begun. The film is adapted from *Spartacus* (1951) by Howard Fast, a novelist, screenwriter, playwright, and historian. Fast himself first tried to adapt his own book because the novel had been optioned by Edward Lewis, the film producer, in 1957, and when the option was running out, Fast conceded a two-month extension in exchange for adapting his book and for a symbolic one dollar. But, according to Douglas, Fast's version was unfit for the cinematic medium, and he asked the blacklisted screenwriter Dalton Trumbo to adapt the novel, using Edward Lewis as a front for Trumbo. The producer, during a meeting with Kubrick and Douglas, expressed his uneasiness at being identified as screenwriter, and the director suggested adopting his name instead of that of Lewis. According to Kubrick, "I directed the actors, I composed the shots, and I edited the movie," so his role was nearer to that of a screenwriter than a producer (Phillips and Hill, 2002: 374). Finally, during shooting, Douglas claimed that Sam Jackson, one of Trumbo's pseudonyms, was the screenwriter. But, before the first release of *Spartacus*, Otto Preminger claimed that Trumbo had the writing credits for *Exodus* (USA, 1960). As a consequence, Douglas listed Trumbo together with the other screenwriters of the film (Phillips and Hill, 2002: 372–375). There was not only a quarrel between Fast and Trumbo about the latter's writing credits, but also between Laurence Olivier (Marcus Licinius Crassus in the film) and Charles Laughton (Sempronius Gracchus). It was Peter Ustinov, who played the role of Lentulus Batiatus and who was also a screenwriter, who made some suggestions to Trumbo to enhance his own role and to balance those of the other two English actors (Phillips and Hill, 2002: 389–393).

Among Kubrick's feature-length films, *Spartacus* is the only one in which the director did not collaborate in writing the screenplay. In his next film, *Lolita*, although he does not share writing credits with Nabokov, he revised his script during the pre-production and production periods. Indeed, the first Nabokov script was about 400-pages and, following the filmmaker's suggestions, the author shortened it by half. But, according to the writer, Kubrick used only 20 percent of his revised script. As in the case of the novel *A Clockwork Orange*, *Lolita* (1955) did not easily find a publisher because of its content. Despite Nabokov's relevance in the literary world, the book was rejected by four American publishers, and it took one year to be published by the Olympia Press in Paris, which specialized in erotica (Phillips and Hill, 2002: 259–261, 216–217). Moreover, it was banned in Australia, Austria, Belgium, Britain, and Burma, but after numerous positive reviews, it was published in the United States in 1958 by Putnam. It was Willingham who first recommended the novel to Kubrick and, when the director and Harris optioned the book, it was already acknowledged as a masterpiece and a bestseller, although it was still considered a scandalous novel. By 1964 *Playboy* reported that two-and-a-half million copies of the book had been sold in the United States alone (Hughes, 2000: 88–89).

As in *Lolita* and *Paths of Glory*, in *Dr. Strangelove, or: How I Learned to Stop Worrying and Love the Bomb* Kubrick collaborated with the source novel's author. The film is adapted from Peter George's *Red Alert* (1958), a book in which the fear of the outburst of a nuclear war is expressed from a serious, dramatic point of view, and in which there are several descriptions of technical military details (Phillips and Hill, 2002: 298–299). According to John Baxter, unlike in Kubrick's previous films, it seems that the director, for this particular adaptation, chose the subject more than the novel. Alastair Buchan, head of the London-based Institute of Strategic Studies, gave the director the idea of making a film about a nuclear war and suggested that he read George's book (Baxter, 1997: 170). But, while Kubrick was collaborating with the novel's author, he thought to transform the melodrama into a black comedy, and he contacted the novelist Terry Southern to help in this task. Indeed, the filmmaker had appreciated the latter's black humor in *The Magic Christian* (1959), a book that he had read following Peter Seller's suggestions. According to the director, when the film was first released, some reviewers had attributed all of the merits of the screenplay to Southern. When *The Loved One* (Tony Richardson, USA, 1965), another black comedy on which Southern and Christopher Isherwood share writing credits, was first released, Kubrick responded to the *New York Times* ad for the film with a press release about *Dr. Strangelove* in which he claimed that he collaborated with Southern from November 16 to December 28, 1962, but that he continued to revise the script during production with the help of George and the actors, especially Sellers (Phillips and Hill, 2002: 339–343).

His next film, *A Clockwork Orange*, was adapted from the novel of the same name by Anthony Burgess, a book that did not easily find a publisher, remained unsuccessful until the film's release, and was later blamed for its violent characters and world. The novel was first published in the spring of 1962, but its first draft had already been written by the end of 1960. In this latter version, Alex, who is the protagonist, spoke a slang that was used, at that time, among "hooligan" groups. Because the novel was set in the near future, the author thought that the slang would soon be outdated and, thus, the setting of the book would become unbelievable. After a holiday spent in Russia, where the authorities seemed to have the same problems with violent young gangs as in England, Burgess had the idea of creating a language called *nadsat*, a word derived from the Russian suffix for "teen," which was constituted by words derived both from Anglo-American and Russian. Because the novel was full of descriptions of crashing, clashing, rapes, and murders, it was not easy to get it published, even if these violent actions were disguised through the use of language. Finally, the book was sold to William Heinemann Ltd. in London and to W. W. Norton in New York. But the latter agreed to publish it only with the clause of omitting the last chapter, during which Alex decides to abandon his gang and his violent behavior to find a wife with whom to have a child and live a quiet life. The publisher thought that this last chapter was inconsistent with the style and structure of the novel and with the protagonist's characterization (LoBrutto, 1998: 336–337). Burgess was not satisfied with this decision, but did not object because he needed money. Indeed, at that time, he thought he was going to die soon because he was diagnosed as suffering an inoperable cerebral tumor. The author, however, criticized this omission for two reasons. First of all, according to him, the book became a fable because it failed to show that human nature can change: "When a fictional work fails to show change, when it merely indicates that human character is set, stony, unregenerable, then you are out of the field of the novel and into that of the fable or the allegory" (Burgess, 2002b: 228). The author wrote, not without irony, and stressing the importance of moral choice:

> But the American publisher's argument for truncation was based on a conviction that the original version, showing as it does a capacity for regeneration in even the most depraved soul, was a kind of capitulation to the British Pelagian spirit, whereas the Augustinian Americans were tough enough to accept an image of unregenerable man. (1998: vi)[2]

Second, the omission of the last chapter disrupted the arithmology of the novel. The book was constituted of three parts, each one divided into seven chapters, so the total number of chapters was twenty-one to symbolize the age of human maturity.

To promote his novel, Burgess agreed to take part in an installment of *Tonight*, a BBC television program, during which the first chapter of the book was dramatized and a discussion about its theme and language was carried out (LoBrutto, 1998: 336). But, despite this opportunity, the novel did not sell well. According to the author, the success of his book had been impeded by two main reasons. Firstly, the program had revealed too much about the story and, thus, instead of exciting curiosity into its potential readers, had already satisfied them. Secondly, the reviewers had not praised the novel. Therefore, before the release of the Kubrick film, the novel had remained almost unknown and, as will be clarified later, Burgess did not ever accept the fact that his book became known and was both appreciated and blamed for its language and violence only after the film's release (LoBrutto, 1998: 338–339).

Unlike *A Clockwork Orange*, *Barry Lyndon* was adapted from a classic book, from William Makepeace Thackeray's *The Memoirs of Barry Lyndon, Esq., of the Kingdom of Ireland*. This novel was first published serially in *Fraser's* magazine between January and December 1844 with the title *The Luck of Barry Lyndon*. Then, significantly revised and with the actual title, the book was published in 1856 in volume two of the author's *Miscellanies: Prose and Verse* (LoBrutto, 1998: 377).

The Shining was adapted from another successful book, *The Shining*, by Stephen King, who is considered, among the coeval authors, one of the more ingenious and, undoubtedly, the most prolific writer of horror novels. The book was first published in 1977, when its author had already become famous thanks to his two previous bestsellers *Carrie* (first published in 1974) and *'Salem's Lot* (1975). Furthermore, the former novel had already been adapted to the big screen (*Carrie*, Brian De Palma, USA, 1976).

Like *Barry Lyndon* and *The Shining*, *Eyes Wide Shut* was adapted from a well-known and appreciated novella: Arthur Schnitzler's *Dream Story*, first published in 1926. Whereas the other adaptations took several years to be realized, this one took about thirty. Indeed, Michel Ciment claimed that the director first spoke to him about this project in the early seventies (2003: 269), and Christiane Kubrick explained: "Stanley was very interested and I didn't want him to be. Then Terry Southern gave him *A Clockwork Orange* ... and Schnitzler was forgotten for a while. But he kept coming back to it." In April 1971, John Calley, a Warner Bros. executive, claimed that the director was going to adapt *Dream Story*. But it was not until December 1995 that Warner Bros. definitively announced the project (James, 1999: 12–20).

While in the case of *A Clockwork Orange, Barry Lyndon, The Shining,* and *Eyes Wide Shut* the filmmaker seemed to have chosen to adapt the novels independent of their public success during the period in which they were first published, and independent of the time in which the stories were set and what their genre was, in the case of *2001: A Space Odyssey* and *Full Metal Jacket,* as in *Dr. Strangelove,* Kubrick seemed to have chosen the genre before the book. It was February 1964, more than four years before the release of the film *2001: A Space Odyssey* and the novel by Arthur C. Clarke, when Kubrick first told Roger Caras, who worked for Columbia Pictures, that he was going to do a science-fiction film. Caras suggested that the director work with Clarke and contacted the writer for him. Clarke received the following telegram: "Stanley Kubrick—*Dr Strangelove, Paths of Glory,* et cetera, interested in doing film on e.t.'s. Interested in you. Are you interested?"; Clarke answered: "Frightfully interested in working with *enfant terrible* stop contact my agent stop" (Schwam, 2000: 15). In March, the filmmaker contacted the writer personally with the following letter:

> DEAR MR. CLARKE: It's a very interesting coincidence that our mutual friend Caras mentioned you in a conversation we were having about a Questor Telescope. I had been a great admirer of your books for quite a time and had always wanted to discuss with you the possibility of doing the proverbial "really good" science-fiction movie. My main interest lies among these broad areas, naturally assuming great plot and character: 1. The reason for believing in the existence of intelligent extra-terrestrial life. 2. The impact (and perhaps even lack of impact in some quarters) such discovery would have on Earth in the near future. 3. A space-probe with a landing and exploration of the Moon and Mars. (Castle, 2005: 372)

It was the writer who suggested the director should adapt his short story "The Sentinel," which had been written in 1948 for a BBC contest (but had not won the prize). It was first published in 1951 by the review *Ten Story Fantasy* with the title "Sentinel of Eternity."

Just as Kubrick contacted Clarke because he wanted to make a science-fiction film, in 1980 he called Michael Herr, author of the Vietnam novel *Dispatches* and writer of the narration in *Apocalypse Now* (Francis Ford Coppola, USA, 1979), because he "was thinking about making a war movie next, but he wasn't sure which war, and in fact, now that he mentioned it, not even so sure he wanted to make a war movie at all" (Herr,

2000: 6). The director and the writer continued to talk endlessly by phone for about three years, until Kubrick happened to read Gustav Hasford's *The Short-Timers*, a Vietnam novel first published in 1979 by Harper & Row. The book had taken seven years to write and two years to find a publisher, but before its distribution the filmmaker had already bought its rights (LoBrutto, 1998: 458). Both Kubrick and Herr were enthusiastic about this novel that became *Full Metal Jacket* in the director's cinematographic version.

The subsequent phase of the pre-production period, the writing of a screenplay, was, for Kubrick, another long, arduous step. Moreover, according to him, the written and the cinematic medium were too different: neither could a film exactly translate words, nor could words explain a film. This is why the director refused, during his whole career, to clarify the messages and meanings of his films. As early as 1959, Kubrick claimed: "Films deal with the emotions and reflect the fragmentation of experience. It is thus misleading to try to sum up the meaning of a film verbally" (Young, 1959: 7). After the release of *2001: A Space Odyssey*, the filmmaker stressed once more the differences between the two media, and the impossibility of conveying through words the experience of watching the film:

> In *Space Odyssey* the mood hitting you is the visual imagery. The people who didn't respond, I know, for want of coming up with a better explanation, categorize as "verbally oriented people" . . . Communicating visually and through music gets past the verbal pigeonhole concepts that people are stuck with.
> You know, words have a highly subjective and very limited meaning, and they immediately limit the possible emotional and subconscious designating effect of a work of art. (Rapf, 1969: 78)

As mentioned above, it seems that since making this science-fiction film Kubrick definitely chose to convey the meaning of his works through a visual and aural spectacle and not, or at least not principally, through dialogue and voice-over. According to Kubrick, silent movies took greater advantage of the potentialities of cinema than did talkies, which rely more heavily on dialogue and voice-over. While silent movies were closer to music and visual arts, talkies seem to depend more upon words as theatre has always done:

> I have a feeling that no one has yet really found the way to tell a story to utilize the greatest potentials that films have . . . I think the silent movies

came closer to it because they weren't trapped in having to present a scene which was essentially a stage type of scene, movies consist of little play scenes. (Clines, 1987: 175)

Thus, according to the director, novels and theatrical plays were constituted mostly by words, while music, visual arts, and the films that are nearer to silent movies than to classical Hollywood talkies could never be conveyed through words. The screenplay, a form that pertains to the written medium and should be a bridge between a book and a film, was, for Kubrick, a form as far from films as novels and theatrical plays were. The meanings and messages of a scene could never be enclosed in a script; only its dialogue and voice-over could be exactly reported:

> The screenplay is the most uncommunicative form of writing ever devised. It's hard to convey mood and it's hard to convey imagery. You can convey dialogue, but if you stick to the conventions of a screenplay, the description has to be very brief and telegraphic. You can't create a mood or anything like that. (Rapf, 1969: 78–79)

Because the gap between the written and the cinematic medium could not be filled in with scripts, the director used to write a prose treatment of the book before composing a screenplay, and to continuously modify his scripts during shooting, often with the actors' help, taking advantage of their abilities and backgrounds. In the prose treatment of the novel or short story, the filmmaker decided if the story should be compressed or expanded or modified in order to fit the length and rules of the cinematic medium. At this stage, he also tried to develop the source book, highlighting those feelings and emotions that he had felt during the first readings, and clarifying every detail so the story could maintain its believability and coherence. These processes took the director a long time; indeed, the pre-production and production periods lasted for years. But Kubrick's films are among those that are able to exploit the greatest potential of the cinematic medium, and to go as far away as possible from the written one. A discussion of the way in which the director worked at adaptations during the pre-production and production periods should elucidate this point.

The relationship between the film *2001: A Space Odyssey* and the novel by Arthur C. Clarke is one of the more complex and interesting ones from the point of view of the process of adaptation, and of the exchanges between the written and the cinematic medium. The film was not adapted from the novel, nor was the novel adapted from the film. The filmmaker and the science-fiction writer collaborated and, from the short story "The Sentinel," they wrote first a prose treatment of the film and then a screenplay. But, during the making of the film, the latter was utterly altered, and the novel was composed following not only the first prose treatment and screenplay, but also the shooting of the film. Kubrick first met Clarke during April 1964. And in April 1968—that is, exactly four years after that date—the director's film and the author's novel were first released. Since their first meeting, the two collaborators strived to create an exciting plot. Clarke erroneously thought several times to have finished his work, but had to continuously revise the novel because the director did not approve of the end and found the book too wordy. What is more, in August 1966, the writer joined Kubrick at Borehamwood Studios where he not only continued to rewrite his novel, but also helped the filmmaker's team as a science consultant and organizer of technical materials (LoBrutto, 1998: 255–320).

While Kubrick strictly collaborated with his co-screenwriter before and during the making of *2001: A Space Odyssey*, he chose to work alone, for the first time in his life, on the scripts of his two subsequent films (*A Clockwork Orange* and *Barry Lyndon*). Indeed, while he contacted Burgess by phone, he did not ask him to collaborate on the screenplay. It took him four months to complete the first draft of the script, and during this period he was aware of the American version only (LoBrutto, 1998: 340). When he came to know about the last chapter, he commented, not unlike the American publisher: "This extra chapter depicts the rehabilitation of Alex. But it is, as far as I am concerned, unconvincing and inconsistent with the style and intent of the book" (Ciment, 2003: 157). As is discussed later, together with other choices by the director, this omission upset the novel's author.

To compose the script, instead of writing the dialogue in a centered column and the description straight across the page, as is the standard format, Kubrick wrote the description in the centered column and the dialogue straight across the page. He privileged description over dialogue, trying to underline what the mood of each scene should be beyond words, and what should not be changed during shooting compared to what could be left to the actors' improvisation (LoBrutto, 1998: 340). There is evidence that he adopted this method for the screenplay of *Eyes Wide Shut*, too (Raphael, 1999: 141). Indeed, at the Kubrick Archive,[3] there is a draft script by Raphael, dated January 26, 1996 (catalogued GB 3184 SK/18/3/7), which is written in this format. This document is preceded by a signed message in which the author specifies: "I am working on at the second half of the script. I hope that I am right in thinking that this is the way you want it to look. It can, of course, easily be 'translated' into the usual script format which you, understandably, are not crazy about."

As in *A Clockwork Orange*, in *Barry Lyndon* the screenplay was just a blueprint. The filmmaker used the text of the novel as continuity for the film. Then, he developed the cinematic equivalent of each scene (LoBrutto, 1998: 377). In an interview he claimed:

> The first draft took three or four months but, as with all my films, the subsequent writing process never really stopped. What you have written and is yet unfilmed is inevitably affected by what has been filmed. New problems of content or dramatic weight reveal themselves. Rehearsing a scene can also cause script changes. (Ciment, 2003: 177)

For example, when the protagonist Barry Lyndon and his cousin Nora Brady walk in the woods, or when they are shown together playing cards, Kubrick asked the actors to improvise the dialogue: "Stanley said to Ryan [who played the main protagonist], 'This is your cousin and you're . . .' Gay Hamilton [who played Nora] recalls, 'And he just turned to me and said, 'So what would you say at that point?' He set a scenario and we pretty well wrote the lines" (LoBrutto, 1998: 397–398). Therefore, the director, in this film, more than in others, seemed to have developed a *canovaccio* that, in the *commedia dell'arte*, was a vague plot outline in which dialogue was summarized in indirect speech and left to the actors' improvisation (Molinari, 1996: 109). If it weren't for his precision and control over all details, a method that, in the end, leaves little, if nothing, to chance, it could be claimed that he worked as in the *commedia dell'arte*. If we compare the following definition of this way of staging spectacles with Kubrick's way of adapting and shooting films, many similarities can be found:

> The subject was chosen, the characters conceived and named, their relations to one another determined, and the situations clearly outlined, all beforehand. The material was divided into acts and scenes, with a prologue. The situations were made clear, together with the turn of action and the outcome of each scene. When this general outline (called also scenario or canvas) was satisfactorily filled out there was left an opportunity for actors to heighten, vary, and embellish their parts as their genius might suggest. (Bellinger, 1927: 153)

As Harris emphasized during an interview, in order to direct his actors, Kubrick took inspiration from Konstantin S. Stanislavsky's method. When actors were ready to play, the director wanted them to know their lines perfectly and to have understood their roles. They should not only have learned their dialogue, but also have been able to live their characters' lives, to feel their emotions. If, despite these conditions being satisfied, the scene was not interesting and/or coherent with the other sequences, the scene, according to the filmmaker, must be rewritten with the actors' help (Ciment, 2003: 202).

When Kubrick began working on *The Shining*, while he exchanged some telephone calls with the novel's author, he did not ask him to collaborate on the script. He chose instead to work with Diane Johnson, a writer and literature professor, expert in gothic novels. Moreover, he refused to read King's adaptation of his own bestseller, which had already been prepared when he first decided to buy the book's rights. The director and the professor worked every day for three months. First, they worked separately, outlining the film, and then they compared the two outlines and discussed each scene. This process was repeated two or three times (LoBrutto, 1998: 433). Johnson, emphasizing that Kubrick did not mix the written with the cinematic medium to translate words through filmic images, claimed: "Kubrick was very sensitive to the story itself. And during the writing stage, he wasn't really thinking about visual effects. In this sense he was very compartmentalized. He thought like a writer, which I found quite unique" (Ciment, 2003: 295).

The production period was long and arduous, too. Indeed, actors were given new versions of the script almost every day, and were told by the filmmaker that those sheets were only suggestions to be developed in front of the camera (LoBrutto, 1998: 433). Similarly, during the making of *Full Metal Jacket*, Kubrick tried to take advantage of his actors' abilities, especially of Lee Ermey's experience as a marine drill instructor in the U.S. Army during the Vietnam War (he played the role of Sergeant Hartman). About 50 percent of Ermey's dialogue came from his improvisations. Furthermore, his having been a real drill instructor allowed him to create on the set the right atmosphere to help the other actors to play their roles (LoBrutto, 1998: 463).

Not only was the production period long and complex, but so was the pre-production period. When the director formally asked Herr to collaborate with him on the script, he had already prepared a detailed prose treatment of the book, which was around 150 pages. Kubrick and Herr discussed the treatment theme by theme. Then the author wrote a first draft of the screenplay in prose and, subsequently, the filmmaker rewrote it. Finally, Herr wrote a second draft that became the final screenplay (Ciment, 2003: 250). The role of Hasford is not as clear as that of Herr. Indeed, the author spoke several times with the director on the phone, but they met only twice. Kubrick asked him to develop some isolated scenes, but only one of them, Cowboy's death, was retained in the final script (Phillips, 2002: 159). Therefore, Kubrick and Herr would have shared screenplay credits, while Hasford was offered a credit for the additional dialogue, but refused, wanting instead to obtain a screenplay credit. This disagreement ended with Hasford's legal victory, and he was credited along with Kubrick and Herr for the screenplay (LoBrutto, 1998: 484).

The history of *Dream Story*'s adaptation is even more long and complex than *The Shining* and *The Short-Timers*. Christopher Baker, an illustrator, was first contacted by Kubrick in 1993 to create a storyboard. His drawings were inspired by late nineteenth century Vienna (Baker 1993). But a year later, when the director first asked Raphael to work with him on the screenplay, he wanted him to transpose the novel from the *fin de siècle* Vienna to modern New York. The author worked with Kubrick on four different drafts of the script, one written by the filmmaker himself, which Raphael defined just a blueprint and described as follows: "The text is jejune and without literary grace. It is almost gauche in its unpretentiousness. Occasionally it is embarrassing" (1999: 177–179). In his memoir about the collaboration with the director, the author seems to restate the old conflict between screenwriter and filmmaker, giving voice to all his bitterness. Indeed, he claims that, although Kubrick seemed to appreciate the sharpness of his dialogue, he did not seem interested in his prose and he thought about the script as a blueprint: "Kubrick has swallowed all the drafts, digested, and regurgitated them" (1999: 178). But, in an interview, shortly after his memoir had been published, asked about how they handled the scenes of married life, Raphael admitted the importance of the actors' contribution and improvisation, and the role of the screenplay as a *canovaccio* that should be enriched with the actors' skills:

> I think he got a lot out of Nicole about how to handle married life ... With Stanley it was "wait and see," and I think that when you're working with someone as interesting and dedicated as Nicole, you don't simply say, "Here's the text, learn it." From this point of view I feel the screenplay, quite correctly, offered opportunities for improvisation. (Ciment, 2003: 270)

The director's personal style of adapting books was the reason for some of his collaborators' concerns: Raphael's polemic about authorship, Hasford's war about writing credits, and the actors' complaints about the rehearsing of one scene. For example, in *Making The Shining* (Vivian Kubrick, UK and USA, 1980) Shelley Duvall and Jack Nicholson (who play the roles of Wendy and Jack Torrance, respectively) recount that they had to repeat scenes several times. Matthew Modine (Joker in *Full Metal Jacket*) complained about this matter in his diary (2005). And Nicole Kidman and Tom Cruise speak of this same experience in the interviews on the DVD of *Eyes Wide Shut*.

But the major polemics about Kubrick's adaptations arose with two authors: Burgess and King, who both expressed their disappointment in the way in which the filmmaker had modified their novels through his personal adaptations. After the first release of *A Clockwork Orange*, both the film and the book became famous and generated harsh polemics. They were not only criticized for the violence that they depicted and for the way in which they described it, but they were also charged with inducing young people to imitate the crimes illustrated in them. Before the first release of the film, Warner Bros. invited Burgess, his wife, and a friend of the couple to a private screening. In his autobiography, the author claimed that his first concern, before watching the film, was that the cuts necessary to adapt the novel could have transformed it into mere pornography. Comparing his novel to Nabokov's *Lolita*, he said, "The writer's aim in both books had been to put language, not sex or violence, into the foreground; a film, on the other hand, was not made out of words. What I hoped, having seen *2001: A Space Odyssey*, was an expert attempt at visual futurism" (2002b: 244). During the screening, after a few minutes, the author's wife and their friend would have left the theatre if Burgess had not prevented them so as not to be discourteous to the director. The author confessed that what immediately struck him was the end of the film, the omission of the last chapter: "A vindication of free will had become an exaltation of the urge to sin. I was worried" (2002b: 245). Unfortunately, Burgess's preoccupations with the public reaction to the film were not groundless. Shortly after the film was released in England, young gangs began to dress like Alex and his *droogs* (friends in *nadsat*) to maraud the streets. Moreover, some murders and rapes were attributed to the violence shown in the film. For example, in the U.S., Arthur Bremmer shot Governor George Wallace and, when the police read his diary, found that he referred to Alex and his *droogs*, and used *nadsat*. In England, an underage girl was raped by a group of boys who sang "Singin' in the Rain" during the abuse, just like Alex, who sings this same song while raping Mr. Alexander's wife. Another underage boy, who claimed to be obsessed with the film, kicked a tramp to death, like Alex and his *droogs* who hit a homeless man. Finally, another underage boy, who was dressed like Alex and his *droogs*, beat a child (LoBrutto, 1998: 368). After these offensive actions took place, the director and the writer were asked by the media to answer publicly to the charges against the film (LoBrutto, 1998: 368). Burgess agreed to participate on a BBC radio program. At the end, Jimmy Savile, the anchorman, asked one member of the audience, who had been in jail for several years, to stand up, and he asked him whether his readings had influenced his violent actions. The man answered positively. Burgess, in his autobiography, commented that he was not only frustrated by the conclusion of the program, which had confirmed all the prejudices against his novel, but also because his book, which had remained almost unknown for a decade, had become so infamous (2002b: 257). In an interview, the author gave expression to all his feelings and resentments: "The book didn't become a bestseller, not for many, many years, but inevitably it has became my most popular book and this I resent. Out of the thirty-odd books I have written this is often the only book of mine which is known, this I resent very much." And:

> I am regarded by some people as a mere "boy," a mere helper to Stanley Kubrick, the secondary creator who is feeding a primary creator who's a great film director. This, I naturally resent, I resent also the fact I am frequently blamed for the various crimes which are supposed to be instigated by the film. (2002a)

Furthermore, in Burgess's novel *Enderby's End or A Clockwork Testament* (1974), the author's fictional *alter ego*, Enderby, lives an experience similar to Burgess's. Indeed, the latter, in his autobiography, comments:

> Enderby's beach restaurant in Tangier has been visited by a Hollywood producer-director, not unlike Kubrick, who gets on the cheap from the innocent poet a film scenario based on Gerard Manley Hopkins's "The Wreck of the Deutschland." This sublime mystical poem is converted, not by Enderby, into a farrago of clerical sex and Nazi violence; nevertheless, Enderby is blamed for being the father of a piece of pornography. He is blamed daily over the phone, as I was for the film of *A Clockwork Orange*. (2002b: 285)

And, after some copycat crimes were attributed to the film, Enderby, much like Burgess, is invited to a TV program where he tries to defend his poem, its cinematic adaptation, and art in general. Moreover, Burgess's play *A Clockwork Orange: A Play with Music*, which is a theatrical adaptation of his own novel, ends as follows: "A man bearded like Stanley Kubrick comes on playing, in an exquisite counterpoint, 'Singin' in the Rain' on a trumpet. He is kicked off the stage" (1998: 50–51).

Despite all Burgess's resentments towards the film, he wrote in his autobiography that "its brilliance nobody could deny, and some of the brilliance was a film director's response to the wordplay of the novel" (2002b: 245). This statement, as is shown in this book, addresses why both the film and the novel are often considered original and innovative works of art. The violent actions in the book—the robberies, the fighting, the murders, and the rapes—are all described by the protagonist through wordplay. Even if the events told are rough and tough, they are recounted in a joyful, lively manner, as if Alex and his *droogs* were performing a ballet. Indeed, the metaphor of dance is almost always present during the description of the most execrable actions. And this metaphor, as mentioned in the Introduction, was translated and emphasized by the director. Kubrick, during an interview, claimed:

> From the rape on the stage of the derelict casino, to the superfrenzied fight, through the Christ figures cut, to Beethoven's Ninth, the slow motion fight on the water's edge, and the encounter with the cat lady where the giant white phallus is pitted against the bust of Beethoven, movement, cutting, and music are the principal considerations—dance? (Houston, 1971: 111)

While the polemics after the first release of *A Clockwork Orange* arose not only between Kubrick and Burgess, but also between them and public opinion, after the first release of *The Shining* the focus was much more centered on the perspectives of Kubrick and King themselves. The writer criticized the director's conception of the genre and his reading of the novel: "Kubrick is pragmatic and rational and has great difficulty conceiving of a supernatural world, so he looked for evil in the characters and made the film into a domestic tragedy with only vaguely supernatural overtones." And, more briefly: "Kubrick set out to make a horror picture with no apparent understanding of the genre" (Norden, 1983: 56). This first critique concerning the genre was mitigated by King himself who, in an introduction to an edition of *The Shining*, wrote:

> My single conversation with the late Stanley Kubrick, about six months before he commenced filming on his version of *The Shining*, suggested that it was this quality about the story that appealed to him: what exactly, is impelling Jack Torrance toward murder in the winter-isolated rooms and hallways of the Overlook Hotel? It is undead people, or undead memories? Mr. Kubrick and I come to different conclusions. (2001: xii)

A second critique of the adaptation derived from the director's choice of the cast: "Nicholson was all wrong for the part, his last big role had been in *One Flew Over the Cuckoo's Nest*, and between that and his manic grin, the audience identified him as a loony" (Norden, 1983). King later bought the rights of his novel from Kubrick and produced *Stephen King's The Shining* (Mick Garris, USA, 1997), a TV miniseries in which the role of Jack Torrance is played by Steven Weber. As will be discussed later, the filmmaker's adaptation, unlike the novel and the author's own adaptation, scares the spectators in a different way, involving different techniques, and does not change the genre, but exploits different aspects of the fantastic-marvelous and horror genre.

These polemics between Kubrick and the novels' authors, between him and his collaborators, especially co-screenwriters and actors, seem to be due to the director's method of adapting books, and to his personal style and vision that infuse and imbue all his work. An artist with Kubrick's will and ability to control every single step and detail of his work could not have been subjected to a studio's rules. Furthermore, studios decide to finance a film on the basis of a screenplay and scripts were, for the director, the most uncommunicative form of writing, unable to convey mood. Interviewed by Jack Hofsess for the *New York Times*, Kubrick explained:

> What happens in the film business is something like this. When a scriptwriter or a director starts out, producers and investors want to see everything written down. They judge the worth of a screenplay as they would a stage play, and ignore the very great differences between the two. They want good dialogue, tight plotting, dramatic development. What I have found is that the more completely cinematic a film is, the less interesting the screenplay becomes, because a screenplay isn't meant to be read, it's to be realized on film. (LoBrutto, 1998: 407)

The way in which the studio system works was incompatible with Kubrick's method of working, and this is one of the main reasons why the director always remained an independent filmmaker.

Chapter Two

PLOT CONSTRUCTION

Ellipses and Enigmas of Unrelated Scenes

Tableaux Vivants and/or Unrelated Episodes, and Ellipses

Kubrick's films are often interpreted through oppositions, "dualities of meaning." For example, Mario Falsetto claims:

> My contention throughout this study is that Kubrick's work revolved around particular dualities of meaning. Most narrative, stylistic, or thematic issues in the films relate, in some way, to the following polarities: subjective/objective, classical/modernist, rational/irrational, empathy/distance, clarity/ambiguity, order/chaos, symmetry/asymmetry, conventional/subversive, surface/depth, what we know and what remains hidden. (2001: xxii)

As mentioned in the Introduction, many other critics read Kubrick's body of work through oppositions. What remains unclear is the use of the expression "dualities of meaning" and the result of the struggle between these meanings. For example, does chaos disrupt order or do they coexist and, if so, how? Does asymmetry destroy symmetry or are they co-present and, if so, how?

Falsetto himself, during his discussion of the section about man-apes in *2001: A Space Odyssey*, substitutes the expression "dualities of meaning" with "levels of meaning":

> As with so much of Kubrick, the scene operates on several levels at once. First, it must work on an almost primal, cinematic level meant for all viewers, this perceptual level is almost tactile in its effectiveness, the sequence

contains other levels of meaning, referring to more cerebral material and other styles of filmmaking, which are clearly not designed to appeal for all filmgoers. The attraction of the sequence and of much else in Kubrick's work is that it holds the interest of both a sophisticated viewer and a more naïve one. (2001: 49)

Roughly following Falsetto, in the last chapter I discuss that, on the one hand, all of the spectators are involved almost physically in a more "immediate" sublime experience that subsequently challenges them mentally in a density of meaning; and, on the other hand, film scholars can also appreciate a less "immediate" level of meaning that criticizes the clichés of classical Hollywood films.

According to Roman Jakobson, language is realized on the paradigmatic axis, the one of the selection, of those relations that happen *in absentia*, and on the syntagmatic axis, the one of the combination, of the relations that happen *in presentia* (2002: 24–27). The speaker or the writer select linguistic entities and combine them in more complex linguistic unities. Usually the principle of equivalence dominates combination. According to this principle, a particular linguistic entity is chosen and adopted instead of another one that could have the same signifying function. But, in poetry, similarity is superimposed on contiguity and, thus, equivalence becomes the constitutive procedure of the sentence. Every reiteration of the same grammatical concept becomes an effective poetical artifice (1985: 345). Similarly, in Kubrick's films the spectators find repetition of shots and scenes and, instead of following the plot development from the beginning until the end, they are impelled to link the episodes and the other narrative and stylistic elements following new, complex paths.

For example, in this chapter I discuss how the plots of Kubrick's films, at a more superficial level, are often full of ellipses and mysteries that remain unsolved and cannot be explained through a causal logic. At a deeper level, the features of classical Hollywood narrative are implicitly undermined and sacrificed in the name of the *auteur*'s style. Indeed, David Bordwell, emphasizing the importance of cause and effect chains in classical Hollywood films, claims that causality is the prime unifying principle (1985). Furthermore, he argues that time is subordinated to the cause and effect chain, and that the *syuzhet* often omits significant durations to show only events of causal importance (Bordwell and Thompson, 1990). In Kubrick's adaptations, instead, the sequences are usually linked through stylistic choices that create an aesthetically superb diegetic world.

The spectators are actively involved in this enigmatic diegesis where the logical laws of cause and effect seem to have been banned. Therefore, they are impelled to find different paths instead of strictly following the development of the plot.

Similarly, in the next chapter I discuss how the *syuzhet* structures are, on the one hand, symmetrical and their end mirrors their beginning, and/or are strongly ordered and divided into parts. This geometry of the plot construction is often emphasized by sequences that evoke one another and by superbly composed images. On the other hand, this order is disrupted by a play of cross-references among scenes and images through the *mise-en-scène* and the montage. These repetitions entrap the audience in a labyrinthine play. The spectators, once more, try to fill in the ellipses and to solve the enigmas, associating those sequences and images that evoke other scenes and shots through stylistic choices. Thus, the audience looks endlessly for new, complex paths.

Therefore, the complexity of Kubrick's films is due, on the one hand, to the fact that the features of classical Hollywood narrative are substituted by other characteristics, which enable the audience to move in a web constituted by different paths, and which roughly coincide with some of the main features of art-film narration; and, on the other hand, the complexity is due to those abstract speculations that are stimulated by sublime experiences.

✦ ✦ ✦

All of Kubrick's adaptations discussed in this book, except for *The Shining*, are characterized by a similar plot construction: their *syuzhet* is often constituted by *tableaux vivants* and/or unrelated episodes, which is to say, by sequences that are separated by explicit, undetermined ellipses (which are gaps whose presence is signaled by the text and during which the time of the story not narrated remains implicit (Genette, 1972: 135–161), which are usually strongly marked through cuts. Indeed, two subsequent sequences often take place in two different settings, the span of time between them is usually not specified, and they may not involve the same characters. What is more, they are often not linked by a cause and effect chain. In this chapter, *2001: A Space Odyssey* and *Full Metal Jacket* are examined as case studies of this *syuzhet* structure. I analyze this particular plot construction in the cases of *A Clockwork Orange*, *Barry Lyndon*, and *Eyes Wide Shut* in Chapter V, where I discuss how it emphasizes the protagonists' passivity.

This *syuzhet* structure characterizes Kubrick's *2001: A Space Odyssey*, but it is neither a feature of Clarke's novel, nor of science-fiction literature and films in general. On the other hand, in the case of *Full Metal Jacket*, this plot construction characterizes both Hasford's *The Short-Timers* and the genre of the book and the film. Indeed, both Hasford's novel and Kubrick's adaptation can be divided into three main parts that take place in different settings and develop different themes, and each part can be divided into unrelated episodes often separated by ellipses. These subdivisions are stressed in the film through the choice of settings and motifs, the use of cinematic techniques, and a greater number of ellipses. Indeed, while the book presents thirty-seven ellipses, in the adaptation there are seventy-one. In both media, these gaps do not omit significant events of the story, and their only function is to emphasize the division among the episodes.

The first part of the novel and the film takes place at Parris Island, in South Carolina, where, at the Marine Corps Recruit Depot, young men are taught to become marine soldiers before being sent to fight in Vietnam. The settings of the second part of the novel are Da Nang and Phu Bai, while the film is set in Da Nang only. The only link between these first two parts is the protagonist Joker (Matthew Modine), who decides to become a war correspondent for the American newspaper *Stars and Stripes*. The adaptation tends to privilege the sections of the book that develop the theme of journalism, while abolishing or compressing those about war, violence, and the relationships among soldiers. The third part of the novel takes place in Phu Bai, Hue, and Khe Sanh, while the film is set in Hue only. In this last part, Joker is sent to fight against the Vietnamese with other soldiers. Both the novel and the film deepen the theme of war, but the adaptation emphasizes this motif through the compression or the abolition of some of the other themes present in the book, such as that of the relationships among soldiers.

These three main parts appear more disjointed in the film than in the novel also because they are shot with radically different styles. For example, the first part is characterized by brief sequences and iterative scenes (which is to say, by sequences that show an action that takes place more than once in the story [Genette, 1976: 161–207]), while the second and the third part are characterized by longer episodes and the use of the Steadicam. When, in the adaptation, marine recruits are shown during their training at Parris Island, the iterative sequences and their alternation with the non-iterative ones are due to and underlined by choices regarding not only the frequency of the story, but also the setting and time of the scenes, and their order. Firstly, the film presents more iterative scenes than the novel and a more stressed alternation between a few, long sequences and a lot of brief, iterative scenes. Indeed, the iterative sequences of the adaptation number thirty-eight, while there are only five in the book. Secondly, with regard to the setting of the scenes, both the novel and the film alternate between indoors and outdoors. But while the novel describes three different indoor spaces, which is to say, the barracks, the dining hall, and the laundry, the adaptation shows only the barracks. As regards the time of the sequences, in the book the emphasis is more on which day of the eight weeks of training the action is taking place, while the film shows in which moment of the day the sequence is happening and, thus, there is a clearer alternation between day and night. What is more, in the adaptation, the scenes set during the night are almost always shot in the barracks, and the spectators become quickly accustomed to the alternation of daily scenes shot outdoors and nightly ones shot indoors. This rhythm is articulated also by the hymns and marches sung by the recruits, and by the extradiegetic music "Parris Island" (by Abigail Mead), in which the strong and repetitive sound of drums dominates all of the other instruments. Moreover, these pieces often accompany more than one sequence, joining them and increasing the feeling of the repetition of similar actions. Finally, with regard to the order of the episode, the film does not translate the few flashbacks that appear in the novel. They could have interrupted not only the alternation between day and night, and the chain of iterative sequences stressed in the adaptation, but also the theme of training. Indeed, there are three flashbacks in the first part of the book, which usually explain the actions and reactions of the characters that, in the adaptation, are not specified either through the dialogue or the voice-over.

The numerous, brief, iterative sequences of the adaptation, which succeed one another with a rhythm articulated not only by the soundtrack, but also by the alternation between outdoors and indoors, and between day and night, are substituted by longer, non-iterative episodes in the other two parts of the film. Indeed, while the first part of the adaptation can be divided into twenty-two episodes, the second one into seven, and the third one into ten. In the novel, instead, the subdivision into sections is more homogeneous among the three parts because the first part is constituted by twenty-one sections, the second one by twelve, and the third one by sixteen. Thus, the differences among the duration of the episodes in the three main parts are emphasized in the adaptation. Furthermore, in the film, the majority of the episodes of the last two parts take place outdoors, in a completely different landscape. The ordered, tidy fields of the Marine Corps Recruit Depot are substituted, in the second part, by a dirty Da Nang street, and a marine base that will soon be destroyed during the Tet Offensive and, in the third part, by a bombarded, destroyed Hue City. While in the second part there are still some episodes shot at night, in the third one only the very last three shots, when the soldiers sing the "Mickey Mouse Club March," take place at night. Moreover, as is discussed in the next chapter, the Tet Offensive in the second part, and the episodes of the third part in which the "grunts" are shown during the fights, are characterized by the use of a Steadicam that seems to capture the soldiers' confusion and fear. The first part, instead, is characterized by tracking shots that often follow the recruits' marches, or Sergeant Hartman's walks while he gives orders to his "grunts" and inspects them.

The same plot construction of *Full Metal Jacket*—which is to say, unrelated episodes that are separated by ellipses and are not linked by cause and effect chains—characterizes a subgenre of Vietnam novels and films. Stefano Rosso (2003), like James C. Wilson (1982), discusses those Vietnam novels that he defines as "postmodern," such as Herr's *Dispatches* and Hasford's *The Short-Timers*, which are written by novelists that he calls "New Journalists." He lists, among the features that characterize this subgenre, plots constituted by several unrelated anecdotes and dispatches that appear absurd and meaningless. These postmodern Vietnam novels are usually written by the soldiers who experienced the war firsthand (and both Hasford and Herr were combat correspondents, left for Vietnam in 1967, and were present during the Tet Offensive in 1968 [LoBrutto, 1998: 458–459]), and are presented either in an autobiographical or in a memoir form. These New Journalists could not depict the Vietnam War through the clichés used to represent the previous world wars because this new conflict could not be associated with the other ones; it was different from a geographical, tactical, and sociopolitical point of view. Indeed, the Vietnam War was mostly fought during limited and brief combats, in which a few men fought against an almost invisible enemy because Viet Cong used to organize ambushes during which a few snipers, hiding in the jungle, overtook an entire platoon. Even if Viet Cong seemed to possess fewer resources than the Americans, they knew their territory, its impenetrable jungle, and its underground tunnels, and had already fought there for years against the French army. What is more, they were used to the weather, with its unbearable heat, its monsoon rains, and its numerous mosquitoes and leeches. Thus, the American soldiers found themselves in a territory and in a war for which they had not been trained (Rosso, 2003). According to James William Gibson (1994), the features of the world wars literature were not only unsuited to describe this new conflict, but were also unable to express the crisis of the American identity, especially that of the white American men that the defeat provoked. Indeed, this war ended the long tradition of American victories, challenging the myth of the political, military power, and superiority of the U.S.. This crisis of cultural identity was also amplified by epochal social changes. Indeed, during the 1960s, the civil rights and ethnic pride movements began to obtain numerous and relevant victories against racial oppression and, during the 1970s and 1980s, the number of immigrants increased heavily. Thus, white American men became an ethnic group of Anglo-Americans among the others, losing their privileges and numerical superiority. Moreover, the feminist movement succeeded in the conquest of formerly exclusive male fields not only in public, but also in private life. And, during the 1970s and 1980s, the U.S. experienced great economic changes, such as the decline of the manufacturing industry and the transformation of the country from a creditor to a debtor nation. Consequently, Americans felt menaced not only in their international roles, but also in their private affairs (Gibson, 1994). Therefore, according to Rosso (2003), the soldiers had to create a new cultural identity and to describe a totally new experience. What is more, they could not rely on any decisive opinion and judgment about it because public opinion was divided between those who thought this war was an inevitable and right decision, and those who believed that the American intervention in Vietnam was unmotivated and wrong. For these reasons, those writers who, more than others, directly felt and experienced this uncertainty and lack of unanimous judgment, strived to find a new style and a new language that could describe this unfamiliar conflict or, at least, that could reflect the difficulty of narrating the unknown and the incomprehensible. Thus, the New Journalists proposed a way of writing that rejected the objectivity of traditional journalism, creating a more immediate writing that did not furnish a coherent narration with contents easy to grasp and judge, but that was enriched with cues that could help the readers to understand the complexity of this new reality.

This plot construction characterizes some Vietnam films, too. This subgenre, much like the postmodern novels, tries to transmit the difficulty of narrating and describing a war that seems meaningless and useless, and that cannot be communicated and shared. Apart from those Vietnam films dedicated to the veterans (e.g., *Gardens of Stone* [Francis Ford Coppola, USA, 1987]), Stefano Ghislotti (1996) subdivides the other Vietnam films into two main groups, which roughly coincide with those described by Rosso and Wilson in the field of Vietnam literature. As realist novels strive to update the clichés of the world wars literature to the new war, the first group of Vietnam films is inspired by classic war films, and shows scenes of fights in which the American heroism is emphasized (e.g., *The Green Berets* [Ray Kellogg and John Wayne, USA, 1968]). Wilson (1982), not unlike Ghislotti, explains that the first Vietnam films, like realist novels, do not investigate the causes and the complexities of the war, but apply the same techniques used in the traditional war films to the Vietnam War, principally for business reasons. Indeed, this war was a new subject and, thus, it caught the audience's interest both for its novelty and for its actuality. When, during the 1960s and early 1970s, the war became unpopular, the film industry stopped the production of these war movies. Finally, when the controversy seemed to be settled, during the late 1970s and 1980s, Hollywood again turned the Vietnam War into a major commercial success. Wilson claims that the most recent Vietnam films describe the American culture as violent and brutal, transforming Vietnam into a senseless world of destruction (e.g., *Apocalypse Now* [Francis Ford Coppola, USA, 1979] and *Platoon* [Oliver Stone, USA, 1986]). Therefore, the features that characterize the construction of the plot of *Full Metal Jacket* are specific to a subgenre of Vietnam films and novels, are present in *The Short-Timers*, and emphasized in Kubrick's adaptation. A succession of unrelated anecdotes symbolizes, in this case, the complexity of the subject, the Vietnam War, and the inadequacy of the narrative techniques of classical war films to represent such a new, complicated theme.

In *2001: A Space Odyssey,* this same *syuzhet* structure mimics the difficulty of thinking about the universe and mankind's role in it. As in *Full Metal Jacket*, trying to understand is no longer possible. The spectators do not strive to comprehend the complexity of the real world and of the fictional one, but do try to speculate about them and their infinite possibilities. This science-fiction film is the furthest one, among Kubrick adaptations, from classical Hollywood narrative, and could not be further from Clarke's novel and short story or from the written medium in general. Indeed, even if the plot of the film and that of the novel are strikingly similar, the film and the book cannot substitute one another. They can be defined as complementary because, while the film is a visual work that conveys the awe and wonder derived from the observation and the imagination of the infinity of time and space, the novel, through speculations about space voyages and extraterrestrial intelligence, tries to inspire awe and wonder. While the spectators of the film are involved in a visual experience in which the mysteries of the universe are never unveiled, but always increased in a crescendo, the readers of the book are entangled in a succession of hypotheses about extraterrestrial life and other universes. This complementarity of the film and the novel was stressed by Clarke himself, who claimed: "I always used to tell people, 'Read the book, see the film, and repeat the dose as often as necessary'" (LoBrutto, 1998: 310). The director's choice of leaving several enigmas unexplained is stressed and increased by his decision to separate some episodes through ellipses, to cut the dialogue, and not to adopt a voice-over. In the novel, the mysteries are usually widely discussed, and often the gaps of the film correspond to explanatory sections.

The ellipses stress the division of the plot of the film into apparently unrelated episodes that take place in different settings and times and present different characters. Moreover, the entire film is divided into four main parts through the titles: "The Dawn of Man," "Jupiter Mission," "Intermission," and "Jupiter and Beyond the Infinite." In the first episode, in an arid, unspecified African landscape during the Pleistocene period, man-apes are almost starving. After the appearance of a monolith, they learn how to use bones as tools and begin to kill and eat tapirs. Then the spectators are shown Dr. Floyd (William Sylvester), who in the year 2001 is traveling by spaceship from the Earth towards a space station near the Moon. Together with other astronauts he reaches Crater Tycho where a monolith has been unearthed, creating powerful magnetic fields. During the men's inspection, the monolith emits a long, deafening noise. The only link between these first two episodes, into which the first part is divided, is the presence of the monolith. In the second part, entitled "Jupiter Mission," the audience is shown two astronauts, Bowman (Keir Dullea) and Poole (Gary Lockwood), inside the spacecraft Discovery that is heading towards Jupiter. Discovery is controlled by the HAL 9000 computer which soon begins to malfunction. Thus, there is no apparent link between these first two parts. During the third one, "Intermission," HAL kills Poole, the three members of the hibernated crew inside the spacecraft, and tries in vain to kill Bowman. This survivor manages to disconnect the computer, and he is then shown a recorded video by Dr. Floyd in which the scientist explains the goal of the mission. Discovery is directed where the radio waves emitted by the monolith on the Moon were aimed. Therefore, this video links, at the end of the third part, the first three parts through the monolith and Dr. Floyd's character. In the last part, "Jupiter and Beyond the Infinite," Bowman reaches the monolith and begins to travel through the Stargate, taking him through space and time, until he lands in a room and is transformed into a star-child, able to float in the universe.

The novel is instead divided by the author into six main parts that are linked through explanatory sections that fill in the gaps left in the plot of the film. For example, in the film, the episode of man-apes is separated from the subsequent one, in which Dr. Floyd, on board the spaceship Orion III, travels towards Space Station 1 near the Moon, through an ellipsis that covers four million years. The image of a bone tossed in the air by Moon-Watcher (Daniel Richter), the leader of the man-apes and the first one to understand how to use the bone as a weapon, is separated only by a cut from the image of an orbiting satellite, which has a shape similar to that of the bone and which floats in space (see Figure 2.1 and Figure 2.2). In the novel, the episode of man-apes ends with a brief description of the evolution from man-apes to men, and the subsequent part is introduced by an account of Dr. Floyd's travel by a jet from Washington to the Florida coast where he goes aboard a spaceship. What is explained in the book—how man-apes progressively became men thanks to several improvements that followed that first conquest of using a tool—is substituted by an ellipsis in the film. This gap in the cinematic medium seems more eloquent than the explanatory chapter in the novel. The graphic match, the visual similarity between the image of the bone and that of the orbiting satellite, seems to suggest to the spectators that the satellite is only another of men's instruments, not unlike that first bone. From that first step during the Pleistocene period, nothing has stopped men's historical evolution. Furthermore, only four million years have passed, a relatively short span of time if compared with the time of the universe. Indeed, both episodes are grouped under the title "The Dawn of Man," as if to underline that men, even if they are able to reach the Moon and the other planets of the solar system, are still at the beginning of their evolution. Men in the year 2001 are still savages, they need to free themselves from their bodies' constraints, from the prison of matter, and to freely float in the universe, across time and space. This is the thought at the core of the film, which induces spectators to speculate about the greatness and infinite nature of the universe, about the possibility of extraterrestrial life and how aliens' evolution could be far greater than theirs. Indeed, Kubrick claimed:

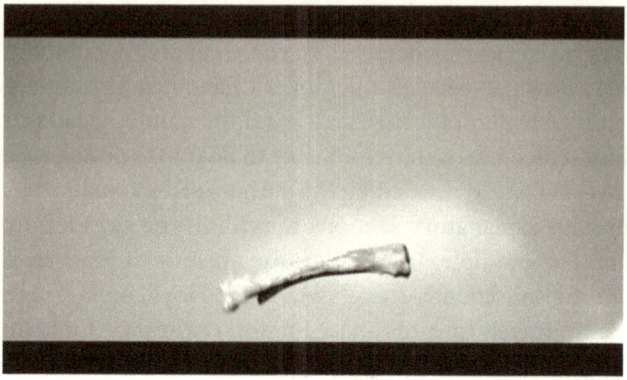

Figure 2.1 A bone tossed in the air by Moon-Watcher during the Pleistocene period.

Figure 2.2 Orion III is traveling from the Earth to the Moon in the year 2001. The two shots are divided by a cut.

I will say that the God concept is at the heart of *2001*—but not any traditional, anthropomorphic image of God. I don't believe in any of Earth's monotheistic religions, but I do believe that one can construct an intriguing scientific definition of God... When you think of the giant technological strides that man has made in a few millennia—less than a microsecond in the chronology of the universe—can you imagine the evolutionary development that much older life forms have taken? They may have progressed from biological species, which are fragile shells for the mind at best, into immortal machine entities—and then, over innumerable eons, they could emerge from the chrysalis of matter transformed into beings of pure energy and spirit. Their potentialities would be limitless and their intelligence ungraspable by humans. (Norden, 1968: 330–331)

The second, main ellipsis of the film divides the part in which the monolith found on Crater Tycho on the Moon emits a noise from the part in which Bowman and Poole are inside Discovery. The spacecraft's destination and the purpose of the space mission are not revealed, in either the film or the novel, until Dr. Floyd explains, to the survivor of the mission and to the audience, the goal of this space travel through a recorded video message. In the novel, the part set on Crater Tycho is followed by a description of how the noise emitted by the monolith was recorded and studied. The purpose of the space mission and the direction of the monolith's radio waves are not specified, but their link is suggested by the sentence that closes the part set on the Moon: "Some immaterial pattern of energy, throwing off a spray of radiation like the wake of a racing speedboat, had leaped from the face of the Moon, and was heading out towards the stars" (Clarke, 1968: 95). In the film, the part set on Crater Tycho ends with a long shot of the astronauts gathered around the monolith that emits a sound, and an extreme long shot in which the Sun, the Earth, and the monolith are aligned. The following part, set on board Discovery, opens with the title "Jupiter Mission. 18 Months Later," and a long shot of the spacecraft. In this case, the geometry of the alignment of planets and the monolith, which closes one part, is followed by the geometry of Discovery, which opens the subsequent part. In an extreme long shot, the aliens' artifact seems to be ready to be launched into the atmosphere. In the subsequent shot, the spacecraft is traveling in space and has the shape of an arrow in its archer's hands, in Bowman's hands, and it could be directed towards a monolith previously shot in the atmosphere and waiting to be reached. In the novel, too, this spacecraft is described through the metaphor of the arrow: "her slender, arrow-like body pointed away from Earth" (1968: 105) and "the spherical pressure-hull formed the head of a flimsy, arrow-shaped structure" (1968: 114).

The third and last main ellipsis of the film divides the part in which Bowman comes to know the purpose of his mission from the part in which the astronaut reaches Jupiter and sees the monolith floating in space. In the novel, this ellipsis is substituted by five chapters, which occupy 9.2 percent of the entire book, in which Bowman's daily life on board Discovery and his thoughts about the monolith and the aliens are described.[1] Whereas in the book the possible readers' arguments are translated and guided through Bowman's thoughts, in the film the possible spectators' reasoning is never specified through words, but only encouraged through images. Indeed, the part in which the astronaut watches Dr. Floyd's message ends with a close-up of Bowman, while the subsequent part opens with the title "Jupiter and Beyond the Infinite" and an extreme long shot of the monolith and Discovery floating in space, with Jupiter and its moons around them. The astronaut's loneliness, his awe and wonder, are suggested by his close-up followed by a title, which indicates where he is directed, and an extreme long shot, which joins the enigmas of the monolith, of extraterrestrial life, and the mysteries of the universe. The insignificance (but also the bravery) of a man is compared with the hugeness and majesty of space and time.

2001: A Space Odyssey is a compelling visual and aural experience. Its plot is mostly constituted by unrelated episodes, which are divided by ellipses and take place in different settings and times, presenting different characters and situations. These unrelated episodes are usually not linked by a cause and effect chain, but by images that evoke one another. The order of the unrelated episodes seems to follow an aesthetic chain rather than a logical one. The audience cannot strictly follow the development of the plot from the beginning until the end, but instead has to find other complex stylistic paths that can link the episodes. Therefore, the spectators, who are actively involved in the contemplation of the beauty of these enigmatic succession of images, are impelled to speculate about the awe and wonder of the diegetic world and, consequently, of the real universe and their role in it. As James Griffith notes, *2001: A Space Odyssey* seems a perfect example to rebut the charge made against the cinematic medium by the critics who follow a fidelity approach. The scholar, observing that Kubrick's film is full of narrative gaps, while Clarke's novel fills in all the ellipses, argues:

> The suggestion here, that the novel greatly simplifies the film, would apparently stand Bluestone on his head. For example, the film portrays thought and intelligence much more subtly than does the novel: Kubrick portrays inspiration, or the birth of thought, in motifs of music, triumphant postures, alignments, and intense eyes; Clarke offers, as a corresponding motif, the image of hitting a bull's-eye. (1997: 225)

Mysteries

In *2001: A Space Odyssey*, ellipses that are not filled in leave several enigmas unexplained. But mysteries that remain concealed are created also through other cinematic techniques, and characterize two other adaptations discussed in this book: *The Shining* and *Eyes Wide Shut*. In this chapter, I analyze some of the main enigmas present in *2001: A Space Odyssey* and *Eyes Wide Shut*. I examine *The Shining* in Chapter V, where I discuss the play between a natural and a supernatural explanation of the events shown in the film.

Some of the main mysteries of Kubrick's science-fiction film pertain to the origin and purposes of the monolith and HAL 9000's behavior. All of these enigmas are in part explained in Clarke's novel through the heterodiegetic narrator (a narrator who is outside the diegetic world [Genette, 1976: 291–310]), and/or through Bowman's fluxes of conscience. There are numerous mysteries in *Eyes Wide Shut*, too: for example, the proposal of two models to bring the protagonist Bill (Tom Cruise) to "where the rainbow ends," the meaning of the password "Fidelio" to gain access into the orgy, the identity of the woman who, at the orgy, offers to sacrifice herself to save Bill, and the cause of her death. Some of these enigmas, such as the two models' proposal and the password, do not appear in *Dream Story*, while the other mysteries seem less emphasized in Schnitzler's novella. Indeed, the readers are often guided by Fridolin's fluxes of conscience that usually reveal his interpretations about his experiences, furnishing possible explanations and hypotheses. On the other hand, the spectators of the film are not accompanied either by a voice-over or by the protagonist's dialogue. Furthermore, they are misled and confused by Ziegler's explanations about the orgy that should have solved the main enigmas (Victor Ziegler [Sydney Pollack] is the protagonist's patient who organizes a Christmas party where Bill meets the two models, and who claims to have been present at the orgy and to know its rules).

In Kubrick's *2001: A Space Odyssey*, the mystery about the monolith—its origin and purposes—is increased thanks to the spectacular way in which it is shown, the music that accompanies its appearances, and the way in which man-apes and astronauts react to it. Whereas, in the novel, as in the short story "The Sentinel," the spell of the monolith is heightened thanks to the explanation of its source and aim. In the film, the monolith is shown in four sequences: each time its appearance precedes great events, and three of the times it is accompanied by the "Dies irae" of György Ligeti's *Requiem* and by the alignment of planets.

Firstly, it appears during the episode of man-apes. Soon after its appearance, Moon-Watcher kills a tapir and eats meat together with his tribe, kills the other group's leader, and freely drinks at the waterhole with his companions. Then, when Dr. Floyd, together with other five astronauts, arrives at Crater Tycho on the Moon to see the aliens' artifact, it emits a very loud and unexpected noise. During the Pleistocene period, man-apes' movements were syncopated, almost uncontrolled, and they emitted loud, guttural sounds. Whereas the astronauts, in the year 2001, remain silent, walk slowly and circumspectly, as if they were approaching a holy place or entering a church. Their reverence in front of an artifact, made by an alien civilization far more advanced than their own, is not conveyed through their physical behavior, as in the case of man-apes, but seems to be rendered by the use of the handheld camera: trembling images convey the astronauts' reverence.

The third time that the monolith appears is when Bowman, alone on board Discovery, reaches Jupiter. The astronaut and his pod are then shown traveling through the Stargate. In the novel, the monolith opens to let the astronaut in, closes behind him, and he begins his travel, as if he entered in a wormhole, a space-temporal door that brings him to a parallel universe. Therefore, in the book, the link between the aliens' artifact and the travel is explained.

Finally, in the film, when Bowman finds himself, lying in a bed in a room, almost dying, the monolith appears at the foot of the bed. This time, the aliens' artifact is not accompanied by the alignment of planets and by the "Dies irae." But soon after its appearance, the astronaut finds himself transformed into a star-child, an embryo who has the power of traveling and floating in the universe. In the novel, when the astronaut becomes a star-child, the aliens' artifact, which appears in front of him when he wakes up, emits noises and patterns of lights to get his attention, to study his mind and modify it. A man is reborn into an immortal baby, and has the power of traveling through space and time and of assuming another form or definitely leaving his body, as the aliens do; the relation between the appearance of the monolith and its effects is made explicit in the book. In the last two shots of the film, instead, the star-child is shown in the universe, first, looking down at the Earth and, finally, into the camera, addressing the spectators on the Earth. His eyes are wide open. His gaze is the gaze of a baby, full of wonder, and this evokes and mirrors the audience's gaze. It is interesting to note that Robin Wood argues that contemporary American cinema and, especially the genre of science-fiction, has often constructed the viewer as childlike, as a wide-eyed child enchanted and hypnotized by images (1986: 163). Thus the star-child could represent the spectators and could guide them to look at the Earth with awe.

He could be another diegetic spectator, together with Bowman during the Stargate, similar to the spectators depicted in the sublime paintings of William Turner and Frederic Edwin Church. Indeed, during the nineteenth century, it was thought that painting could give rise to the sublime because its concreteness could become a sign of the unknown and the incomprehensible. Painters of the sublime taught spectators how to gaze at their paintings, depicting diegetic characters in contemplation of the landscapes in front of them. During the Stargate scene, according to Scott Bukatman (1999), Bowman's close-ups are intercut with images of the Stargate so that the astronaut becomes a diegetic spectator who mirrors the extradiegetic audience.

If, at the end of the film, the spectators rethink the sequences discussed above, paying particular attention to the montage, they could conclude that the monolith helped man-apes to evolve into men and will help men to evolve into star-children. But the monolith is an aliens' artifact and, therefore, men's history is influenced and helped by an extraterrestrial intelligence and will. The monolith becomes an "alien messiah." According to Hugh Ruppersberg, the first alien messiah of science-fiction cinema appeared in *The Day the Earth Stood Still* (Robert Wise, USA, 1951) and, during the 1970s and 1980s, became almost a cultural phenomenon. This personage had a religious connotation, was far more advanced than men, and helped them to save themselves from technology and other characteristics of modern life that could have threatened humanity. The paradox of the alien messiah was that it was the result of civilizations far more technically advanced than the human one, and that it used technology to save humanity from a destruction produced by technology itself (Ruppersberg, 2003). These last considerations could be at the core of *2001: A Space Odyssey*. Indeed, Discovery's mission is compromised by HAL's failures.

In the short story and in the novel, the monolith's mystery is unveiled, its source and aim explained from the beginning. Indeed, in "The Sentinel," through the fluxes of conscience of the protagonist, who is the homodiegetic narrator (which is to say, he is the protagonist of the narration that he produces [Genette, 1976: 291–310]), the readers come to know that the monolith is an aliens' sentinel that should advise its creators when it is discovered by men. In the novel, night after night, Moon-Watcher and other man-apes around the planet are taught lessons by monoliths (Clarke, 1968: 25–26). What is more, an entire chapter is dedicated to some explanations concerning the aliens' artifact. The monolith buried under the Moon's surface is a sentinel that should inform its creators that men have reached a level of evolution that has permitted them to find it.[2] But during the last three million years, aliens evolved, as well as men:

> Now they were lords of the Galaxy, and beyond the reach of time. They could rove at will among the stars, and sink like a subtle mist through the very interstices of space. But despite their godlike powers, they had not wholly forgotten their origin, in the warm slime of a vanished sea. And they still watched over the experiments their ancestors had started, so long ago. (1968: 215–126)

The omniscient narrator depicts extraterrestrials with features that are reminiscent of God in the Christian tradition: they are light, energy, they are immortal, their home is the universe and, despite their magnificence, they care about men, they help and encourage them. Similarly, before this passage, the narrator had adopted the evangelical metaphor of farmers and their harvest to describe the aliens' aim:

> And because, in all the Galaxy, they had found nothing more precious than Mind, they encouraged its dawning everywhere. They became farmers in the fields of stars; they sowed, and sometimes they reaped. And sometimes, dispassionately, they had to weed. (1968: 214)

This is the thought at the core of the film, too, the one declared by Kubrick himself in the *Playboy* magazine interview referenced above. In the film, however, the suggestive power of the God concept is evoked through the use of music that recalls holy chants, the alignment of planets that calls forth the spectacle of a nature created by God, the man-apes' reverent terror and the astronauts' deferential walk that could be compared with the respect of churchgoers, and, especially, through what remains unsaid and unknown, through the mystery that is a condition of the Christian faith (defined as secure belief in God and trusting acceptance of God's will).

In addition to the monolith, the computer HAL 9000 on board Discovery and, particularly, the question of whether he has a conscience and why he has begun to fail and become a killer, enrich the mysteries of the film. In the novel, as in the other cases analyzed above, many questions receive an answer. Both in the book and the film, the computer, which is the brain of the mission because it constantly monitors the spacecraft's functions, advises the astronauts that the unit AE-35, which is a component of the antenna that maintains the connections between Discovery and Mission Control on the Earth, is going to break. But when the astronauts, with the help of HAL's twin computer on the Earth, check the conditions of the unit, they find out that it functions perfectly. The logical conclusion is that the failure is in HAL, and not in the unit, and that the computer should be disconnected. When HAL comes to know about this decision, first he kills Poole, who is outside in space, trying to reposition the unit on the antenna. The computer, moving the mechanical arms of the pod, cuts the tube that keeps the astronaut anchored to Discovery. Then he kills the three members of the hibernated crew through the machines from which their lives depend. Finally, he attempts to kill Bowman in vain. The computer's behavior is explained in the novel and it should have been described in the film, according to some testimonies (Walker, 2000: 187). Moreover, Clarke explained:

> But it would have been almost impossible to have given the logical explanation of just why HAL did what it did. It would have slowed things down too much. So it had to be treated on this sort of naïve and conventional level. Then there was the straightforward matter of dramatic content. One had to have some kind of dramatic tension and suspense and conflict. And HAL's episode is the only conventional dramatic element in the whole film. (Youngblood, 1970: 147)

In the novel, HAL's future behavior is anticipated at the beginning of the mission, well before his failure. "And then, if there was no reply from Earth, he would take what measures he deemed necessary to safeguard the ship and to continue the mission—whose real purpose he alone knew, and which his human colleagues could never have guessed" (1968: 109). Moreover, before Bowman disconnects the computer, a chapter of the novel is entirely devoted to the explanation of HAL's misconduct. The computer knows the aim of the mission, but he cannot share this knowledge with his companions, lying to them instead. He might still have handled this situation but, after having learned about his disconnection, he begins to fear for his life and decides to defend himself and the mission. After HAL is disconnected, when Bowman is traveling alone towards Japetus, these explanations are repeated once more. In the film, neither the dialogue with his companions nor the inflections in his voice express the computer's feelings. Indeed, HAL's voice-over was recorded by Douglas Rain who, during his work, was never shown a screenplay or a scene of the film, so his acting could not reveal to the spectators particulars of the plot (LoBrutto, 1968: 278-279). Thus, even the episode involving the computer, which should have been, according to Clarke's statement cited above, a "conventional dramatic element," becomes a largely visual experience in the film.

While in Kubrick's science-fiction film words do not usually help the spectators to reveal the mysteries, in *Eyes Wide Shut* dialogue seems to be often adopted to increase the enigmas and puzzle the audience. Indeed, the first, unresolved mystery is the meaning of the phrase of the two models, who suggest to Bill to go "where the rainbow ends":

> GAYLE: Where the rainbow ends.
> BILL: Where the rainbow ends?
> NUALA: Don't you want to go where the rainbow ends?
> BILL: Now, that depends where that is.
> GAYLE: Well, let's find out.

The word "rainbow" appears again when the protagonist needs a costume to enter the orgy and rents it from a shop called Rainbow Fashions. Thus, Gayle (Louise J. Taylor) and Nuala's (Stewart Thorndike) phrase could allude to the orgy. What is more, Victor Ziegler will tell the protagonist that the women of the orgy are prostitutes. Therefore, the spectators could think that Gayle and Nuala are not only models, but also prostitutes who are invited by Ziegler to the orgy. But these links are only speculations, which are not corroborated, are hypotheses moved by the play of cross-references that characterizes Kubrick adaptations, as is discussed in the next chapter.

The other mystery present in the film (but not in the novel) is the meaning of the password that the protagonist needs to gain access to the orgy. The magic word, which opens the doors of the mansion where the orgy takes place, is "Denmark" in the book and "Fidelio" in the adaptation. The meaning of "Denmark" can be immediately understood. Indeed, Fridolin, the novel's protagonist, explains that he was on the Danish coast the previous summer. And the readers know, from his wife Albertine's confession, that she was conquered there by a naval officer's gaze, and that she would have left her family to spend even only one night with this stranger. "Denmark" symbolizes Albertine's wished, but unfulfilled betrayal, and her husband's sought, but equally unrealized betrayal. On the other hand, the spectators of the film cannot attribute a clear meaning to "Fidelio." The pianist Nightingale (Todd Field), who plays both during the Christmas party and the orgy, and who tells the protagonist the password, suggests in his dialogue with Bill that it is the title of a Beethoven opera. In *Fidelio*, a woman risks her life to save her husband. Firstly, she disguises herself in male attire to enter the dungeon in which her husband is imprisoned, and when her husband is going to be stabbed, she throws herself between him and his enemy saving her beloved. In this opera, as in the orgy, there is a disguise and a woman ready to sacrifice herself to save a man. In the opera, however, as suggested by its Latin title, the love and fidelity of a wife for her husband move her extreme behavior. She is not an unknown woman who takes part in an orgy. Thus, the choice of this password could be read both as ironic and as a flash-forward to what will happen in the mansion where the orgy takes place. But these connections are, once more, speculations *a posteriori*, which are stimulated and stimulate the numerous cross-references.

Both in the novel and the film the main enigma concerns the identity of the woman who saves the protagonist, as well as the cause of her death. Indeed, as soon as Fridolin/Bill enters the mansion, a woman tries to advise him that his life is in peril. The protagonist cannot recognize her because everybody wears a mask. When the orgy participants find out that Fridolin/Bill is an uninvited guest, they threaten him with punishment. The woman reappears and offers her life instead of the protagonist's. The subsequent night, during his wanderings through the city, Fridolin/Bill reads in a newspaper that a woman was found dead in her hotel room. She probably committed suicide. He goes to the morgue to see the corpse. Fridolin, the novel's protagonist, seems to recognize the woman he met at the orgy:

> And yet at the same time he was conscious that even if it were her face, her eyes, the same eyes that yesterday had gazed into his ablaze with life, he could never know for certain—and perhaps didn't even want to know.... Was it her body? That wonderful, blooming body that yesterday had tortured him with longing? (Schnitzler, 1999: 93–94)

The spectators of the film, instead, are shown Mandy (Julienne Davis), the prostitute who overdosed in Ziegler's bathroom during the Christmas party. But the character of the mysterious woman of the orgy is played by another actress (Abigail Good). Bill, the adaptation protagonist, receives a telephone call from Victor, who invites him to his house, and explains the rules of the orgy and the circumstances of the woman's death. Although Ziegler confirms that Mandy was the woman at the orgy, his dialogue complicates the mystery instead of solving it. Indeed, his words are presented as truth thanks to his role, because he claims to have been present during the orgy and know the participants and the mechanisms of these events, and thanks to his way of speaking and moving, his dynamism is contrasted with the doctor's passivity. Everything induces the spectators to trust him; the sound of his voice and his movements seem determinate and resolute, he gesticulates and moves around the room, and he answers Bill's questions without hesitating. On the other hand, the protagonist does not move, utters less than one third of the words pronounced by Victor, and repeats his words, almost stammering. Behind Victor's words, however, there are some unexplained and illogical facts, and the thriller remains unsolved. Indeed, if Mandy is the mysterious woman, why are their roles played by two different actresses? And how can Victor know that Mandy's hotel room door was locked from within, given the fact that this particular point was not reported in the article? What is more, the choice not to frame Ziegler's face in a medium close-up or in a close-up (there are only three medium close-ups of him versus the eleven medium close-ups of Bill) seems to prevent the spectators from observing his emotions. It is worth noting that Kubrick uses the same actor for different roles in *Fear and Desire*, *Lolita*, and *Dr. Strangelove*. In the first film, each of the two victims is played by the same actor who plays his killer (Kenneth Harp is Lt. Corby and the enemy general, and Stephen Coit is Pvt. Fletcher and the enemy captain). In *Lolita*, Peter Sellers plays Clare Quilty, the TV writer, and Dr. Zempf, the Beardsley High School psychologist. And in *Dr. Strangelove*, Peter Sellers plays Group Captain Lionel Mandrake, President Merkin Muffley, and Dr. Strangelove. In his last film, the director does the opposite, which is to say, he uses two different actresses for one role only, but he still plays with the relationship between character and actor. Similarly, in *Cet obscur object du désir* (Luis Buñuel, France and Spain, 1977), the female protagonist is played by two different actresses (Carole Bouquet and Ángela Molina), and this device thickens the mystery about her love relationship with the male protagonist (Fernando Rey). Furthermore, in the last sequence of the film when the two lovers seem to explain to each other their feelings, loud diegetic music prevents the spectators from listening to their dialogue. Similarly, in *Eyes Wide Shut*, the mystery of the death of the orgy woman is never revealed. Indeed, the scene depicting the confrontation between Bill and Victor presents various inconsistencies. Moreover, the spectators never know what the protagonist thinks about what has happened to him because there is no voice-over and, when he is about to recount to his wife his adventures, the sequence ends before his telling begins.

As in *2001: A Space Odyssey*, in *Eyes Wide Shut* the mysteries are not explained at the end, but multiplied. The succession of unrelated episodes, punctuated by ellipses and enigmas, follows an aesthetic play of cross-references that actively involves the audience in compelling visual and aural experiences. Once more, the spectators are impelled to find new, complex aesthetic paths instead of simply following the chain of events presented in the plot.

Chapter Three

PLOT CONSTRUCTION

A Chaotic Geometry

The unrelated sequences which characterize the plot construction of Kubrick's adaptations are, on the one hand, inserted in symmetrical *syuzhet* structures, in which the end mirrors the beginning, as in *A Clockwork Orange*, *Barry Lyndon*, and *Eyes Wide Shut*, and/or in plots strongly ordered into parts, as in *2001: A Space Odyssey*, *Barry Lyndon*, and *Full Metal Jacket*. The symmetry of the *syuzhet* structure is often emphasized by scenes that evoke one another through the *mise-en-scène* and montage. The geometry of the plot construction is usually evoked by superbly composed images, in which the *mise-en-scène* constitutes a particular order and/or symmetry. On the other hand, this geometry is disrupted by a play of cross-references among sequences and shots. The spectators try to fill in the ellipses and to solve the enigmas, associating those scenes and images that evoke other sequences and shots through stylistic choices. But the gaps and the mysteries remain unexplained. This subterranean aesthetic play of cross-references, which seems to disrupt the symmetrical, ordered superstructure, is symbolized by the image of the maze in *The Shining*, and by those scenes shot with a handheld camera or a Steadicam following the characters' sinuous and/or syncopated movements. On the one hand, this apparent chaos seems, once more, to undermine the features of classical Hollywood narrative and the logic of cause and effect. Indeed, these characteristics are unsuited to explain the cross-references and repetitions. On the other hand, this play actively involves the spectators in visual and aural compelling experiences, in superbly conceived diegetic worlds that charm them with their beauty and challenge them with their enigmatic qualities.

The spectators' effort to follow the play of cross-references and repetitions seems to evoke their attempt to explain the complexity of the real world, finding cause and effect links among events. This same struggle also mirrors their effort to understand the most obscure working of their minds, such as the *déjà vu* that accompanies both daily experiences and nightly dreams. Indeed, Sigmund Freud wrote in a letter to his friend Romain Rolland that, when he visited the Acropolis, he thought of already having been there and he doubted the existence of the Acropolis itself. He called such a feeling "derealization": if the subject feels that a piece of reality is strange to himself, there is a *"déjà vu"* (1936: 233–236). Freud links *déjà vu* to dreams both in *Psychopathology of Everyday Life* (1901: 265) and in *Fausse Reconnaissance (Déjà Raconteé) in Psycho-Analytic Treatment* (1914: 203). In the former text, he reports what Dr. Ferenczi wrote to him: "It seems therefore that *'déjà vu'* can derive not only from day-dreams but also from night-dreams as well" (1901: 266–267). In the latter book, Freud links the feeling of having had the same experience (and/or of having been in the same place before) with a memory of a dream that was forgotten: "Several authorities have argued with this view, and have maintained that the basis of the phenomenon is the recollection of something that has been dreamt and then forgotten. In both cases it would be a question of the activation of an unconscious impression" (1914: 203). In *The Interpretation of Dreams*, he returns again to the problem of *déjà vu*: "In some dreams of landscape or other localities emphasis is laid in the dream itself on a convinced feeling of having being there once before" (1900: 399).

Kubrick's adaptations, thanks to cross-references and repetitions that evoke *déjà vu*, acquire a dreamy atmosphere. This mechanism seems explicitly stressed in his last film, where *déjà vu* is so numerous to have induced some critics to interpret the diegetic world as a protagonist's dream. For example, both Flavio De Bernardinis (1999) and Larry Gross (1999) interpret *Eyes Wide Shut* as a dream. The problem of such a hypothesis is that two questions remain unexplained in these scholars' essays. Indeed, who is/are the dreamer/s? And when does the dream begin and end? My hypothesis is that the film is not Bill's dream, but that it is constructed as a dream thanks to the play of cross-references and repetitions. These features are present in the other adaptations, too, even if they are not as stressed as they are in *Eyes Wide Shut*. The director himself compares films to dreams:

> I think an audience watching a film or a play is in a state very similar to dreaming, and that the dramatic experience becomes a kind of controlled dream ... the important point here is that the film communicates on a subconscious level, and the audience responds to the basic shape of the story on a subconscious level, as it responds to a dream. (Weinraub, 1972: 26)

Symmetries and Order

When Michel Ciment asked Kubrick what had most attracted him to Burgess's *A Clockwork Orange*, the director replied: "Everything, the plot, the characters, the ideas. I was also interested in how close the story was to fairy tales and myths, particularly in its deliberately heavy use of coincidence and plot summary" (Ciment, 2003: 163). Indeed, the symmetries of the plot of the novel and the repetition of sentences were highlighted in the new medium. The symmetries praised by the director occur between the first and the third part of the book. The novel is divided by the author into three parts, and Kubrick's adaptation closely follows the plot of the book, except for the end and a few other scenes. In the first part, the protagonist Alex (Malcolm McDowell) and his *droogs* are free to rob shops, hit and murder people, and rape women. At the end of the first part, the protagonist, after having quarreled with his *droogs* about the leadership of the group, and after having entered into the cat lady's house (Miriam Karlin), a rich madam who lives in a villa in the countryside, is hit by his friends and left defenseless outside the woman's front door. When the police arrive, he is arrested and charged with the violation and, when the lady later dies at the hospital, for her murder. In the second part, Alex is in prison and agrees to commute his detention with the Ludovico treatment. This cure, which consists of being obliged to see violent films after a "drug" is injected into the patient's veins, modifies the criminal's reflexes: the patient, after the treatment, should be compelled towards good by being incapable of committing evil. In the third part, Alex is free and cured, but he happens to meet some of the people who, during the first part, had been victims of his violence and are now eager to deliver retribution. The protagonist is finally compelled to commit suicide, but he survives. The doctors delete the results of the Ludovico treatment, and Alex is again free to commit devilish actions without feeling ill. The novel, unlike the film, ends with a protagonist who, having grown up, decides to change his life and find a suitable wife with whom to constitute a family. The plot of the film is similar to that of the novel and the symmetries of the story of the book are present in the story of the adaptation, too.[1]

The beginning of the last chapter of the novel is curiously similar to the beginning of the first chapter. The events narrated, the order in which they are recounted, and often the phrases used to tell them are similar. For example, here is how the first and the last chapter, respectively, open:

"What's it going to be then, eh?" There was me, that is Alex, and my three droogs, that is Pete, Georgie, and Dim, Dim being really dim, and we sat in the Korova Milkbar making up our rassoodocks what to do with the evening, a flip dark chill winter bastard though dry. (Burgess, 2000a: 3)

"What's it going to be then, eh?" There was me, Your Humble Narrator, and my three droogs, that is Len, Rick, and Bully, Bully being called Bully because of his bolshy big neck and very gromky goloss which was just like some bolshy great bull bellowing auuuuuuuuh. We were sitting in the Korova Milkbar making up our rassoodocks what to do with the evening, a flip dark chill winter bastard though dry. (2000a: 132)

Thus, even if the protagonist has grown up and decided to change his life—that is to say, even if the beginning and the end of the novel are different from the point of view of the story—they are symmetrical from the point of view of the language. In Kubrick's film, there is not this symmetry of language, but the story does end as it begins. Indeed, in the very last sequence Alex, after the effects of the Ludovico treatment have been erased, imagines himself making love to a girl in front of some spectators and claims: "I was cured all right." Therefore, the protagonist seems to have remained enclosed in the symmetrical structure of the plot. Unlike Burgess's protagonist, who, at the end, is able to regenerate himself, Kubrick's protagonist is unable to change his nature. The "happy ending" is sacrificed in the name of the plot.

The director's protagonist also remains entrapped in the superbly composed images and the scenes, which seem similar. For example, the first few shots of the sequence in which Alex and his *droogs* enter Mr. Alexander's (Patrick Magee) home for the first time are similar to the first shots of the scene in which the protagonist goes into this same house for the second time. During these shots, the position of the camera and its distance from the elements of the *mise-en-scène* is the same, as are the movements of the camera. These similarities stress, on the one hand, the symmetries between these two sequences, and between the first and the third part of the film. On the other hand, transforming the latter scene in a *déjà vu*, they increase the dreamy, unreal atmosphere of the film. The protagonist seems entrapped in a dreamy world, where he happens to visit the same places and the same characters twice. Alex is a character of a dreamy, labyrinthine diegetic world, one in which his will and strength are overcome by geometry.

Figure 3.1 Alex and his *droogs* at the Korova Milkbar.

The order also dominates single images in which the protagonist seems, once more, framed in a devilish order at the service of symmetry. For example, in the first sequence of the film, at the Korova Milkbar, Alex and his *droogs* are exactly in the vanishing point of the frame. On their left and on their right, the other customers and the bouncers, as well as the tables and milk distributors (which have the shape of naked women and were modeled on Allen Jones's statues), are composed symmetrically. The camera begins with a close-up of the protagonist, who looks directly into it with a typically Kubrickian stare, and then zooms out until the entire room is in frame (see Figure 3.1). The zoom out, thanks to the symmetry of the *mise-en-scène* and the fact that characters do not move, seems to entrap Alex in the vanishing point. His voice-over directly addresses the spectators, as does his gaze, but his lips and body are still. He seems like a puppet who stares at the public while the ventriloquist speaks for him. He, together with the other characters, seems like a statue among other statues.

Like the protagonist of *A Clockwork Orange* remains entrapped in symmetries, the protagonist of *Eyes Wide Shut* seems enclosed in his own world. Just as Kubrick stressed the symmetrical plot construction of Burgess's novel, he also underlined that of Schnitzler's novella. Indeed, *Eyes Wide Shut* can be divided into two parts. Before and after the orgy Bill visits the same places. In the first part, he begins to wander through New York City, after his wife Alice (Nicole Kidman) confesses to him that she would have left him and their daughter to spend even only one night with a man who had looked at her for a few minutes. He meets several women: Marion (Marie Richardson), the daughter of one of his patients, who confesses her love for him; the prostitute Domino (Vinessa Shaw), who invites him to her house; and the daughter of the owner of a costume rental shop (Leelee Sobieski), who embraces him. Finally, he manages to enter a mansion where an orgy takes place, but he is abruptly expelled, in the process risking his very life. In both media, the protagonist visits Marion/Marianne's apartment, Domino/Mizzi's house, Sonata Café/the coffeehouse, the costume rental shop, and the orgy mansion both before and after the orgy episode. But, unlike the novel, the adaptation shows Bill, following the orgy, again in Ziegler's mansion and in his medical office, which are the other two interiors shown in the first part of the film (other than his apartment). Indeed, the ball, which in the novella is recounted through a narrator's flashback, becomes in the film an episode that takes place in Victor's mansion. The scene (which also takes place in Ziegler's mansion) during which Victor explains to Bill what happened at the orgy does not appear in the novel either. Similarly, while in the first part of the film we are shown the protagonist's medical office, in the book we read about Fridolin's workday through another narrator's flashback. In the second part of the adaptation, another scene is shot again in Bill's medical office, whereas, in the novel, this episode takes place at the polyclinic, a space that is not described in the first part of the book.[2]

What is more, just as the end of *A Clockwork Orange* cannot be considered a "happy ending" like the one written by Burgess, the end of *Eyes Wide Shut* is not as optimistic as that in Schnitzler's book. Indeed, in both media, when the protagonist decides to confess all of his experiences to his wife, she prefers not to listen to the word "forever," unlike a traditional heroine. But the novel ends with the narrator's description of "a triumphant sunbeam coming in between the curtains, and a child's gay laughter from the adjacent room, another day began" (Schnitzler, 1999: 99). On the other hand, the last word of the film is Alice's imperative "fuck":

> ALICE: The important thing is we're awake now and hopefully for a long time to come.
> BILL: Forever.
> ALICE: Forever?
> BILL: Forever.
> ALICE: Let's not use that word. You know? It frightens me. But, but I do love you and you know there is something very important that we need to do as soon as possible.

BILL: What's that?
ALICE: Fuck.

Unlike in the novella, at the very end of the adaptation, the couple is not alone in their bedroom. Alice and Bill are in a toyshop together with other families, lit by artificial light and surrounded by toys that their girl would like to purchase. Therefore, Alice's solution, in this context, seems to assume consumerist connotations. This is underlined also by the diegetic music, the song "Jingle Bells," which seems to emphasize the economic aspects of the Christmas context. Moreover, the credits at the end are accompanied by the extradiegetic music *Jazz Suite, Waltz 2* by Dmitri Shostakovich, the piece that the spectators have listened to at the very beginning of the film. Therefore, the piece that has opened the film ends it encircling, closing in on itself, as if nothing has changed, as if to underscore that the protagonist and the spectators have only enjoyed a gorgeous, magnificent spectacle.

As in *A Clockwork Orange*, in *Eyes Wide Shut* the symmetries of the plot construction are emphasized by some episodes that mirror one another and by some superbly composed images. For example, when the protagonist enters the orgy mansion, the *mise-en-scène* evokes a theatrical play. And when the orgy participants find out that Bill is an uninvited guest, this theatrical play is staged again so as to enclose the protagonist, who remains a victim of these spectacular, superbly composed images. Indeed, the main salon of the orgy mansion, where a strange rite is taking place when Bill enters, has a rectangular plan, one central nave, and two lateral aisles divided from the nave by columns. Like a theatre, it has two galleries over the lateral aisles, and one that connects them over the main entrance. In the middle of the nave are eleven women, assembled in a circle, and at the center is a man with a purple hood. All of the spectators watch the rite from either the nave, the aisles, or the galleries. Taking as a reference point the main entrance, Nightingale is at the opposite side, turned towards the wall, and Bill is on the right, under the gallery, turned towards the middle of the salon. What is more, the purple mask and the women are on a square red carpet on which is reflected a bright circle of light that encloses them, as if they were actors lit on a dark stage. The other masks, like spectators in a theatre, remain in the shadow (see Figure 3.2). In the novel, instead, the main room is rendered more through the light than through its architecture, and the description does not refer either to a particular geometry or to a theatrical play. Indeed, the main saloon is "a dark, dimly

Plot Construction: A Chaotic Geometry

Figure 3.2 The beginning of the orgy.

Figure 3.3 The end of the orgy.

lit, high-ceilinged room, draped with black silk hangings" (1999: 44) "in almost total darkness" (1999: 48). The obscurity that characterizes it is in opposition to the "dazzling light" (1999: 46) and the "brilliantly lit adjacent room" (1999: 48, 50) from which the women reappear completely naked, except for their veils and lace masks. Then the guests, previously dressed as monks, transform themselves into colorful cavaliers, and run to dance with the women. In the book, then, the orgy participants are not spectators but instead are actively involved in a wild dance.

In the adaptation, when Bill is unmasked as an impostor, the representation is repeated. When he approaches the purple mask, who has a blue mask at each side, the spectators enclose the four characters into a circle, delineating a round stage in the same position as before, and lit in the same way. The woman who will sacrifice herself to save Bill is on the gallery. When the stage is constituted, the spectators have taken their positions, and Bill, asked about the password, gives the wrong answer, the play begins as it did at the beginning of the orgy (see Figure 3.3). Again, in the novel, the description does not evoke either a theatrical play or a particular geometry, and there is no similarity between this episode and the one describing the beginning of the orgy.

During both scenes in the film, neither the spectators nor the camera enter into the circle (defined by the eleven women and by the spectators, respectively), as if this circle constituted a stage. Whenever the camera approaches it, it begins to track around it in a counterclockwise direction. During the "plays" we, as spectators, thanks to the movements of the camera, have the impression of being able to see everything, to move everywhere around the stage, as in an Elizabethan theatre where spectators could watch the representation in the yard around the stage and in the galleries. Also, the position of the mysterious woman does not have to confuse us because the gallery over the stage was often used by actors, as in the case of *Romeo and Juliet*. Thus, Bill remains enclosed in the circle that he has gazed upon and entrapped in the spectacle that he has admired. As the symmetrical plot structure entraps him, the geometry of the spectacle at the orgy, which is the very center of the symmetry of the *syuzhet*, encloses him. The structure of the orgy reproduces the superstructure of the plot.

Like Bill, the protagonist of *Barry Lyndon* remains enclosed in the *syuzhet* construction that can be defined symmetrically split into two parts. The center of the symmetry, which coincides with the passage from the first to the second part, is the sequence in which the protagonist Barry (Ryan O'Neal) marries Lady Lyndon (Marisa Berenson), entering into the aristocracy and gaining wealth. The division of the film into two main parts—Barry's rise and fall—is emphasized by the titles. Indeed, the first scene is preceded by the title: "Part I: By what means Redmond Barry acquired the style and title of Barry Lyndon." And the sequence in which Barry marries Lady Lyndon is separated from the previous one by the title: "Part II: Containing an account of the misfortunes and disasters which befell Barry Lyndon." In the first part Barry, for his first love Nora (Gay Hamilton), has to challenge Captain Quin (Leonard Rossiter) to a duel and, after having defeated him, begins to wander through Europe. First, he enrolls in the army and fights during the Seven Years' War, then, when he manages to escape from the army, he meets Chevalier De Balibari (Patrick Magee), and he gets rich playing cards. Finally, he marries Lady Lyndon, a

Figure 3.4 Extreme long shot of Barry's father, on the left, and his adversary, on the right.

Figure 3.5 Extreme long shot of Barry, on the left, and Captain Quin, on the right.

rich and noble widow, and he strives to gain a peerage. But his access into the aristocracy is forbidden by his stepson Lord Bullingdon (Leon Vitali), who fights to preserve his mother's dignity, as well as his family's fortune and name. The end of the adaptation mirrors its beginning: Barry begins and ends his adventures as a wanderer, and the cause of his misfortune is always a woman. In the novel, the plot does not share this symmetry and structure. Indeed, the book is divided into nineteen chapters, and Barry marries Lady Lyndon in the sixteenth chapter—not in the middle of his story, but almost at the end. Moreover, while in the adaptation the duration of the two parts is almost identical (56 percent and 44 percent, respectively), in the book their duration is very different (75 percent and 25 percent).³ Therefore, the director has deliberately changed the construction and division of the *syuzhet* of the novel, emphasizing the rise and fall of the protagonist. What is more, in the book the end does not evoke the beginning because the protagonist is arrested and finishes his days in prison, where he writes his memoirs.

In the film, Barry, like Bill and Alex, is imprisoned in the geometry of the plot because he continuously falls into situations that evoke one another as if they were *déjà vu*. For example, the episodes that show a duel and those that show the birthday and funeral of Barry's son, Bryan (David Morley), are linked thanks to the *mise-en-scène*, the dialogue, and the extradiegetic music. The first scene of the film is made up of an extreme long shot of the duel between Barry's father and another gentleman, during which the camera remains still. Following the order of the plot, during the second duel Barry fights against Captain Quin and they use pistols, as in the first sequence. In both scenes: the duels take place outside, in a wild landscape; Barry, like his father, is on the left of the frame, while their adversaries are on the right; and even if the latter sequence is constituted by several shots, there are four extreme long shots. Indeed, the first shot is a close-up of pistols, then the camera zooms out to an extreme long shot, and, more remarkably, when Barry and Captain Quin shoot, they are framed in an extreme long shot (see Figure 3.4 and Figure 3.5).

During the third duel, Barry fights against Lord Ludd (Steven Berkoff) for money: they use swords and duel outdoors, not in a wild landscape, but among columns and arcs. Again the first shot is a long shot: Barry is on the left of the frame, while Lord Ludd on the right. During the last duel, Barry fights (again with pistols) against his stepson Lord Bullingdon. This scene takes place indoors, in a barn, and is made up of several shots: the first one is a close-up of hands putting a bullet in a pistol, not unlike the first shot of the duel with Captain Quin; and there are two long shots. Other elements that link these sequences are the noises and the music. Indeed, the first and the third sequence discussed above are accompanied by the crows singing, while the second and the fourth scene are accompanied by the same extradiegetic music, *Sarabande*, by G. F. Händel. These similarities, linking all of the sequences in which a duel is staged, stress how Barry seems to be compelled to fight throughout his story. In the novel, instead, the only duel that is thoroughly described is the duel with Captain Quin. Thus, there are no similarities among the protagonist's duels.

In the adaptation, the episodes of Bryan's birthday and funeral also evoke one another aesthetically. Indeed, the seventh shot of the birthday

Plot Construction: A Chaotic Geometry 67

Figure 3.6 Bryan's birthday.

Figure 3.7 Bryan's funeral.

sequence is a *plan américain* of Bryan on a white carriage, which is pulled by white sheep and accompanied by other children. The carriage moves from left to right, and the camera tracks with it and zooms out until Barry and Lady Lyndon appear in front of the carriage, guiding the sheep. The funeral scene is constituted by a long shot of Bryan's coffin on the same white carriage, pulled by the same white sheep. The carriage moves from right to left, and the camera tracks with it and zooms out until some children, who guide the sheep, and the mourning procession, which follows the carriage, appear in frame. The camera then zooms in on Barry and Lady Lyndon who are in front of the procession. These two sequences are different only because the episodes that they show are opposite (a birthday party and a funeral) and because the carriage and, consequently, the camera move in the former case from left to right (following our way of reading), and in the latter case from right to left, emphasizing the difficulty of accepting such a situation (see Figure 3.6 and 3.7). Unlike in the film, the episode of Bryan's birthday party does not appear in the novel, and his funeral is only briefly mentioned.

In the adaptation, the links between these two scenes are stressed also by the stylistic similarities between the two sequences that accompany them. In both cases Barry, sitting on Bryan's bed, recounts a story about a fight against a French regiment. During the scene after Bryan's birthday, Barry recounts the same story before Bryan falls asleep. Barry's mother (Marie Kean) is sitting behind Barry on the bed, Bryan is on the left of the frame, and Barry on the right. During the sequence that precedes Bryan's death, Barry recounts the story again. Lady Lyndon is sitting on the other side of the bed, Bryan is on the right of the frame, and Barry on the left. Therefore, the position of father and son in this scene is specular to that of the previous sequence. Bryan's funeral becomes a *déjà vu* of his birthday party and the latter seems, *a posteriori*, to announce the former. Thus, Barry's story seems to conform to the symmetrical structure of the plot and of the episodes, he seems entrapped within the order of the *auteur*'s diegetic world.

Like *Barry Lyndon*, *2001: A Space Odyssey* has a plot strongly ordered into parts. Indeed, as discussed in the previous chapter, the film, unlike Clarke's short story and novel, is divided by the director into four main parts through titles. These parts seem to evoke both the division of the section about man-apes into four episodes and the four Bowman transformations in the very last scene of the film. Indeed, the section about man-apes is divided into four episodes by fades out and in, and each episode develops a different situation. During the very last sequence, Bowman is progressively shown to get older in three stages, and the last transformation he undergoes is into a star-child. These divisions in the cinematic medium seem to follow a progression: an evolution from man-apes to star-children in the whole film, from man-apes to men in the first section, and from astronauts to star-children in the very last scene. The novel, instead, is divided into six main parts, the episode of man-apes is constituted by six chapters, and Bowman undergoes one transformation only, becoming a star-child. Thus, the last episode of the astronaut's transformation does not echo the first one with man-apes.

Don Daniels (1970/1971) traces a parallel between the symmetries of the plot, and the organization of sonata-allegro form, and the motivic development in symphonic music. He claims that the prologue of the film—that is, the section about man-apes—and some themes developed during these episodes can be interpreted as cinematic equivalents of sonata-allegro form and motivic development in symphonic music. Then, extending the parallel between the cinematic medium and symphonic music to the whole film, the scholar claims that the prologue generates the entire structure of the film, as the opening movement of a symphony introduces the music principles to be developed during the whole composition. Daniels's interpretation seems to be guided by a director's statement in which he claims that "the problem with movies is that since the talkies the film industry has historically been conservative and word-oriented. The three-act play has been the model. It's time to abandon the conventional view of the movie as an extension of the three-act play" (Gelmis, 1970: 90). In all of Kubrick's adaptations discussed up to now, symmetries often furnish another way of interpreting the films. Instead of following the plot along the straight line that, from the outset, leads the spectators towards the end, there are other, more interesting and complex paths that trace a labyrinth of cross-references in which meanings are infinitely multiplied.

As with *Barry Lyndon* and *2001: A Space Odyssey*, *Full Metal Jacket*'s plot, as discussed in the previous chapter, is strongly divided into parts. This order is mirrored by the first part, which is constituted by iterative sequences, and by the atmosphere that envelops the Marine Corps Recruit Depot. This ordered rhythm is emphasized by the equalization of the recruits and the *mise-en-scène* of the barracks. Indeed, all of the recruits have their hair shaven and wear the same uniforms, during the day a green uniform with black combat boots, during the night white underwear and colorful rubber flip-flop shoes. At least at the beginning of the film there is no distinction among them (except for Pyle [Vincent D'Onofrio], who is overweight). This choice seems to be emphasized from the very first sequence, in which the spectators are shown a series of medium close-ups of the recruits as their hair is shaven. Each shot is separated from the subsequent shot by a cut and lasts for a few seconds. The camera does not linger on any recruit in particular, photographing all of them from a straight-ahead angle. Furthermore, none of the faces in frame presents an expression worth noticing. Thus, no recruit is given more importance than another. The sequence introduces the order and discipline of the training camp where all the recruits are transformed into the same perfect marine. The equalization is evident also in the virtual absence of dialogue among them, which does not allow the spectators to know their thoughts and character. Indeed, except for the sequences in which Joker explains to

Pyle how to assemble and disassemble his rifle, how to take care of himself, and how to correctly do the other exercises, the first time that the spectators listen to a dialogue between the recruits is when Pyle explains to Joker that he is afraid of not being able to become a marine, and of being hated by everybody. This sort of dialogue is not frequent in the subsequent scenes. Indeed, the audience hears only Cowboy (Arliss Howard) encouraging Joker to hit Pyle, and Joker and Cowboy speaking about the latter's sister and Pyle. In Hasford's novel, instead, the recruits are differentiated from the beginning. For example, the narrator claims: "A wiry little Texan in horn-rimmed glasses the guys are already calling 'Cowboy'" (Hasford, 1980: 4). The readers can infer that the recruits have already had the time to know each other, and to develop their own nicknames. What is more, in the book, the readers know from the beginning that the narrator is homodiegetic, and can thus distinguish between him and the other recruits: "I laugh. Years of high school drama classes have made me a mimic" (1980: 4). The narrator often gives information regarding his thoughts and about his past. On the other hand, as is discussed in the next chapter, in the adaptation the spectators do not listen to such notions regarding the recruits' character either through the dialogue or the voice-over. Moreover, the spectators only begin to associate the voice-over with Joker at the end of the first part: "Our last night on the island. I draw fire watch."

This order is also mirrored by the *mise-en-scène*. The barracks is rectangular. Along the two longer walls there are two rows of double-tiered metal bunks, and along each of the shorter walls there is a door. The two rows of bunks are symmetrical as are the two doors. Along the two longer walls there are huge, symmetrical windows, from which a white light filters during the day and a light blue light during the night. The walls are green and white—the sheets and the recruits' underwear are white, and the blankets and the uniforms are green. In the novel, apart from the description of the bunks, which corresponds to the images shown in the adaptation, there is no mention about the décor of the barracks. But there is, at the very beginning, a brief allusion to the symmetry that reigns in the college at Parris Island, which is said to be "constructed in a swamp on an island, symmetrical but sinister like a suburban death camp" (1980: 3). Therefore, the choice to highlight the symmetry of the barracks is, once more, an *auteur*'s mark.

In *The Shining*, the geometry of the *mise-en-scène* is symbolized by the corridors of the Overlook Hotel, and by the maze outside it. Davide Manti (2003) writes that the symmetry versus the asymmetry of the architecture of the hotel becomes a metaphor of the mind. Indeed, the buildings that constitute the hotel, unified by the huge roof, are symmetrical, while the corridors inside it are asymmetrical. Thus, the interior of the Overlook symbolizes an evil brain that organizes its inhabitants' lives. Everything outside and inside it is enormous, and the building wants to dominate its characters, not only scattering them in the vastness of its corridors, but also imprisoning them. The building is a body that contains other bodies, like a mind that contains its visions and its paths. But, as is argued in this chapter, the chaos that disrupts the symmetry seems more the result of the use of the Steadicam than the particular architecture of the façade of the Overlook Hotel. What is more, there are other elements of the interior of the hotel that suggest order and symmetry, such as the geometrical design of the carpet and the geometrical disposition of Danny's (Danny Lloyd) toy cars, and the architecture of the Colorado Lounge.

Chaos

In Kubrick's adaptations, the geometrical plot structure, emphasized by the symmetries among sequences and the superbly composed images, is often disrupted. For example, although in *2001: A Space Odyssey* disorder would seem to be banned, there are some images, shot inside Discovery, which seem to introduce a chaotic element in the ordered lives of the two astronauts, Bowman and Poole. Indeed, in some shots the symmetry of their acting is so exaggerated that they seem one, each the specular double of the other. The effort to distinguish between them, and the easiness with which they could be confused, seems to introduce disorder in the organized life of Discovery, and to announce its disruption through HAL 9000. When David is eating and watching a recorded program on a monitor, Frank sits down next to him and begins to eat and watch the program, as his companion is doing. Bowman uses his left hand to eat, while Poole uses his right; David's tray is on his left and his monitor is on his right, while Frank's tray is on his right and his monitor is on his left. Bowman's face is not visible, and his hair is the same color and the same cut as that of Poole (see Figure 3.8). Therefore, if it weren't for their different clothes, one of the two astronauts could have been the reflected image of the other. These shots are intercut with images of HAL's eye. Indeed, the computer is identified through red eyes, which strongly recall the lens of a camera, and which are disseminated throughout the spacecraft and on the pods.

Figure 3.8 Bowman and Poole in symmetrical poses.

When David and Frank speak about HAL's disconnection inside a pod, and the computer manages to understand their words by reading their lips, the two astronauts pose again symmetrically, and these images are, once more, preceded and intercut with shots of HAL's eye. In both scenes, HAL's menacing eye seems to break the symmetry, the invisible mirror between the two astronauts, and it will soon disrupt the bond by killing Poole. Thus, order, in part compromised by the possible confusion between Bowman and Poole, seems to lead to chaos.

The symmetry that dominates Kubrick's films is definitely overwhelmed by the use of a handheld camera or a Steadicam. As discussed in the previous chapter, in *2001: A Space Odyssey* the handheld camera is used when Dr. Floyd and other astronauts approach the monolith on Crater Tycho. The aliens' artifact provokes in the astronauts an excitement that confuses them. And this intellectual uncertainty and agitation is mirrored and emphasized by trembling images.

The intellectual chaos becomes, in *A Clockwork Orange*, physical chaos. The excitement for the unknown possibilities of the universe is substituted by excitement for violence. The handheld camera seems to be used to involve the spectators in the characters' syncopated ballet of violence. For example, when the *droogs* enter Mr. Alexander's house, before Alex begins to sing "Singin' in the Rain" while dancing, a handheld camera seems to underline the shock of Mr. Alexander and his wife. The spectators seem to be encouraged to share their bewilderment, thanks to the confusion created by a quick montage, as well as the *droogs*' speedy movements and the trembling images. But the handheld camera also disrupts the order of the previous shots, when the writer and his wife are shown alone. A handheld camera is also used in the sequence in which the protagonist manages to enter the cat lady's house. When the spectators are shown the living room where the lady is doing her exercises, they see paintings of naked women in erotic poses pinned on the walls, as well as the back of the cat lady (who is assuming a position quite similar to those of the subjects of her paintings). Thus, the woman's pose evokes the paintings around her, and the order in the composition of the image is emphasized by these similarities. But this geometry is disrupted when the cat lady seizes a Beethoven bust and begins to run towards Alex, who grasps a penis statue to defend himself. Indeed, the scene is shot with a handheld camera and is accompanied by *The Thieving Magpie*. The ballet begins: the characters move in circle, the camera follows them around accentuating, with its jolting, their turns, as if they were dancing a waltz. The montage follows the rhythm of the music, stressing the tempo of the scene. Thanks to the handheld camera, the viewers seem to take part in the turnarounds of the character's dance, and the order that dominated this scene is destroyed.

The geometry of *Barry Lyndon* is also violently disrupted by those scenes in which a handheld camera is used. Trembling images seem to annihilate the atmosphere of static perfection that envelops the sequences. For example, Lord Bullingdon and Bryan enter into a room during a concert, the former in his stocking feet, the latter in the former's shoes, slapping his feet and, thus, disturbing the music of the orchestra and the silence of the spectators. In front of everybody, Lord Bullingdon accuses his stepfather, and Barry begins to violently hit him. When the protagonist fights against his stepson, the camera is handheld to underline their rage. Henceforth, Barry's decline will be even more evident: in the subsequent scenes, he is shown alone on a terrace; then, dining alone; and, finally, checking his bills. His desire to gain a peerage becomes impossible. Therefore, the handheld camera has not only destroyed the calm perfection of the concert, but also the protagonist's ambitions. Similarly, Lady Lyndon's agony for the loss of Bryan is underlined through the use of a handheld camera. When she tries to commit suicide, and writhes and groans for her pain, the handheld camera accentuates her grief. A character who has always been shown moving slowly, sumptuously, perfectly dressed and made up, is now in frame in her nightgown, with ruffled hair, and her uncontrolled acting is stressed by the handheld camera.

Unlike in *2001: A Space Odyssey* and in *Barry Lyndon*, where a handheld camera is used economically, and not unlike *A Clockwork Orange*, where it is often used, in the third part of *Full Metal Jacket*, when Joker and the other soldiers fight the Viet Cong in Hue, a Steadicam is operated to emphasize the chaos of war, the "grunts'" bewilderment and fear, and to increase the realism of the sequences. Indeed, Kubrick himself claims: "I was after a realistic, documentary look in the film, especially in the combat footage. Even the Steadicam shots were deliberately made less steady to get a newsreel effect" (Ciment, 2003: 246). For example, in the sequence in which Touchdown (Ed O'Ross), the leader of the protagonist's squad, is shot, a Steadicam is adopted to follow the soldiers. It moves at the same speed as the "grunts," as if it was another soldier. When the squad proceeds under the enemy fire, trying to hide behind rocks and ruins, the Steadicam is kept almost at ground level. When somebody is killed, the camera remains still, as when Touchdown and Hand Job (Marcus D'Amico) are shot. These same stylistic patterns are also used when a sniper attacks the squad. Indeed, apart from a few exceptions, in almost all of the shots in which the camera tracks to keep the soldiers in frame, following their steps, a Steadicam is operated at ground level. During this sequence, as in the previous one, when someone is killed, the camera does not move. Thus, the Steadicam seems like a soldier among "grunts," emphasizing the disruption of the geometry that dominated the first part of the film. But the chaos of war had already pervaded the barracks of the Marine Recruit Depot at Parris Island through the movements of the camera.

Indeed, during some of the sequences shot in the barracks, it is possible to find the disorder, a loss of orientation paradoxically due to their being too ordered. The spectators strive to understand where the sergeant is in relation to the two doors and to the recruits or where the recruits are in relation to one another and to the two main doors. For example, at the beginning of the film, when Sergeant Hartman presents himself and the training course, as in a classical Hollywood film, there is an establishing shot through which the spectators can understand the characters' position in relation to the locale and to one another. There follow shots of each of the main characters, so that the audience gets to know them. But during these shots, the spectators cannot exactly understand where the sergeant is in relation to the two doors and to the other recruits. Indeed, calling the wall where there is the door with the sign "Exit" north-wall, the opposite wall south-wall, and the two longer walls east- and west-wall, respectively, the sergeant, during the first shot walks along the west-wall from north to south, then along the south-wall from west to east, and, finally, along the east-wall from south to north. Therefore, he walks in a kind of circle, returning almost to his initial position, thereby increasing the spectators'

Plot Construction: A Chaotic Geometry 75

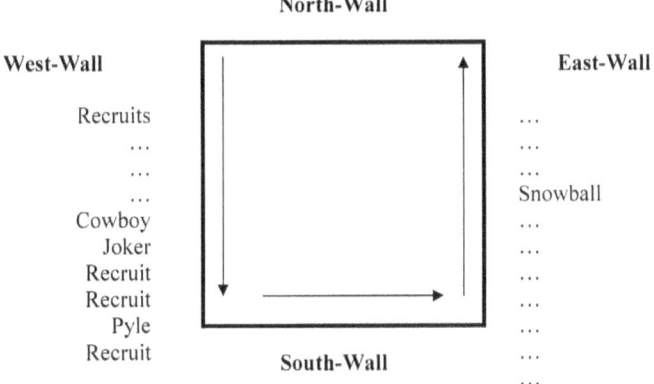

Figure 3.9 The figure reproduces the plan of the barracks. The arrows inside the rectangular symbolize the sergeant's movements. Along the west- and east-wall are the recruits' names in the order in which they first appear in frame.

lack of orientation. During this circle around the barracks, along the west-wall are visible, in the following order, from the north to the south: Cowboy (Arliss Howard), Joker, two other recruits, Pyle, and another recruit who closes the row. Along the east-wall is Snowball (Peter Edmund) (see Figure 3.9). But after some shot/reverse shots between the sergeant and Snowball, the position of the recruits along the west-wall changes. Indeed, in the last shots, from the north to the south, they are, in order: Pyle, another recruit, Cowboy, and Joker who closes the row. Given the fact that the director, up to now, seems to have wanted to increase the spectators' bewilderment, this change does not seem a mistake, but another trick to increase the disorder.

Furthermore, the sequence in which Sergeant Hartman asks Joker if he believes in the Virgin Mary is made up of a tracking shot followed by shot/reverse shots. Once again, during the first tracking shot, both the sergeant and the camera move circularly and, again, the sergeant from the north-wall walks towards the south and back to the north. What is more, the spectators are not shown the barracks from the north- to the south-wall, as in the previous sequences, but from the south- to the north-wall, thus increasing their loss of orientation. Therefore, when the sergeant walks along the barracks, the camera follows or precedes him pretty closely, thus avoiding an establishing shot that could help the spectators understand his position in relation to that of the recruits and the furniture. Furthermore, the sergeant moves in more than one direction during the same shot, and the camera follows or precedes him, thus increasing the spectators' disorientation. And the recruits' position changes. All of these techniques increase a feeling of discomfort, derived from the impossibility of guessing the movements of the camera and the sergeant and the positions of the recruits in a fictional world that would seem ordered. The spectators are tricked by an apparently predictable geometry, which veils the most intricate labyrinths, announcing the chaos of the Vietnam War.

As in *Full Metal Jacket*, where the barracks become a labyrinth, in *Eyes Wide Shut* the straight streets of New York city are transformed, through the film's *mise-en-scène* and montage, into a maze in which the protagonist and the spectators get lost. For example, when the protagonist leaves Marion (without considering the first two shots in which the spectators are shown a street at night in which Bill does not appear), six different streets can be distinguished. The audience has the impression that Bill is walking in a kind of square, returning back to the point of his departure. Indeed, along the first street he is shown walking from the left to the right of the image, along the second from the back to the rear, along the third from the right to the left, and along the fourth from the rear to the back. Actually, from the crossroad where Bill meets Domino, the audience can see the same shops of the first street. But along the fifth street, Bill is walking from the right to the left of the frame, and the shops that can be recognized are on the street which is perpendicular to that on which Bill is walking—not on the same street. The spectators could either conclude that the protagonist's wanderings are not in a square, and that the cuts are not matches on the action, but ellipses; or that the signboards and the façades are a mistake; or this mistake is voluntary, made not only to transform the New York streets into a maze, but also to create an effect of *déjà vu*. There are other cases in which the spectators could either think they are watching an involuntary mistake or experiencing a way in which they are entrapped in the labyrinthine, dreamy atmosphere of Kubrick's New York City. For example, Bill takes a yellow taxi to get from the Sonata Café to Rainbow Fashions. When he speaks to Milich (Rade Serbedzija) through the glass door, however, the audience can see reflected in the glass the signboards of Gillespie's and the Sonata Café. Furthermore, the *auteur*'s diegetic New York City becomes a maze because the streets are usually narrow and deserted, and Bill happens to find himself in new adventures every time that he turns a corner. Every place he visits seems close to each other.

The metaphor of the maze can also be used to describe the corridors of the orgy mansion into which Bill wanders. Indeed, he visits three rooms, walking across three corridors to reach them. Before a mask offers the protagonist the company of a woman, there are only his point of view shots alternated with shots in which he is shown watching erotic scenes. When Bill is walking along a new corridor, which leads him into another room, there is always a dissolve, while the various scenes shot inside the same room are divided by cuts. The use of dissolves and a Steadicam, which flexuously follows the protagonist's glances and wanderings, give the impression of a virtual tour, like wandering inside a labyrinth or a gallery of living paintings. The gorgeous bodies that copulate are always aesthetically settled on tables and chairs; they often constitute perfectly balanced human pyramids, and they repeat the same movements and follow the same rhythm. This journey through the labyrinthine mansion could be compared with those sacred Spanish representations that took place during the *Siglo de Oro*. They were staged on different carts that followed one another along the narrow streets of the boroughs (Molinari, 1996: 134–140). Much like those representations, in Kubrick's film each room seems like a cart, a *tableau vivant* performed to entertain the spectators' eyes.

The Steadicam in *Eyes Wide Shut* does not only follow Bill's wanderings through the corridors of the orgy mansion, but also his wife's dance with the Hungarian stranger Sandor Szavost (Sky Dumont) during the Christmas ball at Ziegler's. The couple moves around and the camera swirls around them, enveloping them, as if it was a tempter serpent that symbolizes Szavost's attempt to seduce Alice. The spectators lose their orientation, do not understand where the couple is in relation to the ballroom. This effect is emphasized by the fact that all of the other characters dance around in couples, and it is introduced by the first shots that show the Hungarian stranger approaching Alice. Indeed, when they meet each other, there is a 180-degree cut. When Sandor begins to talk with Alice, she is positioned on frame left and has her back to the camera, and the man is on frame right facing her. After a cut, the spectators are shown the Hungarian stranger on the left of the frame, facing Alice, and the woman on the right of the frame, facing Sandor. Falsetto comments: "The decision to cross the 180-degree axis and rupture one of the key conventions of classical continuity editing will significantly contribute to the film's oneiric, subjective presentation" (2001: 34). The windings of the couple and the Steadicam are recalled by the sinuous movements of the two models who speak with Bill. They seem, once more, to be two tempter serpents who try to envelop the protagonist. Thus, Bill and Alice remain entrapped

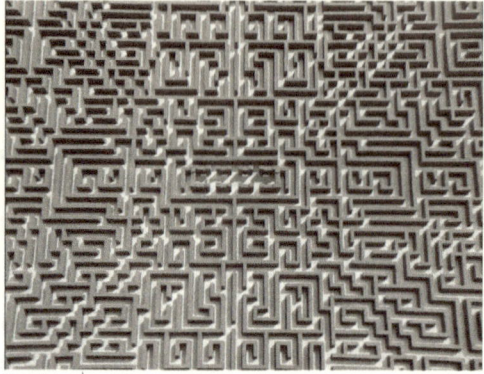

Figure 3.10 First shot of the sequence in which Wendy and Danny walk in the Overlook maze.

Figure 3.11 Shot of the map of the labyrinth.

from the very beginning of the film, and the protagonist continues his nightly wanderings through the labyrinthine streets of New York City and the corridors of the orgy mansion.

In *The Shining*, the labyrinth is not only evoked through the corridors of the Overlook Hotel, but is also represented by a real maze outside the hotel. The Overlook maze was entirely built at Elstree Studios in London, but during the film the spectators are not only shown this maze, but also two other reproductions of it: the map, shown on screen before Wendy (Shelley Duvall) and Danny run inside the real maze for the first time; and the model, on screen when Jack (Jack Nicholson), after having thrown a ball against the wall, goes to look down at it (see Figure 3.10, Figure 3.11, Figure 3.12 and Figure 3.13). It is as if the director would like to suggest to

Figure 3.12 Jack stares at the model of the maze.

Figure 3.13 Map of the labyrinth used during the shooting and shown in *Making The Shining* (Vivian Kubrick, USA and England, 1980).

the audience the secret of the maze, the power of crossing it without getting lost. At the same time, the geometry and symmetry of its paths is endlessly complicated by the use of the Steadicam, and by Jack's point of view or false point of view shot, that ends the last sequence mentioned above. Indeed, the relationship between the last shot of the scene in which Jack stares at the model of the labyrinth and the first shot of the subsequent sequence in which Wendy and Danny walk in the maze is uncertain. If the spectators believe in the supernatural powers of Mr. Torrance, they could interpret the latter shot as a point of view shot; otherwise they could read it as a false point of view shot. In any case, since this choice is left to the audience, it yet again increases their disorientation. What is more, the confusion is multiplied by the fact that the map is different from the model, and there is no other scene that enables the spectators to understand what the real design of the maze is. Finally, the real labyrinth, built and constructed for the shooting, is different both from the map and from the model.

In the film, the maze appears in four sequences: when Wendy and Danny run inside it to play; when Jack looks at the model of the maze in the Colorado Lounge; when mother and child again are shown walking in its paths; and when Mr. Torrance follows his son with an axe to kill him. During all of these scenes, the spectators cannot understand the characters' position inside the maze thanks to the montage and to the use of the Steadicam. Indeed, the shots are divided by cuts, and there often seems to be little continuity between them. Thus, the ellipses prevent the audience from understanding all of the characters' movements. The Steadicam follows their steps at their height, forbidding a wider view of the maze and, consequently, hiding their positions inside it.

The disorientation, which is provoked by the geometry of the labyrinth and the way of filming it, is the same that results from the scenes in which the Steadicam follows Danny riding his tricycle in the labyrinthine corridors of the Overlook Hotel. Indeed, the hotel, constituted of huge, luminous rooms and numerous corridors, becomes a maze when the Steadicam follows Danny at his height along a corridor, and seems to lose him when he turns right or left into another corridor, before reaching him again when the camera turns in his direction. For example, when Danny rides his tricycle through the kitchen and the Colorado Lounge, the camera tracks after him. He rides in the kitchen, then he turns left into a corridor, then left to cross the Colorado Lounge, then left into another corridor and, finally, left again along the kitchen, having ridden in a square. Similarly, before Danny meets the two Grady girls (Lisa and Louise Burns) while riding his tricycle, the suspense generated by the use of the Steadicam at the same height of the boy is greatly increased by the unexpected appearance of the two sisters. The geometry of the corridors of the Overlook Hotel, and of the paths of the maze, thanks to the montage and, above all, to the Steadicam, becomes chaotic, entrapping the characters and the spectators in a play of repetitions and *déjà vu*. All of the tracks seem the same, and this order given by their resemblance and geometry paradoxically brings a feeling of disorientation and *déjà vu* to the spectator.

In Kubrick's adaptations, chaos not only derives from too much order, as in *2001: A Space Odyssey* and *Full Metal Jacket*, or by the use of a handheld camera or a Steadicam, as in all his films, or by the image of the maze, as in *Eyes Wide Shut* and *The Shining*, but also from the play of cross-references among sequences. For example, in *Eyes Wide Shut*, the symmetry of the plot construction is completely disrupted by this play. Indeed, repetitions among scenes are so numerous that they create a dreamy atmosphere of *déjà vu*.

The episode of the Christmas ball at Ziegler's announces that of the orgy, through the presence of the same characters and the movements of the camera. Indeed, Nightingale plays the piano in both cases. Bill is approached by two models at the Christmas party and by two women at the orgy. Mandy, who does not physically play the role of the orgy woman who rescues the protagonist, but who is finally identified as her both at the morgue and during the final confrontation between Bill and Victor, is always naked and is always risking her life. Ziegler, during the last sequence mentioned above, confesses to having been present at the orgy. Finally, as regards the camera movements, the tracking around the stage, which is constituted first by the eleven women and then by the diegetic spectators, seems to evoke the tracking around Alice and the Hungarian stranger while they are dancing. In the novel, except for the fact that both at the carnival party and at the orgy the guests are masked, there is no link between these two episodes.

Similarly, the relationship between the first episode set at the costume shop and that of the orgy is stressed more in the adaptation than in the book. Indeed, the last scene of this episode in the film is shot inside a showroom, depicting Milich's daughter walking backwards and staring at Bill. The implicit availability that the girl seems to show to the protagonist, through her acting, could be thought of as an announcement of that of the orgy women. This consideration seems to be confirmed by the cut that ends this sequence, leaving the girl's desire suspended, and her image impressed in the spectators' mind. In the novel, instead, before Fridolin leaves the shop, the owner's daughter disappears behind a door, and the protagonist implores her father not to do her any harm. Thus, the protagonist, more than aroused by the girl's beauty and availability, seems to be concerned about her welfare. Moreover, in the film, references between this episode and the orgy can be found also in the presence of two Japanese men dressed up as women who seem to anticipate the masked men who dance cheek to cheek, following the notes of "Strangers in the Night," in an orgy room. In the adaptation, the similarities between the two episodes are also emphasized by the camera movements. Indeed, as already discussed, the camera, at the beginning of the orgy, does not enter into the circle made up of the naked women and, at the end of the episode, does not go into the circle formed by the diegetic spectators. Similarly, when Milich's daughter is shown with the two Japanese men in a room at the end of the showroom, the camera does not enter this room. The spectators are shown the entire scene through the glass door, as if the room was a stage and the audience was, together with Bill, spectator of a theatrical comedy. Through this choice, Bill's destiny, together with the audience's, seem to be announced: they will remain only spectators to the orgy, banned from its secrets.

Both in the novel and the film, it is the dream of the protagonist's wife that, more than all of the other episodes, recalls the orgy. The dream of Albertine, the novel's heroine, is longer and more complex than Alice's. Indeed, the former seems a mix of her memories, and of the experiences lived by her husband during his nightly wanderings. Alice's dream, instead, evokes the confession of her unfulfilled desire of infidelity through the mention of the naval officer, and echoes the orgy episode through the nakedness and the copulations:

> Then I was lying in a beautiful garden stretched out naked in the sunlight and a man walked out of the woods. He was, he was the man from the hotel, the one I told you about. The naval officer. He stared at me and then he just laughed. He just laughed at me. He was kissing me and then and then we were making love. Then there were all these other people around us, hundreds of them, everywhere. Everyone was fucking. And then I was, I was fucking other men. So many and I don't know how many I was with.

Thus, in this case, it is the book that accentuates the play of cross-references and *déjà vu* more than the adaptation. For example, in the novel, in Albertine's dream the galley slaves who row Fridolin, his being richly dressed, and the starry, blue sky (Schnitzler, 1999: 62–63) echo the tale recounted at the beginning of the book, the one that their daughter reads before falling asleep. Indeed, both at the beginning of the film and the novella, the protagonist's daughter reads a story. In the written medium, it seems to be a story taken from *A Thousand and One Nights*. In the cinematic version, it is a tale from *A Child's Garden of Verses*, according to an indication in the 1996 script (Kubrick and Raphael, 1996). In the adaptation, the little girl reads: "Before me when I jump into my bed." In the novel, her reading of the tale opens the book with a dreamy atmosphere; it is interrupted by her falling asleep:

"Twenty-four brown slaves rowed the splendid galley that would bring Prince Amgiad to the Caliph's palace. But the Prince, wrapped in his purple cloak, lay alone on the deck beneath the deep blue, star-spangled night sky, and his gaze—' Up to this point the little girl had been reading aloud; now, quite suddenly, her eyes closed. (1999: 3)

These sentences seem to be a prologue of Albertine's subsequent dream. Therefore, at the beginning of the novel, there is a girl who, while reading a dreamy tale, falls asleep, while later on there is her mother who, after having woken, recounts her dream. This play of cross-references is not adapted in the film, and thus it is less emphasized than in the novella. In both media, the female protagonist's dream seems to be a *mise-an-abyme* of the orgy. Alice's dream, more centered than Albertine's (thanks to the simplification of the latter) on her being unfaithful and on the orgy, seems to be another show staged for Bill and the audience. Thus, the orgy episode is endlessly reproduced inside the same work through different methods, both visually and verbally, becoming, as is discussed in Chapter VI, an example of the film's referentiality.

It seems important to note that to interpret Albertine/Alice's dream I have used Freud's concept of *déjà vu*, but I have not read either the dream or the entire story from a psychoanalytical point of view because, although Freud and Schnitzler exchanged some letters and knew and appreciated each other's work, any direct influence of the psychoanalyst upon the author and vice versa is unclear. Indeed, Freud never interpreted Schnitzler's novels and plays, but only briefly cited his *Paracelsus*: "A man of letters, who incidentally is also a physician—Arthur Schnitzler—has expressed this piece of knowledge very correctly in his [play] *Paracelsus*" (1905: 43–44). In a letter, dated May 8, 1906, Freud writes to Schnitzler: "For many years I have been conscious of the far-reaching conformity existing between your opinions and mine on many psychological and erotic problems" (1906). In another letter, dated May 14, 1922, Freud calls Schnitzler his "double," emphasizing the similarities between their works. But he also stresses the differences between their methods and purposes: "So I have formed the impression that you know through intuition—or rather from detailed self-observation—everything that I have discovered by laborious work on other people" (1922). And it is certain that the author read the psychoanalyst's works. Indeed, in 1900, mentioning one of his dreams in his diary, he wrote that it was "exactly one in Freud's *Dream Interpretation*" (Kupper and Rollman-Branch, 1959: 114–115). But he always denied having been inspired by him. When, in 1913, Reik wrote *Arthur Schnitzler as Psychologist* and claimed that Freud's influence was obvious in the author's 1912 story *Beata and Her Son*, Schnitzler strongly opposed his opinion (Kupper and Rollman-Branch, 1959: 114–115).

Usually, the play of cross-references is, in the novel, explicitly stressed by the narrative. Indeed, although the narrator is heterodiegetic, Fridolin's fluxes of conscience and flashbacks are often reported through direct and immediate speech, and the focalization is almost always internal and fixed, anchored to Fridolin (the position of the narrator's eye, and the spaces that this eye can or cannot see are defined by the adoption of a point of view that is called focalization. There is an internal focalization when the narrator's eye is in a character's eye, and the narrator can see only what the character at whom he is linked can see [Genette, 1976: 208–258]). Thus, his obsessions, his considerations, and his thoughts about his adventures mix all the episodes, whose borders merge in his mind. In the adaptation, these cross-references are implicitly translated and emphasized by the *mise-en-scène* and montage, more than by Bill's dialogue.

As already discussed, the chaos, derived from this play of cross-references and other cinematic techniques, implicitly undermines the narrative features of classical Hollywood films analyzed by David Bordwell and Kristin Thompson (1990). To comprehend and appreciate the adaptations, the spectators cannot follow the development of the plots through a causal chain, much like they cannot fill in the ellipses and solve the unexplained mysteries through the logic of cause and effect. To make sense of the enigmatic and chaotic diegetic worlds, they have to pursue the convoluted stylistic and structural choices of the director. As in poetry, in Kubrick's films similarity seems to be superimposed on contiguity and, thus, equivalence almost becomes the structuring principle of the films. Repetitions, *déjà vu*, and cross-references among images, sequences, and episodes, become an effective stylistic and narrative device. Similarly, in the next chapter, I discuss how the use of music in classical narrative sound films, analyzed by Claudia Gorbman (1987), is also subverted in the director's adaptations. Music becomes more eloquent than dialogue and voice-over, and offers another path to understand the complexity of the adaptations. Once more, equivalence seems to dominate not only the combination of words in dialogue and voice-over, but also their selection, and sentences seem to be chosen for their rhythm, as if they were pieces of music. Kubrick's films can be defined as sublime visual poems.

Chapter Four

MUSIC, DANCE, AND DIALOGUE

The Metaphor of Dance

Claudia Gorbman claims that, in classical narrative sound films, music occupies a background role in comparison with other elements, such as characters' actions and dialogue, which usually aid in the progression of the story.

> The classical narrative sound film has been constituted in such a way that the spectator does not normally (consciously) hear the film score. Music being non-narrative and non-representational takes a back seat, as it were, to the viewer's principal object of attention—the story, the characters: the diegesis . . . The spectator tends to be conscious of discourse (elements, including music, that enunciate the story) only insofar as it "transgresses" or "interrupts" story (that which is enunciated). (1987: 31)

One of the main features of music in classical narrative sound film is, according to Gorbman, its "inaudibility" because music should "subordinate itself to dialogue, to visuals—i.e., to the primary vehicles of narrative" (1987: 73). However, in Kubrick's adaptations, music is not only foregrounded, becoming audible, but it also helps the progression of the story, often moving and motivating characters' actions, as in the case of *A Clockwork Orange*. What is more, music is an indispensable element in the creation and development of the metaphor of dance. Through this expression I define the sequences in which the characters' movements and/or the montage follow the rhythm of music. The scenes seem to emanate from music itself, and the *mise-en-scène*, the editing, and the music enrich and transform one another.

In what follows, I discuss how and why this metaphor is used in *2001: A Space Odyssey*, *A Clockwork Orange*, and *Full Metal Jacket*. In the case of the second film, I also address the scenes in which the protagonist's actions are guided by music. Finally, to underline how much the metaphor of ballet is a constant in Kubrick's last six adaptations, I briefly cite relevant sequences of *Barry Lyndon*, *The Shining*, and *Eyes Wide Shut*.

2001: A Space Odyssey is a sublime visual and aural experience about the wonders of space and celestial bodies, as well as the beauty of man's technological achievements. The slow, graceful movements of spaceships, accompanied by classical music, evoke the prettiness and almost weightlessness of classical dancers. The awe of the universe and technology is rendered through a ballet, which increases the joy and excitement provoked by this cinematic experience. The spacecraft peacefully float and revolve in a space full of celestial bodies, accompanied by slow camera movements, a harmonious montage, and Johann Strauss's *Blue Danube* waltz. This metaphor of dance does not appear in Clarke's novel, and it is therefore a feature that pertains only to the cinematic adaptation. As both Brooks Landon (1999) and Scott Bukatman (1999) argue, in science-fiction cinema the spectacle sustains the film, special effects characterize it, and, above all, the narrative stops to let the spectators appreciate and contemplate special effects. On the contrary, science-fiction literature remains primarily a narrative medium. I suggest that in Kubrick's film the narrative does not stop when the metaphor of dance appears, but rather advances. The development of the story, at least as it is understood in classical narrative Hollywood films, does not seem to be the director's principal concern. Kubrick seems more interested in a new kind of narrative that, thanks to special effects, involves the spectators in a visual and aural experience. In this respect, the metaphor of dance becomes a "meta-metaphor" of the dance of the spectators' minds. In Clarke's novel, when the narrative stops and a description about celestial and mechanical bodies begins, the readers are not involved in a ballet of the mind. Indeed, Clarke's prose is more concerned with narrative, descriptions of several phenomena, and possible explanations of them. He seems to adopt a scientific approach towards the mysteries of space, while Kubrick seems to choose a poetical, musical point of view. As discussed in the two previous chapters, the awe and wonder of space and time are evoked in the novel through descriptions and scientific hypotheses. In the film, however, the sublime is more immediately evoked through peculiar cinematic techniques. For example, *The Blue Danube* waltz accompanies the first two sequences set in space: when the spaceship Orion III travels from the Earth towards Space Station 1 near the Moon; and when a moonship travels from the space station towards Clavius Base on the Moon and lands inside it. The dance is not only evoked by the choice of music, but also by the slow camera movements and montage; the shape and movement of Space Station 1, which seems constituted by a pair of dancers, of matching wheels slowly revolving; the shape of the moonship, which seems like a ball slowly floating, a dancer approaching a group of other dancers; and the shape of Clavius Base, which opens the arms of its cupola in the middle of its concentric structure to welcome the new dancer moonship.

Aboard Orion III and the moonship, the dance continues thanks to the weightless movements of the hostesses. Indeed, when Dr. Floyd is asleep, his arm and his pen freely dance in the air, and the hostess, walking gracefully thanks to "grip shoes," grasps the pen as if she was catching a balloon. The magic of this scene is that the experience of moving in the absence of gravity is conveyed through a few shots, and is depicted like an ancient waltz. In the novel, the description of the hostess's walk stresses the technique involved in the possibility of walking in zero gravity and the difficulty of moving. There is neither magic nor dance:

> There was a slight buoyancy about her steps, and her feet came away from the floor reluctantly as if entangled in glue. She was keeping to the bright yellow band of Velcro carpeting that ran the full length of the floor—and of the ceiling. The carpet, and the soles of her sandals, were covered with myriads of tiny hooks, so that they clung together like burrs. (Clarke, 1968: 50–51)

In another sequence in this episode, another hostess appears from a door inside a tunnel, walks up a wall, and, upside down, disappears into a door opposite to the one from which she entered. She walks slowly, gracefully, as if she was performing an acrobatic exercise. She rotates around a tunnel, a circumference, as a moon rotates around its planet.

This same magic, the gracefulness and the weightlessness that are the attributes of dance, also characterizes the first scenes set inside the centrifuge of Discovery. Indeed, this spacecraft has a slowly rotating centrifuge, which allows the astronauts to live in a gravity similar to that of Earth. During the first sequence set inside Discovery, the spectators see Poole jogging around the centrifuge. First they see him moving around, as if the camera was still, and then they seem to follow him, as if the camera was rotating with him. Finally, in the following scene, while Bowman is having breakfast and watching a recorded program on a video, Poole comes out from a door in the opposite direction and reaches the other astronaut. Bowman and Poole freely move around a circumference, as if they were hamsters inside their wheels. Unlike hamsters, however, they can walk upside down, apparently violating physical laws. Their movements, those of the camera, and the rotation of the centrifuge, accompanied by the *Adagio* from Aram Khatchaturian's *Gayaneh* ballet suite, seem, once again, like an acrobatic dance in which the dancers challenge the weight of their bodies, in which the set slowly rotates to follow their choreography. Unlike the film, the book describes this device through its technical data and then by its physical accessibility: "The equatorial region of the pressure-sphere—the slice, as it were, from Capricorn to Cancer—enclosed a slowly-rotating drum, thirty-five feet in diameter. As it made one revolution every ten seconds, this carousel or centrifuge produced an artificial gravity equal to that of the Moon" (1968: 113). The following phrases close the depiction of the device, describing how the astronauts can enter into it:

> But normally it was left running at constant speed, for it was easy enough to enter the big, slowly turning drum by going hand-over-hand along a pole through the zero-gee region at its centre. Transferring to the moving section was as easy and automatic, after a little experience, as stepping on to a moving escalator. (1968: 114)

Instead of the dance of the film—the ease and naturalness with which the astronauts live and move inside the centrifuge—the readers of the novel have to deal with technical data. In the cinematic medium, the *mise-en-scène* and montage seem to emanate from the music that transforms the movements of celestial and mechanical bodies into a ballet. And this dance, creating a sublime experience, seems either to stimulate or to echo the ballet in the spectators' mind.

In *A Clockwork Orange,* the metaphor of dance, more than just involving the spectators in a peaceful contemplation of the awe and wonder of the diegetic world, entangles them in an excited, syncopated succession of violent scenes. As discussed in the previous chapter, the slow camera movements and montage are substituted by the frequent use of a handheld camera and a rapid montage. The images seem to emanate from music. But the melodious rhythm of *The Blue Danube* waltz is substituted by the faster liveliness of Beethoven's Ninth Symphony and Rossini's *The Thieving Magpie*. The metaphor of ballet is no longer a "meta-metaphor" of the dance of the audience's mind, and of the power of their thought to speculate about a sublime experience, but becomes a "meta-metaphor" of violence itself. Fights, murders, and rapes ascend the role of works of art.

Unlike *2001: A Space Odyssey*, the metaphor of dance characterizes the novel *A Clockwork Orange*, too, and is emphasized in Kubrick's film. As already discussed, this metaphor is developed in the book through wordplay constituted by *nadsat*, using repetition, onomatopoeia, and rhyming words. For example, the sequence in which the *droogs* find Billyboy's gang raping a woman, followed by the gangs fighting each other, was filmed in a deserted theatre that was the old casino at Taggs Island, where Fred Karno made his fame and fortune creating Fred Karno's Circus. Furthermore, the scene is shot like a theatrical performance. Indeed, the first shot is a medium long shot of a painted still life; the camera then zooms out and tilts down towards Billyboy's gang, which is trying to immobilize a woman and undress her on the stage of the theatre. The scene seems like a play, not only because it takes place on a real stage, but also because the characters' movements follow the music of *The Thieving Magpie* and, on the stage, a pink mattress is prepared for the rape. What is more, Alex and his *droogs* watch the scene from the dark of the parterre, like the spectators of the film, while the stage is lighted. But the protagonist and his friends soon become part of the play. The music does not stop while they advance tidily in a row, emerging from the shadows, keeping the same distance one from the other, stopping the scene, and taking part in the new act. When the woman leaves the stage, the new act begins. Each member of the gangs is filmed hitting a *droog* of the opponent group. The impression of a staged play is maintained thanks to the montage, which follows the rhythm of *The Thieving Magpie*. When Alex whistles to advise his friends that the police are arriving, the show ends. In Burgess's novel, as mentioned in the Introduction, the homodiegetic narrator adopts the metaphor of dance to recount how he fights against the other group's leader: "It was stinking fatty Billyboy I wanted now, and there I was dancing about"; "And, my brother, it was real satisfaction to me to waltz—left two three, right two three—and carve left cheeky and right cheeky" (Burgess, 2000a: 14–15).

Later, when the gang enters Mr. Alexander's home, and the protagonist begins to give orders to his friends (to terrorize the writer and his wife, and to destroy the house), he sings and dances to "Singin' in the Rain," and his movements follow the rhythm of his words. Yet again, the sequence seems like a performance. In the novel, the narrator once more adopts the metaphor of dance. Alex first describes how Dim beats Mr. Alexander with the following words: "he went grinning and going er er and a a a for this veck's dithering rot, crack crack, first left fistie then right." Then he reports how Mr. Alexander's wife is terrorized: "and then she started letting out little malenky creeches, like in time to the like music of old Dim's fisty work." Finally, he recounts how Georgie and Pete react when they see Dim hitting Mr. Alexander: "They went haw haw haw, viddying old Dim dancing round and fisting the writer veck so that the writer veck started to platch like his life's work was ruined, going boo hoo hoo with a very square bloody rot." To complete the description of Dim beating Mr. Alexander, he says: "with old Dim still dancing round and making ornaments shake on the mantelpiece" (2000a: 19).

It is worth noting that the expression "ballet of violence" is adopted by some critics to describe scenes shot in slow motion during which violent actions occur. For example, commenting on the cinema of John Woo, Tony Williams, Robert Hanke, and Tom Tunney, respectively, adopt the expressions "violence and choreographed ballet (his ritual blood baths)" (Williams, 1997: 78); "hyperkinetic choreography of gun violence and explosive pyrotechnics" (Hanke, 1999: 41); and "musical-like choreography and the overall rhythmic quality of the destruction" (Tunney, 1993: 47). What is more, Woo himself claims: "I was very influenced by musicals, like *Singin' in the Rain* and *West Side Story*, and dancers like Fred Astaire and Gene Kelly. They have the rhythm of life, and I shoot action scenes just as though they were dance sequences" (Woo, 1993: 52). Similarly, to describe Sam Peckinpah's style, Marc Crispin Miller argues: "It is this cynicism that lies behind Peckinpah's [highly stylized and heavily publicized] treatment of violence. His obsessive rendering of violence into gross lethargic ballet heightens our vicarious experience of it, makes it less of a kick and more of an indulgence . . ." (1975: 5–6). Stacey Peebles claims that Arthur Penn was the first director to use this technique in the final sequence of *Bonnie and Clyde* (USA, 1967):

> Stephen Prince notes that "subsequent filmmakers might take slow motion ballets of blood to much greater extremes, but Penn was the first American filmmaker to conjoin multicamera filming, montage editing, and slow motion systematically in the visualization of screen violence" (Prince, 2000: 135). Penn himself has stated that in this scene he wanted to show "two kinds of death: Clyde's to be rather like a ballet, and Bonnie's to have the physical shock." (Labarthe, 1972: 169)

Peebles argues that two years later this technique was adopted by Peckinpah in *The Wild Bunch* (USA, 1969) and by the 1980s and 1990s it became a common practice. She cites Woo's *Face/Off* (USA, 1997) and the Wachowski Brothers' *Matrix* (USA, 1999) as examples (Peebles, 2004). In *Full Metal Jacket,* each time the sniper shoots at a soldier in Joker's squad, slow motion is used. But neither the montage, nor the characters' movements follow the rhythm of the music and, thus, I have not described these shots through the metaphor of dance. By contrast, I have defined a ballet of violence in *A Clockwork Orange,* where the violent scenes seem to emanate from music itself. In *Face/Off,* however, the scene in which Castor Troy (Nicolas Cage) and his gang are attacked by the police, led by Sean Archer (John Travolta), in their hiding place, could also be described through the meaning I have given to the expression "ballet of violence." Indeed, when the song "Somewhere over the Rainbow," to which Castor Troy's little son is listening through earphones, becomes audible to the audience, the montage and the characters' performance seem to follow the rhythm of the music thanks to the use of slow motion, as in Kubrick's adaptation.

There are some scenes of *A Clockwork Orange* in which not only do Alex's performance and the montage follow the rhythm of the music, but also the protagonist's thoughts and actions are moved by music itself. It is as if music guides and controls Alex—as if it were playing the role of the director himself. Indeed, the protagonist often acts rashly, as if he was being directed either by Kubrick or by the music. This feature, together with the plot construction, stresses Alex's passivity, as is argued in the next chapter. Similarly, in the novel, music is often cited and described and is, in several cases, the very cause of Alex's behavior. Indeed, in the book, as in the film, there are six scenes during which the protagonist acts in response to the music he listens to. For example, when a lady sings at the Korova Milkbar and Dim laughs, Alex hits him for his behavior because his *droog* is not able to appreciate the lady's voice and the words she sings (Burgess, 2000a: 22–23). This protagonist's reaction will be the reason for his later discussion and fight with his friends. Later, when Alex goes back home for the first time, he masturbates and has visions while listening to music. Thus, his pleasure and imagination, his mind and body are moved by music (Burgess, 2000a: 26–27). The subsequent day, while the protagonist is walking with his *droogs,* after their discussion about money and leadership, he hears a piece of music coming from an open window and he begins to hit his friends, instinctively driven by music, without thinking, but in a manner obedient to the charm of the notes (Burgess, 2000a: 40). Finally, when Alex is submitted to the Ludovico treatment for the second time, the documentaries of Hitler's parades and the bombardments of the

Second World War are accompanied by the Ninth Symphony, and the protagonist revolts against this use of his favorite composer's piece (Burgess, 2000a: 85). After the Ludovico cure, Alex associates his physical sickness and nausea not only with violent actions, but also with the Ninth Symphony specifically. Indeed, when Mr. Alexander induces Alex to commit suicide, he obliges him to listen to this piece (Burgess, 2000a: 123–124). The protagonist is compelled to attempt suicide by music and, thanks to the music, the other characters and the spectators later comprehend that he is cured, that the effects of the Ludovico treatment have been erased. When the Minister of the Interior (Anthony Sharp) pays him a visit at the hospital to induce him to support the government, the Ninth Symphony is played to symbolize the new agreement between Alex and the government, the protagonist's complete recovery, and his new visions of violence. Alex, while listening to this piece, has new violent thoughts and thus, once more, his mind is stimulated by music (Burgess, 2000a: 132).

In the scenes described above, music guides the protagonist's behavior and actions in both the book and the film. But there are many differences between the two media because the musical pieces cited and described by Burgess are almost always different from those used by Kubrick. The major difference between the novel and the film is that, in the book, many of the composers and pieces are often invented by the author, while, in the film, the only names and songs invented are those cited in the music shop. In his essay, Rabinowitz claims that Kubrick could have asked a composer to invent pieces that could have followed Alex's descriptions and reactions or he could have chosen existent music, as he ended up doing. Rabinowitz suggests that there are three reasons for Burgess's choice. First of all, because the book is set in the near future, composers and pieces that do not exist will be never out of fashion. But it must be observed that classical music will be never out of fashion either. Indeed, Burgess often cites pieces of classical music, and the majority of the music chosen by Kubrick are classical pieces rearranged by Wendy Carlos and Rachel Elkind. Secondly, the readers are able to imagine and appreciate the music only through the protagonist; they strictly depend on him because the pieces are described by him, as the homodiegetic narrator, and guide his actions and visions. Thirdly, while the music of the novel follows and highlights Alex's feelings, that of the film is at the service of the images. Thus, while music is for Burgess the end—that is to say, while the novel is about music, for Kubrick music is a means. His film uses music. Rabinowitz criticizes what he considers the director's misinterpretation of the book (Rabinowitz, 2003). But an adaptation should not necessarily have to be subordinated to its source and judged according to its fidelity. What is more, the film is dominated by the metaphor of dance, which is to say, acting, camera movements, and montage follow the rhythm of the music, and often the protagonist seems like a dancer moved by music itself. Thus, it can be claimed that often images emanate from music, as in the case of *2001: A Space Odyssey*, and music becomes an indispensable element to transform the violence depicted into a ballet.

As in *A Clockwork Orange*, in *Full Metal Jacket* there are two scenes in particular during which violence is represented as a ballet. When the protagonist and the other soldiers of his squad are hunched down beside a low wall at the outskirts of Hue, after an enemy attack, a three-man television crew tracks in front of them. The three men proceed in a row, closely following one another, and walking almost at ground level. Their movements seem to follow the extradiegetic song "Surfin' Bird" (by A. Frazier, C. White, T. Wilson, Jr., and J. Harris, 1963), while diegetic noises of firing fill the air. The "grunts" play in front of the camera, joking about their situation:

JOKER: Is that you, John Wayne? Is this me?
COWBOY: Start the cameras. This is *Vietnam: The Movie*!
EIGHTBALL: If Joker is John Wayne, I'm a horse!
DONLON: T. H. E. Rock can be a rock!
T. H. E. ROCK: I'll be Ann-Margret!
DOC JAY: Animal Mother can be a rabid buffalo!
CRAZY EARL: I'll be General Custer!
RAFTERMAN: Who'll be the Indians?
ANIMAL MOTHER: We'll let the gooks play the Indians!

This sequence is referential because the cinematic medium is cited in the diegesis, and the diegetic actors imagine playing roles in an imaginary intradiegetic film about Vietnam, the same war depicted in the diegesis. Moreover, the techniques used to direct this intradiegetic film mirror those adopted by the director of the diegetic film. Indeed, the three men operate a handheld camera, as Kubrick often does. And the crudeness of a battleground is filtered through the metaphor of ballet. In the novel, neither this metaphor nor the camera crew appear, but the dialogue among the soldiers of the cinematic medium is directly adapted from the written medium (Hasford, 1980: 98–99). Thus, in the book, too, there is a citation of the cinematic medium, and the novel displays its referentiality.

The violence of one of the last scenes of the film, when Joker finds himself in front of the sniper, is also rendered through the metaphor of dance. Indeed, the sequence is shot in slow motion, and the two characters' movements seem to follow the rhythm of the extradiegetic piece "The Suspended" (by Abigail Mead, 1987). When the sniper listens to the noise of Joker's gun, she turns around jumping, and her long black hair twirls in the air, as if she was a dancer performing her last pirouette. The violence of the scene is filtered through the metaphor of dance, not unlike the sequence from *A Clockwork Orange* discussed above, when Alex punishes his *droogs* by wounding and throwing them in a river. Indeed, this sequence is filmed in slow motion, too, and the characters' acting, the camera movements, and the montage follow the rhythm of *The Thieving Magpie*. Similarly, in *The Short-Timers*, the "grunts" are attacked on two occasions by two different snipers. During both episodes the shots fired by the snipers and the soldiers are rendered through the onomatopoeic word "*bang*," written in italics. For example, during the first sniper's attack, when Rafter Man manages to kill the enemy, the narrator describes the scene as follows:

> *Bang*. Rafter Man is firing his M-16. *Bang*. *Bang*. The sniper lowers her weapon. She looks at Rafter Man. She looks at me. She tries to raise her weapon. *Bang*. *Bang*. *Bang*. *Bang*. *Bang*. Bullets shock flesh. Rafter Man is firing. Rafter Man's bullets are punching the life out of the sniper. The sniper falls off the roof. (1980: 117)

Apart from the repetition of the onomatopoeic word "*bang*," it is interesting to note all of the other repetitions that I have underlined above, the assonance between "shock flesh," the adoption of an asyndeton style (which is to say, the lack of a coordinating conjunction before the last item in a series), and of simple and brief sentences. Thus, even in the written medium, there is a tendency to underline the sound effect of the scene. The author's choice is emphasized by the director through the metaphor of dance.

The metaphor of ballet, which characterizes these two scenes in the last part of the adaptation, seems to be introduced during the first part of the film, when the recruits are taught to become perfect marines at Parris Island. They are prepared to fight mostly through marches. They march outdoors during the day and indoors during the night, and they always sing following the rhythm of their steps. Only in two cases they are accompanied by background extradiegetic music (a repetitive sound of drums).

And, in the very last march, during graduation day, when they pass in front of the diegetic spectators, they are accompanied by the "Marines' Hymn." In almost all of the other cases, it is Sergeant Hartman who sings the first phrase, and then the recruits repeat it in chorus. As it is discussed later, the sergeant's words seem meaningless, but they exactly match the rhythm of the recruits' marches, and they are full of repetition, like a nursery rhyme. As an example, here is the sergeant's first song:

SERGEANT: Mama and Papa were laying in bed.
CHORUS: Mama and Papa were laying in bed.
SERGEANT: Mama rolled over and this is what she said.
CHORUS: Mama rolled over and this is what she said.
SERGEANT: Oh, give me some.
CHORUS: Oh, give me some.
SERGEANT: Oh, give me some.
CHORUS: Oh, give me some.
SERGEANT: P.T.
CHORUS: P.T.
SERGEANT: P.T.
CHORUS: P.T.
SERGEANT: Good for you and good for me.
CHORUS: Good for you and good for me.
SERGEANT: Mmm, good.
CHORUS: Mmm, good.
SERGEANT: Mmm, good.
CHORUS: Mmm, good.

In the novel, the songs sung by the recruits are reported in italics. In two cases they sing indoors before sleeping (1980: 10–12), and in two other cases they sing outdoors while they are marching, as in the adaptation (1980: 13, 25). In two cases the songs of the cinematic version are directly taken from the novel (1980: 12, 13). And, in all of these cases, the phrases of the songs are meaningless and full of repetition. Kubrick seems to have emphasized these features of the written medium, lengthening each song, increasing their number, and almost always linking them to marches. Thus, the repetition of words are highlighted in the cinematic medium through the repetition of the recruits' movements.

Significantly, during the very last sequence of the film, the soldiers are shown walking outdoors at night and singing the "Mickey Mouse

Club March" (by Jimmie Dodd, 1955). Joker's voice-over comments: "My thoughts drift back to erect-nipple wet dreams about Mary Jane Rotten Crotch and the great homecoming fuck fantasy. I am so happy that I am alive in one piece and short. I'm in a world of shit, yes. But I'm alive. And I'm not afraid." Words are unsuitable to explain such a new, incomprehensible war. Words become repetitive and meaningless, and their sound and musicality become more important than what they signify. The protagonist's phrases that close the film have a simple construction, are full of repetition, and are accompanied by a children's march. Words are used as music is and could be substituted by it. Indeed, the frequency with which the metaphor of ballet appears suggests that images are more linked to music than to dialogue. Similarly, the novel closes with the following paragraph, full of repetition (the underlining is mine):

> We hump <u>back</u> down the trail.
> <u>Back</u> on the hill, <u>Sorry Charlie</u>, our bro, will laugh at us one more time; <u>Sorry Charlie</u>, at least, will greet us with a smile.
> Putting our minds back into our feet, we concentrate our energy into taking <u>that next step, that one more step, just one more step</u>.... We <u>try very hard not to think</u> about anything important, <u>try very hard not to think</u> that there's no slack and that it's a long walk home.
> There it is.
> I wave my hand and Mother takes the point. (1980: 180)

The repetition is emphasized in the film through music and acting, through the "Mickey Mouse Club March" and the "grunts'" march.

The metaphor of dance, which, to be fully realized in the cinematic medium, needs to be supported not only by dialogue, but also by *mise-en-scène*, montage, and, above all, music, seems to be present in the written medium through the use of onomatopoeia, repetition, assonances, and an asyndeton style. This metaphor can be stressed in the adaptation thanks to the very structure of the medium, which is able to reproduce, through different techniques, the same ideas and concepts in the different arts that constitute it. In both *A Clockwork Orange* and *Full Metal Jacket*, Kubrick fully develops the literary style of the authors of the adapted novels. Furthermore, the metaphor of dance, which is also present in *2001: A Space Odyssey*, even if it does not appear in Clarke's prose, seems to be a feature of the way the director creates his works. Indeed, he seems to be constantly looking for the synchronization of all cinematic techniques, so that each of these elements could follow the same rhythm, in a perfect balanced ballet. Even if the metaphor of dance is not as emphasized in the three other films discussed in this book, there is always at least one scene during which his characters are filmed while dancing.

In *The Shining*, ghosts from the thirties dance in couples in the Gold Room of the Overlook Hotel, following the diegetic piece "Midnight, The Stars and You" (by Jimmy Campbell, Reg Connelly, and Harry Woods, 1932) played by a band. In King's *The Shining*, the narrator describes the songs sung by the band or cites their titles: "the smooth sounds of some postwar band"; "the band swung into 'Mood Indigo'"; "the tune was 'Tuxedo Junction,' with a lot of mellow sax in it but not much soul"; "the band music, now doing a swing version of Lennon and McCartney's 'Ticket to Ride'" (2001: 384, 389–391). But the emphasis is less on the ball, and more on the description of the "beautiful woman" with whom the protagonist dances and the conversation they have. Unlike the protagonist of the adaptation, that of the novel does not remain a passive spectator of the dance. In *Barry Lyndon*, Nora Brady and Captain Quin dance together with other couples in a field in Ireland at the sound of the traditional, diegetic music of "Piper's Maggot Jig." Thackeray does not describe the ball, but emphasizes that, although Nora goes to the dance with Barry, she does not dance with him, but only with the other officers (1999: 24–25). In *Eyes Wide Shut*, Alice first waltzes with a Hungarian stranger at the Christmas party, while two models, moving like serpents, try to envelop her husband in a ballet of allurement. Then, at the orgy mansion, the metaphor of dance dominates almost all of the scenes. Indeed, the strange rite with the purple mask and the eleven women, which takes place when the protagonist enters into the orgy mansion, is accompanied by the diegetic music "Masked Ball" (by Jocelyn Pook, 1997). When Bill visits the other rooms, women and men copulate following the rhythm of the diegetic piece "Migrations" (by Jocelyn Pook and Harvey Brough, 1997), and men dance in couples following the diegetic notes of "Strangers in the Night" (by Bert Kaempfert, Charles Singleton, and Eddie Snyder, 1966). Unlike King and Thackeray, Schnitzler, as discussed in the previous chapter, describes both the ball at the carnival party in which husband and wife take part, and that at the orgy mansion.

In these films the three male protagonists are not involved in the dances. This remark seems to emphasize both their passivity and their role as spectators, as is argued in the next chapter. They seem to suggest to the audience how to look at the gorgeous spectacle that takes place in front of their eyes. They recall, once more, the diegetic spectators painted in contemplation of the sublime landscapes of William Turner and Frederic Edwin Church.

The metaphor of dance is used for different purposes in the Kubrick adaptations discussed in this book. In *A Clockwork Orange* and *Full Metal Jacket*, it seems to translate the play of language, used by the authors of the adapted novels, to convey, respectively, the harshness of rapes, murders, and fighting, and the cruelty of a new, incomprehensible, and controversial war. Through the metaphor of ballet, violence becomes, in these films, a work of art. In *2001: A Space Odyssey*, this metaphor conveys the awe and wonder derived from the contemplation of celestial and mechanical bodies, of the infinite possibilities of the universe, and of mankind's role in it. In *The Shining, Barry Lyndon,* and *Eyes Wide Shut*, it helps in the creation of a spectacle performed for the enjoyment of the eyes of the diegetic and the extradiegetic audience. In all of these films, the metaphor of dance is a means through which the director exploits the possibilities of the cinematic medium, so that all its elements follow the same rhythm. The succession of images seems to directly emanate from music; music is foregrounded, becoming audible.[1]

The Music of Language

It's not a message that I ever intend to convey in words. *2001* is a nonverbal experience ... I tried to create a visual experience, one that bypasses verbalized pigeonholing and directly penetrates the subconscious with an emotional and philosophical content. To convolute McLuhan, in *2001* the message is the medium. I intended the film to be an intensely subjective experience that reaches the viewer at an inner level of consciousness, just as music does; to "explain" a Beethoven symphony would be to emasculate it by erecting an artificial barrier between conception and appreciation. You are free to speculate as you wish about the philosophical and allegorical meaning of the film—and such speculation is one indication that it has succeeded in gripping the audience at a deep level—but I don't want to spell out a verbal road map for *2001* that every viewer will feel obliged to pursue or else fear he's missed the point. (Norden, 1968: 328)

According to the director's statement cited above, *2001: A Space Odyssey* cannot be explained through words, and words are not an essential element of his film. He defines it as a "visual experience," and he compares it to music. Among Kubrick's adaptations, *2001: A Space Odyssey* seems the furthest from the written medium and, thus, the one that relies less than the others upon dialogue. Nonetheless, I argue that all of the adaptations discussed can be compared to music. Even in films such as *A Clockwork Orange* and *Barry Lyndon*, which adopt a voice-over, and which would seem to convey more information about the characters and the story through dialogue, sentences are often chosen for their musicality. And Kubrick adaptations can be defined as visual poems.

The case of *2001: A Space Odyssey* is emblematic. The director complained to the co-screenwriter because dialogue was too wordy. That is why he chose to cut it, and to eliminate the use of a voice-over. Indeed, in the film there are little more than forty minutes of dialogue, out of the 139-minute running time, and there is no voice-over to explain the ellipses and the enigmas. Initially, Kubrick planned to adopt a voice-over to introduce the section about man-apes, and to open the film with a ten-minute black-and-white prologue during which scientists and astronomers were to express their opinions about the possibility of extraterrestrial life (LoBrutto, 1998: 280). But these devices were dropped, as the images did not need to be accompanied by verbal explanations. Instead, the film became a visual experience during which the spectators were free to interpret the images, as if they were listeners of music.

The episode in which HAL 9000 kills the three members of the hibernated crew on board Discovery and is then disconnected by Bowman seems particularly significant in relation to the use of dialogue in this film. The three hibernated astronauts are kept alive thanks to machines controlled by the computer, and their physical status is continuously shown through layouts projected on monitors. The scene opens with a close-up of the computer's red eye, followed by a long shot of Discovery from HAL's point of view. This opening is followed by shots of HAL's eye, alternated with shots of the hibernated men, and of the videos that monitor their physical status. The spectators' worst suspicions come true, and the monitors show layouts of physical status progressively flatter and flatter, accompanied by the following signs: "Computer Malfunction," "Life Functions Critical," and "Life Functions Terminated." The scene closes, as it opened, with a close-up of HAL's eye. This killing is rendered more atrocious and disturbing by its silence. What is more, the silence and the speed that characterize these deaths are in contraposition with the verbosity and slowness of HAL's disconnection. Indeed, the computer continues to speak, trying to dissuade its killer, to arouse his pity. HAL first begins to defend its position using the art of rhetoric:

> Just what do you think you're doing, Dave? Dave, I really think I'm entitled to an answer to that question. I know everything hasn't been quite right with me, but I can assure you now very confidently that it's going to be all right again. I feel much better now. I really do. Look, Dave, I can see you're really upset about this. I honestly think you ought to sit down calmly, take a stress pill, and think things over. I know I've made some very poor decisions recently, but I can give you my complete assurance that my work will be back to normal. I've still got the greatest enthusiasm and confidence in the mission and I want to help you.

He adopts expressions like "everything hasn't been quite right with me" and "I've made some very poor decisions recently" to describe the killing of four astronauts, as well as the attempt to kill Bowman. Moreover, he attributes his criminal behavior to the banal fact that he was not feeling very well ("I feel much better now"). Furthermore, he tries to persuade the astronaut that he should not take hasty decisions ("you ought to sit down calmly, take a stress pill, and think things over"), as if it was Bowman who needed to reflect. Then HAL's speech becomes a prayer full of repetition and pauses, as if he was a child trying to excuse himself after misbehaving:

> Dave stop. Stop, will you? Stop, Dave. Will you stop, Dave? Stop, Dave. I'm afraid. I'm afraid, Dave. My mind is going. I can feel it. I can feel it. My mind is going. There is no question about it. I can feel it. I can feel it. I can feel it. I'm afraid.

At the end, when almost all of his memories have been disconnected, HAL introduces himself and sings a childish song full of rhymes:

> Good afternoon gentlemen. I am a HAL 9000 computer. I became operational at the HAL plant in Urbana, Illinois, on the twelfth of January 1992. My instructor was Mr. Langley and he taught me to sing a song. If you'd like to hear it I can sing it for you. It's called "Daisy." "Daisy, Daisy. Give me your answer, do. I'm half crazy. All for the love of you. It won't be a stylish marriage, I can't afford a carriage. But you'll look sweet, upon the seat of a bicycle built for two."

Switching off the computer's last chips becomes like killing a harmless, undefended being. In *2001: A Space Odyssey*, words no longer characterize human beings, but rather the machine. Indeed, on board Discovery, Bowman and Poole utter 1,022 words, while the computer alone utters 921 words. What is more, the two astronauts speak together only when they decide to disconnect HAL, while the computer communicates with both of them. Men are able to appreciate mysteries and the beauty of space and technology, they are able to grasp the wonder of the unknown, of the inexpressible, while the machine can only appreciate what can be translated into words, what can be codified.

In both *A Clockwork Orange* and *Barry Lyndon*, as opposed to *2001: A Space Odyssey*, dialogue is used more often, and a voice-over is adopted to convey information about the story. Indeed, these two adaptations are not as full of mysteries as Kubrick's science-fiction film. But they are still full of ellipses. Indeed, dialogue and, especially, voice-over either explain events when they are already happening, as in the case of *A Clockwork Orange*, or foretell them, as in *Barry Lyndon*. Thus, the characters seem passive because they seem involved in new episodes without having chosen them, like plastic dolls moved from one setting to another by their architect. This metaphor could be adopted to describe the use of the zooming technique in *Barry Lyndon*, where the characters are often statically disposed in the *mise-en-scène*, and their perfect arrangement in the setting is emphasized by zooming in and out. What is more, in this film, the protagonist's passivity is stressed by the director's choice of changing the homodiegetic narrator of the adapted novel into a heterodiegetic voice-over. Thus, Barry's life is commented on and often foretold by an omniscient, third-person voice-over that seems to operate as the zooming technique does. It encloses the protagonist in the diegetic world, leaving him with no chance to free himself from his destiny. In *A Clockwork Orange*, the voice-over is homodiegetic, as in the novel, but Alex comments on events when they are already happening. Thus, paradoxically, his voice-over stresses his passivity.

In these two adaptations, dialogue and voice-over seem to have a further function. Sentences, which, in the majority of cases, are directly translated from the adapted novels, seem to be chosen for their sound and musicality. Indeed, Burgess invented *nadsat* for his novel using onomatopoeic and rhyming words, and repetition. Kubrick not only adopts this style for his dialogue and voice-over, but he also emphasizes it through the metaphor of ballet.

Furthermore, the author's book is rich in metaphors, and the director exploits them. For example, when a lady sings at the Korova Milkbar, the voice-over says: "And it was like, for a moment, O my brothers, some great bird had flown into the milk bar, and I felt all the malenky little hairs on my plot standing endwise, and the shivers crawling up like slow, malenky lizards, and then down again" (also in Burgess, 2000a: 22). When Alex goes back home for the first time, and he listens to the Ninth Symphony, the voice-over comments: "Oh, bliss! Bliss and heaven! It was gorgeousness and gorgeosity made flesh. It was like a bird of rarest spun heaven metal. Or like silvery wine flowing in a spaceship, gravity all nonsense now" (also in Burgess, 2000a: 26). At the music shop, as Alex invites two girls to his house to listen to music, he says: "Come with Uncle and hear all proper. Hear angel trumpets and devil trombones" (also in Burgess, 2000a: 34). When Alex speaks with Mr. Deltoid (Aubrey Morris) and the latter asks him "Do I make myself clear?", the former replies, "As an unmuddied lake, sir. As clear as an azure sky of deepest summer" (also in Burgess, 2000a: 30). This same dialogue is repeated at the very end of the film, between the Minister of the Interior and the protagonist, to seal their agreement (this dialogue is not used at the end of the novel). Almost all of the metaphors that appear in the adaptation are used to describe music and its effect upon Alex. Dialogue and voice-over seem to be shaped around music, which is often the cause of the protagonist's behavior, and which is not only audible, but also foregrounded. This feature is stressed in the diegesis of the film through Alex's words when he comments upon the use of the Ninth Symphony during the Ludovico treatment:

> VOICE-OVER: Then I noticed, in all my pain and sickness, what music it was that, like, cracked and boomed. It was Ludwig Van. Ninth Symphony, fourth movement.
> ALEX: Stop it! Stop it! Please, I beg you! It's a sin! It's a sin!
> DOCTOR: Sin? What's all this about sin?
> ALEX: That! Using Ludwig Van like that. He did no harm to anyone. Beethoven just wrote music.
> DOCTOR: Are you referring to the background score? . . .
> ALEX: But it's not fair. It's not fair I should feel ill when I hear Lovely, Lovely Ludwig Van. (also in Burgess, 2000a: 85)

Significantly, the doctor defines the Ninth Symphony as "background score," a definition that does not appear in the book, while for Alex, the diegetic spectator in this case, and for us, the extradiegetic audience, this music is foregrounded.

Whereas in *A Clockwork Orange* dialogue and voice-over are characterized by a play of language, which often imitates music, and by metaphors, which are mostly used to describe music itself, in *Barry Lyndon* the rhetorical figure that seems to recur more often is dramatic irony. According to Manfred Pfister, there is a dramatic irony

> when the internal and the external communication systems conflict with each other. This always happens whenever the superior awareness of the audience adds an additional layer of meaning to either the verbal utterance or the non-verbal behavior of a figure on stage in such a way as to contradict or undermine the meaning intended by that figure. (1993: 56)

In Kubrick's adaptation, dramatic ironies are realized thanks to a contrast between the voice-over's claims and the characters' dialogue and actions. In the majority of cases, these incongruities are emphasized by the *mise-en-scène* and have a humorous effect. For example, during the very first scene, when the duel between Barry's father and another gentleman is shown, the voice-over states: "Barry's father had been bred, like many sons of genteel families, to the profession of the law. There is no doubt he would've made an eminent figure in his profession had he not been killed in a duel which arose over the purchase of some horses" (almost as in Thackeray, 1999: 5). The fact that Barry's father comes from the upper-class and is educated to start a promising occupation seems in contraposition to the fact that he risks and loses his life only to obtain some horses. The voice-over's sarcasm can be appreciated by the spectators because they are not allowed to grow fond of this character. Indeed, Barry's father is shown only once in an extreme long shot.

When Barry leaves the German girl (Diana Körner) with whom he has spent some days, they greet each other in a bucolic *mise-en-scène*, saying "I love you." But the voice-over sardonically comments:

> A lady who sets her heart on a lad in uniform must be prepared to change lovers pretty quickly or her life will be a sad one. This heart of Lischers was like many a neighboring town that had been stormed and occupied many times before Barry came to invest it. (also in Thackeray, 1999: 76)

The camera slowly zooms out from a medium close-up of the two characters until part of the landscape also appears in frame, as if to reappraise the intimacy between the two characters.

After the marriage of Barry and Lady Lyndon, the voice-over ironically claims:

> Her Ladyship and Barry lived, after a while, pretty separate. She preferred quiet, or to say the truth, he preferred it for her being a great friend to a modest and tranquil behavior in woman. Besides, she was a mother, and would have great comfort in the dressing, educating, and dandling of their little Bryan. For whose sake it was fit, Barry believed that she should give up the pleasures and frivolities of the world leaving that part of the duty of every family of distinction to be performed by him. (also in Thackeray, 1999: 243–244)

But Lady Lyndon is shown with thoughtful and bored expressions, motionless in the static perfection of the *mise-en-scène* and of her pompous dresses. First, she is shown on a sofa with her two sons; then, playing the harpsichord with Mr. Runt (Murray Melvin) and Lord Bullingdon; and, finally, playing cards with Mr. Runt and two other ladies. Meanwhile, Barry is shown kissing and embracing two ladies.

Thus, in both *A Clockwork Orange* and *Barry Lyndon*, a rhetorical figure taken directly from the adapted novel is translated into the cinematic medium and highlighted. In the case of the former film, metaphors are stressed through the use of diegetic and extradiegetic music, and in the case of the latter adaptation irony is emphasized through the voice-over and the *mise-en-scène*.

As in *2001: A Space Odyssey*, where the computer HAL 9000 paradoxically speaks more than the two astronauts Bowman and Poole, in *The Shining* the dialogue between the protagonist Jack or his son Danny and the ghosts of the Overlook Hotel, and between Danny and his imaginary friend Tony, constitutes 23 percent of the dialogue of the entire film. What is more, the dialogue between Jack and the ghosts, or between Danny and Tony, seems more eloquent and significant than that among the Torrances. Indeed, the dialogue among the three members of the family seems, in the majority of cases, meaningless and full of repetitions. For example, when Jack speaks with Danny in his bedroom about the Overlook Hotel, their dialogue is full of repetition, either the father repeats the sentences of his son or vice versa. And Jack curiously repeats the sentences uttered during the previous sequence by the two Grady girls when they invite Danny to "come and play with us. Come and play with us, Danny. Forever and ever and ever."

> JACK: How's it going, Doc? <u>Having a good time</u>?
> DANNY: Yes, Dad.
> JACK: <u>Good</u>. <u>I want you to have a good time</u>.
> DANNY: <u>Do you like this hotel</u>?
> JACK: I do. I love it. Don't you?
> DANNY: I guess so.
> JACK: <u>Good</u>. <u>I want you to like it here</u>. I wish we could stay here <u>forever and ever and ever</u>. (my underlining to highlight the repetitions.)

What is more, the features that characterize the dialogue of this adaptation—that is to say, its meaninglessness and repetition—increase towards the end, when Jack begins to adopt incomprehensible, almost crazy behavior towards his family, becoming a menace to them. For example, Wendy finds the manuscript of Jack's novel, but the pages are made up of the same sentence written repeatedly: "All work and no play make Jack a dull boy." What changes is only the type of the printed letters. Yet again, the signifier seems more eloquent than the signified. The meaning, which is usually conveyed through the signified of sentences, is now conveyed through an image of them. When Jack finds out that Wendy is reading his manuscript, they begin to quarrel and their discussion is an endless repetition of meaningless words. As in the case of the dialogue between father and son, either the husband repeats his wife's words or vice versa:

> JACK: <u>How do you like it</u>? <u>How do you like it</u>? What are you doing down here?
> WENDY: <u>I just wanted to talk to you</u>.
> JACK: Okay. <u>Let's talk</u>. <u>What do you want to talk about</u>?
> WENDY: <u>I can't really remember</u>.
> JACK: <u>You can't remember</u>.
> WENDY: No, I can't.
> JACK: <u>Maybe it was about</u> Danny?
> WENDY: <u>Maybe it was about</u> him. <u>I think we should discuss Danny</u>. <u>I think we should discuss what should be done with him</u>.
> JACK: <u>What should be done with him</u>?
> WENDY: I don't know.

JACK: I don't think that's true. I think you have some very definite ideas about what should be done with Danny. And I'd like to know what they are.
WENDY: Well I, I think maybe he should be taken to a doctor.
JACK: You think maybe he should be taken to a doctor? When do you think maybe he should be taken to a doctor?
WENDY: As soon as possible?
JACK: As soon as possible?
WENDY: Please.
JACK: You believe his health might be at stake.
WENDY: Yes.
JACK: And you are concerned about him. And are you concerned about me?
WENDY: Of course I am.
JACK: Of course you are! Have you ever thought about my responsibilities?
WENDY: What are you talking about?
JACK: Have you ever had a single moment's thought about my responsibilities? Have you ever thought for a single moment about my responsibilities to my employers? (my underlining to highlight the repetitions.)

Then Wendy begins to threaten Jack with a bat and implores him not to do her any harm, while her husband orders her to stop swinging the bat. These brief sentences are repeated several times, until the wife manages to hit him and take him to the storeroom where, once more, he repeats endlessly the same phrases. Jack's last lines of dialogue, when, with an axe in his hand, he is determined to exterminate his family, mimic the fairy story of "The Three Little Pigs":

JACK: Come out come out wherever you are.
WENDY: I can't get out! Run! Run and hide! Run! Quick!
JACK: Little pigs, little pigs, let me come in. Not by the hair on your chinny-chin-chin. Then I'll huff and I'll puff and I'll blow your house in!
WENDY: Please! Don't! Don't! Stop it!
JACK: Here's Johnny! Hello? Anybody here? Hello? Anybody here? Anybody here? Danny-boy! I'm coming! I'm coming Dan! I'm coming! (my underlining to highlight the repetitions.)

Thus, at the end of his adventure, when he is completely controlled by the supernatural forces of the Overlook Hotel, the protagonist's words become childish, not unlike the last sentences and song recited by HAL in *2001: A Space Odyssey*. More than advancing the story or furnishing information about its development, language seems to be used as a comment on the images. Language could be compared to a musical accompaniment.

In *Full Metal Jacket*, as in *The Shining*, the dialogue of Sergeant Hartman and the other soldiers is meaningless and full of repetition; it is also rich with scurrilous metaphors and slang expressions. As discussed in Chapter II, according to Stefano Rosso (2003), these features characterize those Vietnam novels that he defines as postmodern. First of all, the language is insufficient to link the reason and the emotion both of the writer and of the readers, and to create a relationship between the sight and the comprehension of the characters. From a strictly grammatical point of view, there is a lot of repetition and hyperbole, the slang of the sixties is adopted to involve the readers, and obscene language is used to capture the dialogue among the soldiers. This foul language is the best choice to convey strong emotions without falling into romance, is more compatible with the masculinity exhibited by the soldiers, and is in strong opposition with the bureaucratic language of the "lifers," who are those characters who occupy the highest ranks of the military organization. The slang used by the "grunts" often conveys black humor, which completely abolishes the seriousness of the realistic novels, deriding the soldiers' actions that were described in heroic, self-sacrificial terms. Rosso claims that this kind of language is so exclusive and so particular that it often becomes difficult for the readers to understand. The goal of this slang is to underline how a group of soldiers becomes a self-sufficient entity that tends to exclude everybody else: not only their families and women, but also the other "grunts" who are not marines. The scholar also states that this language is used in the dialogue among the soldiers in opposition to the bureaucratic phrases adopted by the military vertexes. In Hasford's novel, however, characters like Sergeant Gerheim (Sergeant Hartman [Lee Ermey] in Kubrick's film) adopt the same expressions of the soldiers. There seems to be no difference between the language of a private and that of another marine of a higher rank. This language seems to constitute a code that could be read as a metaphor of the difficulty to describe this new, incomprehensible, and controversial war.

In the cinematic medium, these features seem to be emphasized thanks to Lee Ermey's overacting, the speed with which he pronounces his sentences, and his loud voice. Indeed, the musicality of his speeches is stressed thanks to his acting, thus his words are not dissimilar from the songs sung during the marches. It is worth recalling that this actor was first chosen by Kubrick as a technical advisor because he served in the Marine Corps for eleven years, where he rose to the rank of Staff Sergeant and did two tours of Vietnam. The director decided to give him the part of Sergeant Hartman after having seen him while he was showing the actors playing the recruits how they should perform their parts (Modine, 2005). Moreover, "Full Metal Jacket," a rap version of Sergeant Hartman's phrases, rearranged by Abigail Mead (pseudonym of Vivian Kubrick, one of the filmmaker's daughters) and the guitarist Nigel Goulding, debuted at the second position in the UK Top Forty in 1987 (Hughes, 2001: 235–236). The first time that Sergeant Hartman speaks in the film is when he quickly walks around the barracks, surveying the recruits:

> SERGEANT: I am Gunnery Sergeant Hartman, your senior drill instructor. You will speak only when spoken to. The first and last words out of your <u>sewers</u> will be "Sir!" Do you <u>maggots</u> understand?
> RECRUITS: Sir, yes, sir!
> SERGEANT: I can't hear you. Sound off <u>like you got a pair</u>.
> RECRUITS: Sir, yes, sir!
> SERGEANT: If you <u>ladies</u> leave my island, if you survive recruit training, you will be a <u>weapon</u>, a <u>minister of death praying for war</u>. But until that day you are <u>pukes</u>! <u>The lowest form of life on Earth</u>. <u>You are not even human fucking beings</u>! You are only <u>unorganized grab-asstic pieces of amphibian shit</u>! Because I am hard you won't like me. The more you hate me the more you'll learn. I am hard but I am fair! There is no racial bigotry here! I do not look down on niggers, kikes, wops, or greasers. Here you are all equally worthless! My orders are to weed out non-hackers who do not pack the gear to be in my beloved Corps! Do you <u>maggots</u> understand that?
> RECRUITS: Sir, yes, sir!
> SERGEANT: Bullshit! I can't hear you!
> RECRUITS: Sir, yes, sir! (my underlining to highlight metaphors and similes.)
> (also in Hasford, 1980: 4–5)

The phrases "Do you maggots understand?," "I can't hear you," and "I'm hard" are repeated twice. The sentences are brief, have an asyndeton style, and an elementary grammatical construction that sometimes is repeated, as in the refrains of songs. For example, the "if phrase" is repeated: "If you ladies leave my island, if you survive recruit training, you will be . . ."; "I am" is repeated three times: "Because I am hard you won't like me," "I am hard but I am fair!" The language is obscene, but is full of metaphors and similes. Indeed, the recruits' mouths become "sewers," and they are called "maggots," "ladies," "pukes," "the lowest form of life on Earth," "not even human fucking beings," and "unorganized grab-asstic pieces of amphibian shit." After the training, they will become instead "weapons" and "ministers of death praying for war." It could be claimed that language does not seem to be used to convey more information in less time, but to lengthen and vulgarize a few concepts about the recruits' discipline during their training.

The difficulty of choosing the right expressions to describe the Vietnam War is clearly stressed in the second part of the film, when Lieutenant Lockhart (John Terry) corrects the articles written by his war correspondents, giving them advice about how to use words and phrases:

LIEUTENANT: "Diplomats in Dungarees. Marine engineers rebuild Dong Phuc villages . . ." Chili, if we move Vietnamese they are evacuees. If they come to us to be evacuated they are refugees.

CHILI: I'll make a note of it, sir.

LIEUTENANT: "NVA Soldier Deserts After Reading Pamphlets. An NVA regular who realized his side would lose deserted after reading Open Arms pamphlets." That's good, Dave. But why say "NVA regular"? Is there an irregular? How about NVA soldier?

DAVE: I'll fix it.

LIEUTENANT: *The Lawrence Welk Show* will be on TV in two weeks. Dave, do words on it. "Not While We're Eating. NVA learned not to interrupt meals of marines on a search-and-destroy mission." We have a new directive from M.A.F. on "search and destroy." Substitute "sweep and clear" in place of "search and destroy." Got it?

DAVE: Got it. Very catchy.

LIEUTENANT: And Joker, where's the weenie? The kill. The grunts must have hit something.

JOKER: Didn't see them.

LIEUTENANT: I've told you we run two basic stories here. Grunts who buy toothbrushes and deodorant for gooks, "winning of hearts and minds." And combat action resulting in a kill, "winning the war." You must have seen blood trails, drag marks?

JOKER: It was raining, sir.

LIEUTENANT: That's why God passed the law of probability. Rewrite it with a happy ending, say one kill.

JOKER: A sapper or an officer. Which?

LIEUTENANT: Whichever you say. Grunts like reading about dead officers.
JOKER: Okay, an officer. How about a general?
LIEUTENANT: You'd like our guys to read the paper and feel bad? In case you didn't know this is not a popular war. Our job is to report the news that the "why-are-we-here" civilian newsmen ignore.

From this dialogue, it seems that both the soldiers' attitude towards the war and public opinion are influenced by rhetoric. There is a wide gap between the language of Sergeant Hartman and that of the "grunts'" and the rhetoric of Lieutenant Lockhart and that of the war correspondents. In the former case, repetition, vulgar slang, elementary grammatical construction, metaphors, and similes transform information into a fanciful refrain. In the latter case, each word is carefully chosen and imposed to depict a war that must be approved by public opinion, and in which the soldiers must believe.

The difficulty and, often, the inappropriateness of language to convey meaning seems to be stressed by the homodiegetic voice-over, directly translated from the homodiegetic narrator of the adapted novel, which is seldom used in the adaptation and, when it appears, gives only a little information about the time and place in which the events shown are happening. The first time that the spectators hear the voice-over is in the first part of the film, when the recruits are shown while training, after Sergeant Hartman's dialogue cited above: "Parris Island, South Carolina. The United States Marine Corps Recruit Depot. An eight-week college for the phony-tough and the crazy-brave." In this case, the voice-over furnishes information about the setting and time (also in Hasford, 1980: 3). Again, in the first part, when, for the last time, the recruits are shown training before graduation day, Joker claims:

> Graduation is only a few days away and the recruits of Platoon 392 are salty. They are ready to eat their own guts and ask for seconds. The drill instructors are proud to see that we are growing beyond their control. The Marine Corps does not want robots. The Marine Corps wants killers. The Marine Corps wants to build indestructible men, men without fear. (also in Hasford, 1980: 19–20)

These sentences do not only give information about time, but also about the results of the training. Recruits are described as "salty," "ready to eat their own guts and ask for seconds," "killers," and "indestructible men, men without fear." The substantive "men" recurs twice and in contraposition with the noun "robots." But, during the training, Sergeant Hartman's purpose seems to have been to transform the recruits into the same killing machine, like a copy of HAL 9000. These sentences could be interpreted as a sign of the difficulty of using the right words to convey meaning. In the second part, when the audience is shown the marine base in Da Nang for the first time, the voice-over says: "Tet. The Year of the Monkey. Vietnamese Lunar New Year's Eve. Down in Dogpatch, the gooks are shooting off fireworks to celebrate" (also in Hasford, 1980: 37). These words inform the spectators about the setting and time. In the third part, before the protagonist and his fellow soldier Rafter Man visit a mass grave, the voice-over comments: "The dead have been covered with lime. The dead only know one thing. It is better to be alive." Thus, Joker neither comments on death in general, nor on the victims of the war, but instead he makes an ironic observation. Once more, language seems inappropriate to describe the effects of such a strange and cruel war. The goal of the voice-over at the beginning of the very last episode, before the protagonist's squad leaves for a new mission, is again to furnish information about place and time: "Intelligence passed the word down that during the night the NVA had pulled out of our area to positions across the Perfume River. Our squad is sent on patrol to check out the report" (also in Hasford, 1980: 77). At the end of this sequence, Joker's words end the film:

> We have nailed our names in the pages of history—enough for today. We hump down to the Perfume River to set in for the night. My thoughts drift back to erect nipple wet dreams about Mary Jane Rottencrotch and the great homecoming fuck fantasy. I am so happy that I am alive, in one piece and short. I'm in a world of shit . . . yes. But I am alive. And I am not afraid. (also in Hasford, 1980: 154)

These phrases not only furnish information about the setting, but also about the protagonist's state of mind. Unlike a classical hero, Joker is not satisfied because his platoon has just killed a sniper avenging some of his fellows or because he is fighting for his country, but because he is still alive and has a chance to go back home. Therefore, the phrases pronounced by the voice-over furnish information about the setting and time or, if they are enriched with a protagonist's personal opinion, they do not express a judgment about the war, but only an ironic or anti-heroic gag.

In *2001: A Space Odyssey*, *The Shining*, and *Full Metal Jacket*, repetition of words and sentences seems to emphasize the difficulty of using language to convey meaning. In Kubrick's last adaptation, *Eyes Wide Shut*, language is a deceit, a joke. Repetitions are used to increase the mysteries and ellipses that cannot be filled in. The protagonist remains enclosed in a labyrinthine diegetic world thanks not only to the plot construction, but also to words and sentences repeated endlessly. He does not really communicate with the other characters, but he repeats their phrases as if he is trying to understand them, to think about their signified. The result is that their meaning remains unexplained and their signifier, their sound, and their musicality become more important. Thus, language, once more, seems to be used like music.

For example, during the Christmas party at Victor Ziegler's mansion, when Bill is summoned upstairs by his guest because the prostitute Mandy has overdosed, the doctor, to resuscitate her, repeats endlessly the same sentences:

> BILL: Mandy, <u>can you hear me</u>, Mandy? <u>Can you hear me</u>? <u>Move your head if you can hear me</u>. <u>Move your head if you can hear me</u>, Mandy. <u>There you go</u>. <u>You can hear me</u>. <u>Can you open your eyes</u> for me? Mandy, can you do that? Let me see <u>you open your eyes</u>. <u>There you go</u>, <u>come on</u>. <u>Come on</u>, <u>look at me</u>. <u>Look at me</u>. <u>Look at me</u>. <u>Look at me</u>. <u>Look at me</u>. <u>Look at me</u>, Mandy. <u>Good</u>. <u>Good</u>. (my underlining to highlight repetitions.)

To resuscitate her, he only uses these repetitions, instead of touching her or consulting with her. In fact, during all of his adventures, Bill continues to repeat the words and sentences pronounced by his interlocutors. Even with his wife, at the beginning of their discussion about the Christmas party, he repeats the phrases used by her, as if he was trying to grasp their meaning:

> BILL: <u>What</u>? <u>What are you talking about</u>?
> ALICE: <u>I'm talking about the two girls</u> that you were so blatantly <u>hitting on</u>.
> BILL: I wasn't <u>hitting on</u> anybody.
> ALICE: Who were they?
> BILL: They were just a couple of models.
> ALICE: And where <u>did you disappear to with them</u> for so long?
> BILL: Wait a minute. <u>I didn't disappear with anybody</u>. (my underlining to highlight repetitions.)

During the scene with the prostitute, Domino, it is she who approaches and invites him to her house; he only follows her, repeating her sentences as if he could not understand them, as if he spoke another language:

DOMINO: Going anywhere special?
BILL: No, I'm just taking a walk.
DOMINO: How'd you like to <u>have a little fun</u>?
BILL: I'm sorry?
DOMINO: <u>Have a little fun</u>? <u>I just live right down there</u>. Would you like to <u>come inside with me</u>?
BILL: <u>Come inside with you</u>?
DOMINO: It's a lot nicer in there than it is out here.
BILL: <u>You live in there</u>? (my underlining to highlight repetitions.)

Similarly, when he goes back to Domino's, and finds her roommate, Sally, who tells him that Domino is HIV-positive, Bill repeats her phrases:

BILL: So <u>do you have any idea</u> when you expect Domino back?
SALLY: No. <u>I have no idea</u>.
BILL: <u>You have no idea</u>?
SALLY: No. Well. To be perfectly honest, <u>she may not even be coming back</u>.
BILL: <u>She may not even be coming back</u>?
SALLY: I.
BILL: You.
SALLY: I think there's something that I should tell you.
BILL: Really?
SALLY: But <u>I just don't know, I don't know</u>.
BILL: <u>You don't know</u>? Well, what is it?
SALLY: <u>I don't know</u> whether to tell you this. <u>Why don't you have a seat</u>? Ok? <u>Let's sit down</u>. <u>I don't quite know how</u> to say this.
BILL: <u>You don't quite know how</u>? (my underlining to highlight repetitions.)

These are only a few examples of how the protagonist, instead of really communicating with the other characters, expressing his ideas and thoughts, repeats endlessly their words and sentences. On the one hand, this feature emphasizes Bill's passivity, as is argued in the next chapter; on the other hand, it increases the mysteries because the spectators are not allowed to know what the protagonist thinks. Furthermore, the repetition seems to underline the difficulty of conveying Bill's mental odyssey through language alone. In *2001: A Space Odyssey*, words cannot explain the infinite possibilities of the universe and mankind; in *The Shining*, they cannot describe a supernatural world; in *Full Metal Jacket*, they cannot translate the complexity of the Vietnam War; and finally, in *Eyes Wide Shut*, words cannot convey the nuances of the human mind. Communication through language becomes impossible. Thanks to repetition, words lose their signified and remain only with their signifier, almost mimicking music.

In Kubrick's adaptations, music becomes audible and images seem to emanate from it. Dialogue and voice-over are used, in the majority of cases, as music is. Indeed, they are adopted for their rhythm, for their signifier, and not for their signified. Much like images, sequences, and episodes evoke one another, words are repeated in characters' dialogue and voice-over. Once more, similarity is superimposed on contiguity, and equivalence becomes the structuring principle, not only of shots, scenes, and episodes, but also of soundtracks. Everything seems to be subordinated to music and language becomes one of the instruments in the director's visual poems. Furthermore, music contributes to create a sublime spectacle that takes place in front of protagonists who often remain motionless and inarticulate. Their dialogue does not convey the meanings of their experiences, of the gorgeous *mise-en-scène* that unrolls before their eyes. Words can only try to reproduce the rhythm of the spectacle, joining and enriching Kubrick's orchestra. Thus, music, dialogue, and voice-over emphasize the characters' passivity that, as is discussed in the next chapter, is one of the features that help to create the dreamy atmosphere that envelops *A Clockwork Orange, Barry Lyndon, The Shining,* and *Eyes Wide Shut.*

Chapter Five

DREAMY WORLDS

KUBRICK: There is a very wide gulf between reality and fiction, and when one is looking at a film the experience is much closer to a dream than anything else.

—(Houston, 1971: 111)

What are truly characteristics of dreams are only those elements of their content which behave like images, which are more like perceptions, that is, than they are like mnemonic presentations . . . we shall be in agreement with every authority on the subject in asserting that dream hallucinates—that they replace thoughts by hallucinations. Dreams construct a situation out of these images, they represent an event which is actually happening, as Spitta puts it, they dramatize an idea.

—(Freud, 1900: 50)

A Clockwork Orange, Barry Lyndon, The Shining, and *Eyes Wide Shut* seem to be shrouded in dreamy atmospheres. The director's first concern does not seem to have been to realistically depict the extradiegetic world, but, rather, to break the illusion of reality, to create a diegetic world as far as possible from the extradiegetic world, even if the latter world is often cited in the diegesis, as is argued in the next chapter.

This dreamy atmosphere is manifest in the very first scenes of *A Clockwork Orange, The Shining,* and *Eyes Wide Shut*. As already discussed, the first film opens with a close-up of the protagonist who, in an imaginary pub in an unspecified future, looks directly into the camera, while his voice-over addresses the spectators using *nadsat*. The *mise-en-scène* clearly indicates to the audience that the diegetic world is imaginary, unreal, and that the rules that dominate it are dissimilar from those that govern the extradiegetic world (see Figure 3.1). *The Shining* opens with aerial footage that seems, from the very beginning of the adaptation, to invite the spectators to wonder about a natural or a supernatural explanation of the diegesis. The camera follows the protagonist's car, which is reaching the Overlook Hotel in the mountains of Colorado on a deserted road that verges a savage lake. But, in the very first shot, Jack's Volkswagen is not in frame and the camera moves forward, towards an island in the middle of the lake. During this same sequence, first, the camera moves forward passing the car and, then, when the Volkswagen enters into a tunnel, the camera moves forward past the mountain, and the car enters again in frame only when it comes out from the tunnel. Thus, the camera movements are not strictly linked to the car's movement, and the spectators begin to wonder whether the camera represents an evil, supernatural presence that flies over the protagonist. This effect is emphasized by the second piece of the fifth movement of the extradiegetic piece *Symphonie Fantastique* (by H. Berlioz, 1830, rearranged by Wendy Carlos and Rachel Elkind in 1980). The fifth movement represents a witches' sabbath, and the second piece is a burlesque parody of the "Dies irae," the Gregorian hymn for dead men. Thus, an uncanny presence, evoked by the camera movements, is stressed by the extradiegetic piece that recalls witches and death. Similarly, in the very first shot of *Eyes Wide Shut*, Alice undresses, but in the next sequence, the spectators are shown Alice as she is dressing for a Christmas party. Thus, the very first shots do not seem to be linked in a chronological chain. In this case, the montage introduces a dreamy element.

The dreamy atmosphere that characterizes Kubrick's adaptations results from features that also appear in dreams. For example, the director's films are constituted by *tableaux vivants* and/or unrelated episodes, which are usually separated by ellipses and are full of unexplained enigmas. I have shown how much a cause and effect logic is often unable to fill in the ellipses and solve the mysteries. In *The Interpretation of Dreams*, Freud claims that the sequences that constitute dreams cannot be linked in a causal chain: "Dreams are disconnected, they accept the most violent contradictions without the least objection, they admit impossibilities, they disregard knowledge which carries great weight with us in the daytime" (1900: 54). Citing Strümpell, he argues that in dreams "there is an eclipse of all the logical operations of the mind which are based on relations and connections." Similarly, citing Spitta, he claims that "ideas that occur in dreams seem to be completely withdrawn from the law of causality." And, finally, citing Sticker, he adds that in dreams the "logical relations between ideas" disappear (1900: 57).

I have already discussed how the cross-references among the unrelated episodes and/or *tableaux vivants*, and among single images, disrupt the order created by the symmetrical plot structures and the geometry of the *mise-en-scène*. Scenes and shots, which recall and foretell previous and subsequent sequences and images, evoke *déjà vù* that, according to Freud, is a feature common to both the waking and dreaming life. These characteristics, together with plot structures that are symmetrical and/or are ordered into parts, and the near meaninglessness of dialogue and its repetition, contribute to the creation of protagonists who often remain passive spectators of their diegetic worlds.

It seems worth stressing that Kubrick is often accused of being a misanthrope because almost all of his characters seem to lack depth.[1] For example, Janet Staiger, discussing the audience's reaction of *A Clockwork Orange*, claimed: "Kubrick was described as something of an amoral 'god-figure' or a misanthrope" (2000: 93–124). It is the director himself who, answering to this charge, distinguished between life and art. Indeed, as Tony Pipolo remembers: "Surprised—and perhaps wounded—by accusations that his films were cold and misanthropic, he once quipped, 'You don't have to make Frank Capra movies to like people'" (2002: 5). Claiming that Kubrick's protagonists seem to lack complex characterization does not imply that the director hated men. An analysis of a film is not necessarily linked to a psychological judgment about its filmmaker. Moreover, how can a director, who has to work and collaborate with a lot of people, be a misanthrope? And yet: "Critical judgment gives way to attaches on the man: his move to England—where he could have more control over his films than he could in Hollywood, and protect his private life—is termed 'reclusivity'; his painstaking care with each film is judged 'obsessional'. These are then declared the keys to the cynicism of his films" (Pipolo, 2002: 6). Paradoxically, the director's unwillingness to speak with critics and journalists, and his serene, private family life augmented the myth of an isolated, reclusive artist who preferred the quiet hermitage of the English countryside to the glamorous world of Hollywood. As already discussed, however, the choice to live in the English countryside, far from being dictated by some director's mania or aversion to social and public life, seems to have been mostly guided by his desire to work in an ideal environment. Kubrick's decision to grant few interviews, and to collaborate with few critics and journalists, was inspired by his total devotion to his art, and to his profound belief that the meanings and messages conveyed through the cinematic medium could not be translated into words. An analysis of the director's protagonists should lead to an interpretation of his body of work, and not of Kubrick the man. It still can be argued that Kubrick's protagonists seem in contraposition with their perfect worlds. Where do the superbly constructed diegetic worlds come from? As already emphasized, in *2001: A Space Odyssey* mankind seems to be helped by the aliens. In *The Shining*, as will be discussed later, the supernatural has a leading role. In any case, an artist can choose to represent people who behave in a particular manner, without believing that everybody acts in the same way. Is it possible to deduce, from an analysis of Frank Capra's films, that this director strongly believed that in our world everybody is altruistic or ready to be redeemed? The mistake lies, once more, in the confusion between art and life, and diegetic and extradiegetic worlds.

In what follows, firstly, I discuss the passivity of the three protagonists of *A Clockwork Orange*, *Barry Lyndon,* and *Eyes Wide Shut*. I stress their roles as both puppets and wanderers in a diegetic world in which they remain entrapped, often unable to cope with the succession of experiences that imprison them. They usually appear to be passive spectators of the events that befall them, as if they have dreamt their worlds and experiences. There are echoes here of Freud, who suggests that "the finished dream strikes us as something alien to us. The strangeness cannot be due to the material that finds its way into their content, since the material is for the most part common to dreaming and waking life" (1900: 48). Freud underlines the dreamer's passivity towards her dreams, explaining that both the authority of the self is reduced, and mental activities do not order the flux of thoughts during sleep: "Sleep signifies an end of the authority of the self. Hence falling asleep brings a certain degree of passivity along with it." And: "Falling asleep at once involves the loss of one of our mental activities, namely our power of giving intentional guidance to the sequence of our ideas" (1900: 50, 54). Finally, I discuss why the spectators of *The Shining* hesitate between a natural or supernatural interpretation of the events on screen, and what the uncanny features of the film are, and I link the notions of supernatural and uncanny both to dreams and fairy tales. I then consider this in relation to concepts regarding the horror genre.

Protagonists' Passivity

In *A Clockwork Orange*, *Barry Lyndon*, and *Eyes Wide Shut*, the plot construction mirrors the intricacies and mysteries of human life, respectively, in the future, during a brief period of Alex's youth; in the past, following Barry's life for almost its entire duration; and in the present, during a few days of Bill's middle-age. Thus, in only three films, Kubrick has represented human life in almost every aspect. But all three of his protagonists wander, and it is this wandering that seems to link them, and to describe the human condition as it is represented by the director, a complex journey that cannot be interpreted through a cause and effect chain.

These protagonists seem compelled to be wanderers, as is Charles Baudelaire's *flâneur*. In "The Painter of Modern Life," the French writer compares convalescence, as it is described in Edgar Allan Poe's "The Man of the Crowd" (1840), to childhood: "Convalescence is like a return towards childhood" (1863: 8). Both a convalescent and a child can feel the same excitement experienced by a *flâneur* when he happens to find himself in the crowd:

> The crowd is his element, as the air is that of birds and water of fishes. His passion and his profession are to become one flesh with the crowd. For the perfect *flâneur*, for the passionate spectator, it is an immense joy to set up house in the heart of the multitude, amid the ebb and flow of movement, in the midst of the fugitive and the infinite. To be away from home and yet to feel oneself everywhere at home; to see the world, to be at center of the world, and yet to remain hidden from the world—such are a few of the slightest pleasures of those independent, passionate, impartial natures which the tongue can but clumsily define. The spectator is a prince who everywhere rejoices in his incognito. The lover of life makes the whole world his family, just like the lover of the fair sex who builds up his family from all the beautiful women that he has ever found, or that are—or are not—to be found; or the lover of pictures who lives in a magical society of dreams painted on canvas. Thus the lover of universal life enters into the crowd as though it were an immense reservoir of electrical energy. Or we might liken him to a mirror as vast as the crowd itself; or to a kaleidoscope gifted with consciousness, responding to each one of its movements and reproducing the multiplicity of life and the flickering grace of all the elements of life. He is an "I" with an insatiable appetite for the "non-I," at every instant rendering and explaining it in pictures more living than life itself, which is always unstable and fugitive. (1863: 9–10)

As Baudelaire's *flâneur* is a spectator of the crowd, Kubrick's protagonists seem to be spectators of their dreamy diegetic worlds. But they are not passionate. The *flâneur*'s joy of fusing himself with the crowd is substituted by the reverence, awe, and wonder of the director's characters who, even if they are attracted by their worlds, cannot find in it either a family or a home. They often remain passive wanderers, spectators of a sublime experience in which they cannot find an active role.

Both the first and the third part of *A Clockwork Orange* are constituted by unrelated episodes because in each of them Alex is shown in different settings, committing different criminal actions that are not announced either by the dialogue or the voice-over. There are some exceptions. Before going to the cat lady's house, Alex and his *droogs* are shown in a pub while they are discussing this visit. While the protagonist is walking together with his gang along a riverside, before throwing Dim and Georgie into the river and wounding Dim with his knife, the voice-over announces his intentions. When Alex, after the Ludovico treatment, wakes up in a room and is obliged to listen to the Ninth Symphony, before throwing himself out of the window, the voice-over claims that he is going to commit suicide. Finally, after the suicide attempt, before the spectators are shown that the protagonist is still alive, the voice-over anticipates that he survives. In all other cases, however, the voice-over almost always describes a situation that is happening, after the spectators have already been shown the new setting and the beginning of the new action. In the first and in the third part of the novel and the film, the protagonist seems to wander because the homodiegetic narrator does not announce his plans and purposes. Alex seems to find himself in new places and situations without having chosen them. But the passage from one section to the next is more pronounced in the book than in the adaptation. Indeed, in the former case, the narrator almost always introduces a new episode through a few words or phrases. For example, when the protagonist and his gang leave a pub, before hitting a homeless person, the narrator explains that they meet him outside the pub. In the film, however, the spectators are shown Alex and his *droogs* sitting at a table in the Korova Milkbar and, after a cut, they are shown already approaching a drunken homeless person who is lying on the ground. The ellipses that in the film stress the passage from one episode to the next, are filled in the book by a few words or a few sentences. Thus, Kubrick's adaptation emphasizes the plot construction of the first and the third part of the novel, which is constituted by unrelated episodes, through the introduction of ellipses that separate the sections, and the choice of showing a new action *in media res*. As discussed in the previous chapter, the episodes cannot usually be linked in a cause and effect chain; they are united through a ballet of violence, and the protagonist of the film seems more passive than in the novel. He seems to be more in service of the plot. This latter feature is also due to the symmetrical plot structure, the similarities among sequences, and the superbly composed images that seem to entrap Alex. A close analysis of the plot of the film leads to a reading of the protagonist that is different from that proposed by the majority of critics. He no longer seems "more alive than anybody else" and he no longer "makes you root for his foxiness, for his crookedness," as, for example, Pauline Kael claims (1972: 135).

Alex's passivity is not only underlined through the plot structure, but also thanks to the metaphors of dance and theatre. Indeed, he often acts as if he was moved by music itself, as if music guided and inspired him. What is more, his performances, the camera movements, and the montage often follow the rhythm of the music. Thus, music becomes a symbol of the director's aesthetic that commands his protagonist. This interpretation of Alex as a puppet is also corroborated by the metaphor of theatre. Indeed, in many sequences, the protagonist seems to exhibit his role as an actor, and the film displays its artificiality and reflexivity, as is argued in the next chapter.

The adaptation's awareness of being a work of art, in which violence becomes an aesthetic performance, is manifest also in the scenes in which some cinematic techniques, such as ultra-wide-angle lenses and accelerated or slow motion are implied to break the narrative fluidity. For example, the scene in which Alex makes love with two girls he met at the music shop becomes ironic thanks to the high-speed motion and the music. In an interview, Kubrick himself claims: "It seemed to me a good way to satirize what had become the fairly common use of slow motion to solemnize this sort of thing, and turn it into 'art'. The *William Tell Overture* also seemed a good musical joke to counter the standard Bach accompaniment" (Ciment, 2003: 151–152). This sequence, according to the director's statement, becomes a charge (that is to say, a satiric imitation, which recounts a vulgar subject through the imitation of the noble style of the hypotext, explicitly manifesting its status as an imitation [Genette, 1997: 29–36]).[2]

When Alex and his *droogs* are walking along a river, the protagonist, inspired by the diegetic piece *The Thieving Magpie*, hits Georgie and Dim, and throws them into the water. The whole sequence is shot in slow motion, and the soundtrack is constituted by the diegetic music only. The speed of the scene and the absence of noises and dialogue break the narrative fluidity. Moreover, Alex overacts, adopting a Kubrickian stare and looking twice directly into the camera. Similarly, when Alex runs outside the cat lady's house and his *droogs* are waiting for him to take revenge, the scene in which Dim hits the protagonist in his face with a bottle of milk is filmed in slow motion. This speed, which symmetrically evokes the sequence discussed above, in which it is Alex who beats Georgie and Dim, breaks the narrative fluidity once again. Finally, the very last scene of the film, when the protagonist imagines himself making love to a woman, is filmed in slow motion and is accompanied by the diegetic Ninth Symphony. In this case, Alex's thoughts are like a parody of the classical clichés of Hollywood films (a parodic hypertext changes the meaning of the hypotext through a minimal transformation, it modifies its subject without modifying its style [Genette, 1997: 29–36]). This feature stresses once again the unreality of the adaptation and its reflexivity, together with the protagonist's role as a puppet moved by music that symbolizes the director's aesthetic.

The unreality of the film and, in particular, its dreamy atmosphere are stressed by the point-of-view shots that adopt ultra-wide-angle lenses. The characters look directly into the camera, addressing both the protagonist and the audience, and their faces are distorted. The characters become caricatures of themselves, as if they were speaking animals in a fairy tale.

While the succession of sequences in *A Clockwork Orange* are linked by the metaphor of dance, in *Barry Lyndon* the aesthetic that dominates the scenes seems to be that of the eighteenth-century paintings. Each sequence is a *tableaux vivant* frozen in its perfection. Milena Canonero, costume designer together with Ulla-Britt Söderlund, claims that the director was inspired by some painters of the eighteenth century, such as Thomas Gainsborough and Joshua Reynolds, for the English part, and Adolph von Menzel for the scenes shot by candlelight (Masi, 1990). The actors are perfectly composed inside the frame and, in the majority of the sequences, they move sumptuously, slowly, as if to represent the noble perfection of the aristocracy. What is more, they are often lit by a soft, warm candlelight that increases the similarities between the images and the eighteenth-century paintings.[3] The smooth, slow tracking shots allow the spectators to follow the characters' genteel and mannered movements, and the zooming in and out allows them to peacefully frame an object or a character emphasizing it, without disrupting the calm perfection of the entire sequence. Mario Falsetto claims that this "tactic is analogous, in a certain way, to the act of looking at a painting. The eye is often drawn to a detail before the viewer experiences the entire canvas" (2001: 58).

Moreover, each *tableaux vivant* is separated from the previous one through an ellipsis. Indeed, both the first and the second part of the film can be divided into fifty episodes and at the end of each of them there is an ellipsis. Thus, Barry continuously finds himself in new settings and situations, not unlike the protagonist of *A Clockwork Orange*. But while Alex abruptly finds himself in *media res*, and the spectators cannot guess through either the dialogue or the homodiegetic narrator what situation he will be involved in, the future of the protagonist of this costume drama is often announced by the voice-over, which is that of a heterodiegetic narrator. Indeed, there are sixteen flash-forwards given by the voice-over narration. And the more important events in Barry's life are pre-announced, such as his future as a wanderer after the duel with Captain Quin, or how vain his attempts to gain a peerage after his marriage with Lady Lyndon will be, or the death of his beloved son Bryan.

According to Michael Klein and Gillian Parker (1981), while in the first part of the film, during Barry's rise in society, the voice-over is ironic, in the second part, during the protagonist's decline, his irony is counterbalanced by dramatic events, musical intensity, camera style, and the beauty of the photography. In the first part, superbly composed images, which reproduce eighteenth century paintings, depict characters as they would like to be represented. But the ironic voice-over and musical comments, together with reverse zoom shots, distance the audience. In the second part, irony is substituted by pathos and tragedy through dramatic events and music, and a different use of camera movements that engage the audience's sympathy regarding the characters' misfortunes. Scholars argue that Barry becomes an emblem of modern alienation, and the themes of Thackeray's novel are updated by Kubrick's adaptation. Similarly, Neil Sinyard (1986) argues that both the editorial comments of the novel, and the use of voice-over and reverse zoom shots in the film, suggest that both Thackeray and Kubrick take a superior attitude towards their fictional worlds and characters. But while the author can be defined as a social satirist, and the novel a satire on snobbery, the director can be claimed to be a social scientist, and the film an accurate depiction of the difficulty of social mobility and survival against a hostile fate. Not unlike these scholars, I argue that the voice-over, together with other cinematic devices, stresses the protagonist's passivity and, consequently, the dreamy atmosphere that envelops the diegetic world: these are features that characterize Kubrick's style.

In *A Clockwork Orange,* the plot structure is not so dissimilar from that of Burgess's novel, because it only emphasizes the succession of unrelated episodes through the use of ellipses that divide them. In *Barry Lyndon,* however, the *syuzhet* construction could not be further from that of Thackeray's book. Indeed, in the novel, which is autobiographical, the homodiegetic narrator links all of the episodes through his point of view. The narrator's opinions and will are so strongly affirmed that Barry alone seems to shape his future, even if he often has to deal with misfortune and chance. What is more, the episodes of the book that are not adapted fill in the gaps left by the film, and contribute to the construction of a protagonist who seems the only actor of his life. Indeed, in the novel Barry seems more resolute because he is involved in more adventures and, through deceits and trickeries, he often manages to obtain what he wants. For example, the protagonist of the book kills several characters during the war, whereas in the adaptation he is never shown while killing somebody. What is more, while Barry in the novel has complicated love affairs, during which he uses all of his wit to win his lovers' hearts, in the adaptation Barry has fewer and relatively easy sentimental relations.

The plot construction of *Barry Lyndon* characterizes *Eyes Wide Shut,* too, where the unrelated episodes, separated by ellipses, constitute a succession of *tableaux vivants* of modern love affairs. Bill's passivity is emphasized, as is Barry's, by the plot construction, but also by the dialogue and the absence of a voice-over. Indeed, the protagonist often repeats the words and sentences uttered by other characters, and his dialogue does not express his opinions.

In *Eyes Wide Shut,* as in *A Clockwork Orange,* the protagonist's passivity is also stressed by the almost claustrophobic succession of episodes that always show him in another setting, in another situation, as if his wanderings through the city were guided by an invisible hand, as if he were a puppet moved from one place to the next. In Schnitzler's novel, almost all of the episodes have a symmetrical structure because when the protagonist enters an interior, he has to cross rooms before arriving at the room in which the main action takes place and, when leaving, he has to repeat his path in reverse. By contrast, in the film Bill, before entering the main room, has to cross other rooms but, as soon as the main action takes place, the sequence ends and the spectators are shown a shot of a street or the protagonist in another interior. Moreover, in the book the main episodes are divided by sections in which the protagonist is described while he is walking along a street to reach the next interior. These sections are filled with Fridolin's fluxes of conscience, so the readers understand what he thinks about his experiences. In the adaptation, instead, the protagonist appears to be more passive. Indeed, his fluxes of conscience are never reported either through his dialogue or a voice-over. The spectators remain entrapped in mental wanderings, as the protagonist remains enclosed in the labyrinthine succession of the episodes.

What is more, in order to stress Bill's passivity, there are a number of scenes in which the protagonist's dialogue and/or actions are interrupted by another character or event. For example, during the Christmas ball at Ziegler's mansion, when the protagonist is speaking with the piano player, Nick Nightingale, their conversation is interrupted by a man at Ziegler's service who summons Nick. Later on, Bill speaks with two models, Gayle and Nuala, and their conversation becomes intriguing and mysterious. But a man at Victor's service—the same one who before had called the pianist—summons Bill upstairs, where Mandy, a prostitute known by Ziegler, has overdosed. During his nightly wanderings, both in the novel and the film, the protagonist meets a prostitute who asks him to go home with her. In the book, it is the protagonist who first tries to resist her, then, when he begins to make love to her, she resists. In the film, as soon as Bill and Domino begin to kiss each other, the protagonist's mobile phone rings. It's Alice, and Bill is interrupted once more.

Moreover, as already discussed, Bill's passivity is particularly emphasized by the dark, deserted, and labyrinthine streets of Kubrick's Greenwich Village, and by his point of view shots when he wanders through them and, later, through the numerous corridors of the orgy mansion. For example, the scene in which Bill meets a group of boys along the street who push and scoff at him seems to anticipate his confrontation with the orgy participants. In both cases, the protagonist does not react; he only looks at them, remaining physically isolated from the group of other men. In the orgy mansion, Bill does not take part in the sexual play. As he wanders through the corridors and rooms, the audience is shown the spectacle through his point of view and, when he is discovered, he is isolated from the other participants. When he meets the group of boys, he does not react to their provocations. He only looks at them, and the spectators are shown the scene from his point of view. When one of the boys bumps into him, the group and Bill exchange their position along the street, and the camera changes its position to maintain the protagonist's point of view and to emphasize his loneliness against the group's camaraderie. In the novel, as in the film, on the one hand, Fridolin does not react to the boys' affront, trying to remain physically far from them by only staring at them. On the other hand, the protagonist of the book, unlike that of the adaptation, compares himself to the boys through two flashbacks about his student days during which he took part "in a few fencing-matches," and he "had even been prepared to duel with pistols" (Schnitzler, 1999: 22–23). What is more, through his flux of conscience about the dangers of his work, he seems to convince himself that he is far more courageous than the boys: "And what about his profession! Dangers on all sides and at every moment—it was just that one tended to forget about them" (1999: 23). Thus, in the novel, the protagonist's physical passivity seems to be counterbalanced by his mental activity.

Kubrick's protagonists are usually passive wanderers. They are as passive as dreamers and thus their passivity, as discussed above, stresses the dreamy atmosphere that pervades their diegetic worlds. But they are also wanderers, a feature common to the characters of both dreams and fairy tales. The following passage—in which Freud compares the experience of Odysseus, who, far from home, finds himself naked and dirty in front of Nausicaä and her maidens, to an anxiety-dream—suggests a comparison between Kubrick's heroes and Ulysses himself:

> There can be no doubt that the connections between our typical dreams and fairy tales and the material of other kinds of creative writing are neither few nor accidental. It sometimes happens that the sharp eye of a creative writer has an analytic realization of the process of transformation of which he is habitually no more than the tool. If so, he may follow the process in a reverse direction and so trace back the imaginative writing to a dream. One of my friends has drawn my attention to the following passage in Gottfried Keller's *Der grüne Heinrich* (Part III, Chapter 2): "I hope, my dear Lee, that you may never learn from your own personal experience the peculiar and piquant truth of the plight of Odysseus when he appeared, naked and covered with mud, before the eyes of Nausicaä and her maidens! Shall I tell you how that can happen? Let us look into our example. If you are wandering about in a foreign land, far from your home and from all that you hold dear, if you have seen and heard many things, have known sorrow and care, and are wretched and forlorn, then without fail you will dream one night that you are coming near to your home; you will see it gleaming and shining in the fairest colors, and the sweetest, dearest and most beloved forms will move towards you. Then suddenly you will

become aware that you are in rags, naked and dusty. You will be seized with a nameless shame and dread, you will seek to find covering and to hide yourself, and you will awake bathed in sweat. This, so long as men breathe, is the dream of the unhappy wanderer; and Homer has evoked the picture of his plight from the deepest and eternal nature of man." (1900: 246–247)

This description of Odysseus recalls Alex when, after having being beaten by his former *droogs*, happens to find himself in front of Mr. Alexander's home. It evokes also the scene when Barry, with his amputated leg, permanently leaves England in the company of his mother. In particular, it recalls Bill when he has to take off his mask in front of the other orgy participants, and he is asked to undress himself. While Homer's hero, as with those in fairy tales, is not only active, he is also moved by a precise task, and often acts with the help of a friendly diegetic world. On the other hand, Kubrick's protagonists usually wander in a hostile world without a definitive goal. Indeed, Jack Zipes, citing Max Lüthi, claims that the hero of a magic folk tale is "a wanderer charged with carrying on a task" (2006: 4). And Marie-Louise Tenèze suggests:

> It is the relation between the hero—who is explicitly or implicitly, but always assured of aid in advance, guaranteed—and the difficult situation in which he finds himself during the course of action that I propose as the constitutive criterion of the genre. The hero of the magic folk tale ventures, alone and far from his familiar surroundings, to the perilous fringe of an exceptional experience capable of supplying him with a "personal provision of power," his insertion into the world—and thus, there is a magic solution to the absurd and desperate endeavor to leave the social order which is played out in the universe of fiction. (1970: 23–24)

In Kubrick's adaptations, the protagonists do not gain access into their diegetic worlds at the end of their adventures, instead remaining passive listeners and spectators. In the very last sequence of *A Clockwork Orange*, Alex again plays the role that he had played in the first part of the film. He is still a criminal whose violent thoughts are inspired by diegetic music. Barry, without a peerage and money, goes back to his country with his mother. And an astonished Bill listens to his wife's imperative and simple solution to their matrimonial crisis.

The similarities and differences between the director's films and fairy tales are emphasized in *The Shining*. Indeed, in this adaptation, when the play between a natural and a supernatural explanation of the events is finally resolved, that is to say, when the audience is finally oriented towards a supernatural answer, the protagonist Jack is not supplied with a "personal provision of power," and there is no "magic solution" to his effort to abandon his family by annihilating it. When Jack is finally "inserted" into the supernatural world of the Overlook Hotel, and the audience accepts a supernatural explanation, he definitively loses his place in his family in a natural world, and he dies. In Kubrick's *The Shining*, unlike in fairy tales, the supernatural is not taken for granted. To believe in it the protagonist has to struggle and, as soon as he becomes an element of this world, he remains enclosed in it. In this film the struggle of lone wanderers, such as Alex, Barry, and Bill, is symbolized by the struggle between two parallel worlds.

As Baudelaire's *flâneur* feels compelled to fusing himself with the crowd losing his identity, becoming a mirror that reflects it, the director's protagonists are attracted by the spectacle of their worlds. A ballet of violence, a sequence of eighteenth century *tablaux vivants*, and a living gallery of gorgeous bodies move Alex, Barry, and Bill, respectively. Jack is attracted by the ghosts of the past of the Overlook Hotel, by the marvelous. Unlike Baudelaire's *flâneur*, but like the director's other protagonists, he never finds either a home or a family in the supernatural world by which he is charmed. He struggles to follow the ghosts, as Poe hastens to follow the man of the crowd, but in the end they both have to succumb in front of the unknown, of the mystery: *"er lasst sich nicht lessen—*it does not permit itself to be read. There are some secrets which do not permit themselves to be told" (Poe, 1840: 207).

The Fantastic, the Uncanny, and the Horror Genre in *The Shining*

According to Tzvetan Todorov, a text must fulfill the three following conditions to be defined as fantastic:

> First, the text must oblige the reader to consider the world of characters as a world of living persons and to hesitate between a natural and a supernatural explanation of the events described. Second, this hesitation may also be experienced by a character; thus the reader's role is so to speak entrusted to a character, and at the same time the hesitation is represented, it becomes one of the themes of the work—in the case of naïve reading, the actual reader

uncanny | fantastic-uncanny | fantastic-marvelous | marvelous

Figure 5.1 Figure to distinguish among the uncanny, the fantastic, and the marvelous.

identifies himself with the character. Third, the reader must adopt a certain attitude with regard to the text: he will reject allegorical as well as "poetic" interpretations. These three requirements do not have an equal value. The first and the third actually constitute the genre; the second may not be fulfilled. (1975: 33)

According to the first condition, a text can be defined as fantastic as long as its readers cannot decide whether what happens to the characters is the product of their imagination, is an illusion of their senses, or is part of their reality. In the former case, the laws of the world described do not change, but rather coincide with the physical laws of our own world. In the latter case, the laws of the diegetic world no longer coincide with those of the extradiegetic world, and the imaginary world is moved and governed by laws unknown to us. In the former case, the text is defined uncanny, in the latter marvelous. The Russian formalist develops Figure 5.1 in order to better visualize the differences among: the fantastic in its pure state; the fantastic-marvelous, in which, after an initial hesitation, the readers opt for a supernatural explanation of the events; the marvelous; the fantastic-uncanny, in which the audience finally opts for a natural answer; and the uncanny. The fantastic in its pure state is symbolized by the line that divides the fantastic-uncanny from the fantastic-marvelous (1975: 44).

I would like to argue that both King's novel, as well as Kubrick's film, can be defined fantastic-marvelous tales because both the readers of the novel and the spectators of the film hesitate, at least at the beginning, between believing in a natural or supernatural explanation of the events described and shown, while, towards the end, they have to dismiss the natural solution and follow the supernatural one. But the question of whether to believe or not to believe is stressed more in the adaptation because it is carried on for a longer period of the narrative and remains always instilled in the audience.

After a comparison between the story and the plot of the novel and those of the film, and a discussion of the episodes of the book that were not directly adapted in the film, it is possible to claim that the majority of these events instill in the readers the suspicion that the Overlook Hotel is a haunted place, which obeys rules unknown to our own world. For example, the first main event that seems inexplicable in our physical laws, and that was not adapted in the film, is that of the wasps' nest. Jack finds a wasps' nest on the roof; after having killed all the wasps inside it with a bug bomb, he gives it to Danny. During the night the wasps in the nest on the boy's bedside table come out and sting him. The other main episodes of the novel, which were not adapted and which instill in the readers the doubt that the Overlook Hotel is haunted, are those concerning: the extinguisher; the hedge animals; the clock under glass, which seems to come alive; and the man dressed as a dog, who scares Danny and impedes him from crossing the corridors of the hotel.

If I discuss the events that were adapted but slightly changed from the novel, I come to the same conclusions. First of all, I examine Danny's character and, in particular, his capacity to speak with Tony, an "imaginary" friend. In both the novel and the film, it seems to be Tony who tells Danny what will happen in the future through images and direct speech. In the book, Tony seems to be physically present when Danny has his visions, and he speaks like all the other characters. For example, the first time that he appears in the novel he calls Danny, and he is described as being physically present, not far from the boy: *"Danny . . . Dannee'* He looked up and there was Tony, far up the street, standing by a stop sign and waving" (King, 2001: 33). In the adaptation, Tony seems more like an invention of Danny's mind because, when the boy speaks with him, he moves his index finger to represent him, and he speaks like a ventriloquist to report his words. Thus, both in the novel and the film, the readers and the spectators should wonder whether Tony is only the product of Danny's imagination or a real presence who lives outside the boy's fantasy, and whose existence follows different rules from those that govern our own world. But the spectators of the film should be more inclined towards a natural explanation, while the readers of the novel towards a supernatural one. The same thing occurs with Danny's "visions" that, as the narrative advances, reveal themselves to be flash-forwards. In the novel, they are more numerous, more varied, and more detailed, while in the film, the boy always sees the same simple images: blood coming out from elevators; two sisters, who are the two Grady girls, murdered by their father Grady (Philip Stone), the former winter caretaker of the Overlook Hotel; and the word "redrum" written in red lipstick on a door, which will later be written by Danny himself. What is more, the young protagonist of the book "reads" the thoughts of different people, and he holds a conversation with Hallorann, the cook of the hotel who can shine, without uttering a word. In the film, instead, the only sentence that Hallorann (Scatman Crothers) communicates by thought to Danny (and the spectators, but not the characters, can hear because it is recited while Hallorann is speaking about something else and in Hallorann's voice) is the following: "How'd you like some ice cream, Doc?" Moreover, in the adaptation, the boy only once reads his father's thoughts, foreseeing that he has obtained the job as winter caretaker of the Overlook Hotel, and that he is about to call home to announce the news. Therefore, in the case of Danny's capacity to read the thoughts of others and communicate by thought with Hallorann, while the readers of the novel should be inclined towards a supernatural answer to the young protagonist's abilities, the spectators of the film should (at least at the beginning, before Danny begins to call Hallorann in Miami to help him) be inclined towards a natural explanation of his powers.

Continuing the discussion of events in the novel that were adapted but slightly changed, Danny and then Jack enter room 217, the room about which Danny had had lots of horrible premonitions, and about which Hallorann had already alerted him. Danny finds a dead woman in the bathtub who stands up and tries to strangle him. Jack does not see her, but he does feel a hand touching his back in the bathroom; then he smells the scent of soap; and, finally, he feels a presence in the bathtub who is trying to reach him, and who is trying to open the door of room 217 while he is already in the corridor. This episode was adapted by Kubrick, but in the film the spectators see the son entering into room 237, followed by the effect of his transgression—that is, the boy scared, with bruises on his neck—but they never see him together with a dead woman. The spectators see only the father with a woman. Thus, once more, the audience of the adaptation should hesitate believing a natural or supernatural explanation of the event, because the encounter between Jack and the woman is not corroborated on screen by an encounter between Danny and the woman. On the other hand, the readers of the novel should be more inclined towards a supernatural interpretation of the episode because both father and son see and/or feel the same presence.

Both in the book and the film, the only character who the readers and the spectators can rely on is Wendy. Indeed, even if the readers and the spectators accept the idea that Danny has special powers, and often sees things that happened in the past or will happen in the future, the episodes that involve him could only be visions, invisible for characters who cannot shine. If, on the other hand, they believe that the boy's imagination is too fervid, Danny is an even more unreliable character. Jack is as untrustworthy as his son. Indeed, the readers and the spectators do not know whether what he sees is due to the fact that he is schizophrenic or to the fact that he is possessed and moved by the Overlook Hotel. Thus, when Wendy begins to see and hear strange things—when she begins to believe—the readers and the spectators begin to believe in a supernatural explanation of the events. Wendy is the character who represents the audience's hesitation between a natural and a supernatural answer to the episodes; she symbolizes the play of the fantastic genre. Entrusting the readers' and the spectators' role to a character is a condition (which may not be fulfilled) of the fantastic discussed by Todorov and already cited above. In King's novel, Wendy begins to believe that something strange is happening, which is not due to her husband's behavior, when she, together with Jack and Danny, hears noises coming from the elevator that seems to go up and down. In the adaptation, towards the end Wendy sees two masks, followed by Grady with a wound in his head, speaking to her and drinking, and then blood coming out of the elevators. Thus, in the film, the confirmation of a supernatural explanation of the events—of what father and son had experienced early on in the adaptation—arrives later in the development of the story.

Finally, the endings of the book and the film are completely different: while in King's novel the supernatural dominates the end, in Kubrick's adaptation the supernatural constitutes only an epilogue. Indeed, in the former case, the fact that Jack is possessed by the Overlook Hotel, which is alive with all its ghosts, becomes manifest. Danny manages to speak with Jack inside the monster, and Jack begins to hit himself. The hotel then tries to possess Hallorann in order to convince him to kill Wendy and Danny, but he resists its power. Finally, the Overlook Hotel explodes with Jack inside it and, to underline the fact that the hotel was haunted, Hallorann shines about a strange creature that represents the Overlook Hotel and that comes out from the Presidential Suite. In the film Jack, after having killed Hallorann with an axe, dies frozen in the maze, while attempting to kill Danny. In the very last sequence, in frame there is a photograph pinned on the wall of the Gold Room, in which Jack is together with the other participants at a ball in 1921. The image of Jack frozen in the maze, which closes the previous sequence, together with this photograph, which closes the film, raises more questions rather than just offering a supernatural

Episodes of the novel that are not adapted in the film	Wasps' nest.	
	Extinguisher outside room 217.	
	Hedge animals.	
Episodes of the novel that are adapted in the film, but slightly changed	**Novel**	**Film**
	Tony is described physically present and speaks through direct speech.	Danny moves his index finger and speaks like a ventriloquist to communicate with Tony.
	In room 217: Danny sees a woman; Jack feels a woman's presence.	In room 237: the spectators aren't shown Danny in the room with the woman, but only Jack.
	Wendy listens to noises coming from the elevator and finds confetti and a mask on its floor early in the plot.	Wendy sees inexplicable things only at the end of the story.
	Danny speaks with Jack inside the monster; the Overlook Hotel tries to possess Hallorann; the hotel explodes and Hallorann sees a strange creature coming out.	Jack dies frozen in the maze; he is present in a photograph from 1921.

Figure 5.2 Episodes of the novel that are not adapted, and that are adapted but slightly changed, which induce the readers to believe earlier than the spectators of the film in a supernatural explanation of the events.

explanation of the events as opposed to a natural one, as in the case of the book. Thus, in Kubrick's film, the play of to believe/not to believe continues until the very end because, when the supernatural seems to have been claimed, when Wendy and the spectators begin to believe that the laws of the Overlook Hotel are not the laws of our own world, Jack dies in a natural, simple way, and the haunted hotel and its ghosts do not help him (although the supernatural is suggested by the photograph). While in the novel, the play between to believe/not to believe—typical of the fantastic-marvelous—ceases, in the adaptation it continues until the very end.

Many episodes and motifs of the film that do not appear in the book were added to increase the uncanny features of the adaptation. It is Kubrick himself who, in some interviews, cites Freud and, especially, his concept of the uncanny, as the main source of inspiration for *The Shining*:

> About the only law that I think relates to the genre is that you should not try to explain, to find neat explanations for what happens, and that the object of the thing is to produce a sense of the uncanny. Freud on his essay on the uncanny wrote that the sense of the uncanny is the only emotion which is

more powerfully expressed in art than in life, which I found very illuminating. (Castle, 2005: 462)

In 1919, in his essay on this subject, the psychoanalyst begins his discussion from definitions reported in some dictionaries and finds that, in some cases, the German words *heimlich*, which means homely, and *heimisch*, which means native, coincide with their opposite, with *unheimlich*, which means something not known and unfamiliar (1919: 220–226). Analyzing Hoffmann's *The Sand-Man*, Freud lists some of the situations during which the feeling of the uncanny is evoked. For example, one of his alumnnus, Otto Rank, in 1914, in his essay on the double, claims that the double, which derives from the primary narcissism that dominates children and primitive men, has a positive meaning because it is identified with something, like the soul, which saves the body from death. Freud claims that, when primary narcissism is surmounted, the double no longer has a positive meaning, but becomes an uncanny signal of death. Indeed, it no longer represents the soul, but the double of the ego, the conscience, which observes and judges the ego. What is more, always in the later stages of the ego's development, all of the possible, but unfulfilled futures to which men are still attached are grouped under the concept of the double. As in the case of the double, the other situations that evoke uncanny feelings in Hoffmann's tale refer to phases that pertain to former stages of the ego's development—to phases that were surmounted—but that are evoked by the tale. Among these episodes there is, for example, the repetition of the same thing, when this repetition introduces the idea of fate rather than chance, suggesting that mysterious, occult powers could govern life. These examples pertain to the principle of the "omnipotence of thought," which coincides with the primitive, animistic conception of the universe, which is still shared by children and which, in the later stages of the ego's development, is surmounted, but could come back, producing uncanny feelings, if it is stimulated by situations like those cited above. Therefore, the uncanny is something repressed that recurs, something familiar that had become unfamiliar through repression, but that comes back (1919: 226–245).

Freud closes his essay distinguishing between the uncanny that derives from those beliefs, shared by primitive men and children, which were surmounted; and the uncanny that derives from infantile complexes, such as the castration complex and womb-phantasies. He also distinguishes between reality and fiction. Indeed, he claims that the uncanny deriving from beliefs surmounted works in real life and in fiction if the setting is material reality, but it does not work in fiction if the setting is arbitrary and artificial. By contrast, the uncanny deriving from infantile complexes works both in real life and in fiction, but it is not as frequent in real life as the other type of uncanny (1919: 245–252). Thus, using Todorov's terminology (but putting it in inverted commas so as not to confuse what the Russian formalist means with the genre "uncanny" with what Freud defines as uncanny): if a tale pertains to the "uncanny" genre, the uncanny can derive both from beliefs surmounted and from repressed infantile complexes; if a tale pertains to the "marvelous" genre, the uncanny can derive only from repressed infantile complexes. Regarding the "supernatural," the psychoanalyst emphasizes that, in this type of tale, the uncanny can derive both from beliefs surmounted and repressed infantile complexes, as long as the author does not manifest that his tale is "marvelous." Thus, in Kubrick's *The Shining*, which, until almost the very end, pertains to the "fantastic" genre, the uncanny can derive both from beliefs surmounted and from repressed infantile complexes.

Freud's essay on the uncanny clearly affected the director's adaptation, as several uncanny features described by the psychoanalyst appear in the episodes and themes of the film that were not adapted from the novel. For example, in Kubrick's adaptation, the double is evoked by Danny's "imaginary" friend Tony; by mirrors; and by the photograph that shows Jack in 1921. When Danny speaks with Tony, he moves his index finger and speaks with a strange, modified voice, making it seem that Tony lives inside Danny. Indeed, if the spectators believe that Tony is not a creation of the boy's imagination, he is nonetheless a being who needs Danny's body to speak, so is in effect Danny's double. If the audience believes that Tony is a creation of the boy's imagination, Danny has a double personality; he is again a double, but in another sense.

Moreover, mirrors and images reflected are numerous. For example, when Danny speaks with Tony for the first time, he is looking at himself in the mirror of his bathroom. From a medium shot of Danny, the camera tracks in on his reflection in the mirror, ending in a close-up of him. Later, when Wendy brings Jack his breakfast at the hotel, he looks at himself into the mirror. The first signs of his madness begin to appear because he seems to have already lost the notion of time. Indeed, he is awakened at half-past eleven by Wendy, and asks her what time is it. Similarly, when father and son speak about the Overlook Hotel, in frame there is a *plain américain* of Jack and his image reflected in the mirror. He seems already sick because he looks absentminded. As discussed in the previous chapter, when he asks Danny whether he likes the Overlook Hotel, Jack says: "I wish we could stay here forever and ever . . . ever." Significantly, when Jack enters into room 237, there is a close-up of him embracing and kissing a naked, young, beautiful woman; the camera then pans from left to right on the reflected images of them in a mirror, revealing that the girl has become old and decayed. The mirror seems to have the magical power of reflecting reality and its dangers. Similarly, when Danny repeats "redrum" and writes it on the door in red lipstick, through Wendy's point of view there is a long shot of the door with the word "murder" reflected in the mirror. Thus, the true meaning of the word "redrum" is revealed through a mirror. Finally, mirrors are present in the shots filmed at the bar of the Gold Room, when Jack drinks and speaks with Lloyd (Joe Turkel), and in the shot in the bathroom of the Gold Room, when he speaks with Grady. In this case, the presence of mirrors seems to highlight the double life of the Overlook Hotel.

Furthermore, as already mentioned, the last shot of the film is a medium close-up of Jack in a photograph pinned on a wall of the Colorado Lounge. The camera then tilts down until in frame appears the sign "July 4th Ball 1921." Therefore, the protagonist has always been at the service of the hotel and has always been identical to himself, but he was also a father, a husband, a teacher, and a man who hoped to become a writer. Jack was a double and had a double life.

Among beliefs surmounted, Freud also cites the repetition of the same things when this repetition introduces the idea of fatality (the idea that mysterious, occult powers could govern life). What is more, he argues that, when repetition becomes uncanny, it evokes the dreamer's feeling of impotence:

> The factor of the repetition of the same thing will perhaps not appeal to everyone as a source of uncanny feeling. From what I have observed, this phenomenon does undoubtedly subject to certain conditions and combined with certain circumstances arouse an uncanny feeling, which, furthermore, recalls the sense of helplessness experienced in some dream-states. (1919: 235–236)

Thus, the dreamy atmosphere of Kubrick's adaptation is not due only to supernatural elements and some cinematic techniques, but also repetition. This latter motif is evoked, for example, by the repetition of Danny's visions discussed above or when Wendy looks at Jack's paper she finds that hundreds of sheets are full of the same sentence: "All work and no

Episodes and themes of the film that are not adapted from the novel	
Double	**Tony**: Danny moves his index finger and speaks like a ventriloquist to communicate with Tony.
	Mirrors, for example: 1. when Danny speaks with Tony for the first time; 2. when Jack is in room 237 with the woman.
	Photograph: Jack is present in a photograph from 1921.
Repetition of the same things	**Danny's visions**: 1. blood coming out of the elevators; 2. the two Grady girls; 3. the word "redrum."
	Jack's work: "All work and no play make Jack a dull boy."
	Labyrinth: 1. maze; 2. corridors.

Figure 5.3 Episodes and themes of the film that are not adapted from the novel, and that introduce uncanny features.

play make Jack a dull boy." And, as already discussed, characters often repeat the other characters' words. Furthermore, the maze and the corridors of the Overlook Hotel introduce the idea of repetition, because the paths of the maze and the corridors of the hotel are all the same, as already argued. In his essay on the uncanny, Freud writes about one of his uncanny experiences that evokes the theme of the labyrinth. He was walking in a deserted, provincial town in Italy, when he found himself in a narrow street. He hastened to leave it, but he found himself back in it two other times (1919: 236).

In what follows, I analyze Noël Carroll's definition of the horror genre, and I link it to Todorov's study of the fantastic (Todorov, 1975). Carroll gives the following definition of the horror genre:

> Assuming that "I-as-an-audience-member" am in an analogous emotional state to that which fictional characters beset by monsters are described to be in, then: I am currently art-horrified by some monster X, say Dracula, if and only if
> 1) I am in some state of abnormal, physically felt agitation (shuddering, tingling, screaming, etc.) which
> 2) has been caused by
> a) the thought: that Dracula is a possible being; and by the evaluative thoughts: that
> b) said Dracula has the property of being physically (and perhaps morally and socially) threatening in the ways portrayed in the fiction and that
> c) said Dracula has the property of being impure, where

> 3) such thoughts are usually accompanied by the desire to avoid the touch of things like Dracula. (1990: 27)

Therefore, according to Carroll, a being, to be defined horrific, must be physically threatening and impure. And a monster "is impure if it is categorically interstitial, categorically contradictory, incomplete, or formless" (1990: 32). According to Carroll, if the monster is not impure, but only physically threatening, the tale cannot be defined horror, but a tale of dread. The scholar, to distinguish tales of dread from horror stories, specifies that

> these events are construed to move the audience rhetorically to the point that one entertains the idea that unavowed, unknown, and perhaps concealed and inexplicable forces rule the universe. Where art-horror involves disgust as a central feature, what might be called art-dread does not. (1990: 42)

Consequently, I can add that horror stories are a subgenre of tales of dread because, if, from the first definition of horror stories reported above, we delete condition 2a, which states that the monster must be impure, we obtain the definition of tales of dread.

If we compare Carroll's study of horrific beings to Kubrick's *The Shining*, we can claim that only the two Grady girls and the woman in the bathroom of room 237 are horrific beings. They are indeed physically threatening; the two Grady girls threaten Danny by asking him to play with them forever, while the woman tries to strangle Danny and to hold Jack. They are also impure because they transgress the categorical distinction between living/dead. Lloyd, Grady, and the other guests at the masked ball, and the two masks seen by Wendy, are not horrific beings because, although they transgress the categorical distinction between living/dead, they do not seem to be physically threatening. More numerous are the horrific beings described in King's *The Shining* because, in addition to those shown in the film, we must add all of the beings that are both physically threatening and impure, such as the wasps; the extinguisher; the hedge animals; the man dressed as a dog; and the Overlook Hotel itself because, when it explodes, Hallorann sees a strange creature, which represents the Overlook Hotel, coming out of the Presidential Suite. Jack's character needs to be discussed alone. Indeed, both in the film and the novel he is physically threatening, but while in the film he is not

Horrific beings	
Novel	**Film**
Woman in room 217; Two Grady girls.	
Wasps; Extinguisher; Hedge animals; Man dressed as a dog; Overlook Hotel; Jack.	

Figure 5.4 Horrific beings in the novel and in the film.

impure and, consequently, he cannot be considered a horrific being, in the novel—at least at the end—he can be considered an impure and horrific being. When, in King's novel, Danny understands that Jack is possessed by the Overlook Hotel, he manages to speak with his father inside the monster, and Jack begins to hit himself. Thus, in the novel Jack is like Dr. Jekyll and Mr. Hyde; he becomes a horrific being. After these considerations, we can claim that while King's novel can certainly be defined as a classic horror tale, Kubrick's film is not a typical example of the genre, although it can be defined as horror.

To relate his study to Todorov's analysis about the fantastic, Carroll claims that not all of the fantastic-marvelous tales are horror stories. But, with a few observations, the two studies can be related more closely. Indeed, Todorov argues that a tale can be defined fantastic-marvelous when, after a hesitation between a natural and a supernatural explanation of the events, the characters and the readers must accept a supernatural explanation, and must believe that the physical laws of the world described are not those that govern our own world. A tale can be defined as marvelous if, from the beginning, the physical laws of the diegetic world are different from those of the extradiegetic world, and are accepted from the characters and from the readers. According to Carroll, the world described in a tale of dread is characterized by unknown, unavowed laws. I have discussed how horror stories can be considered a subgenre of tales of dread. Therefore, tales of dread and, consequently, horror stories, can be considered a subgenre of the

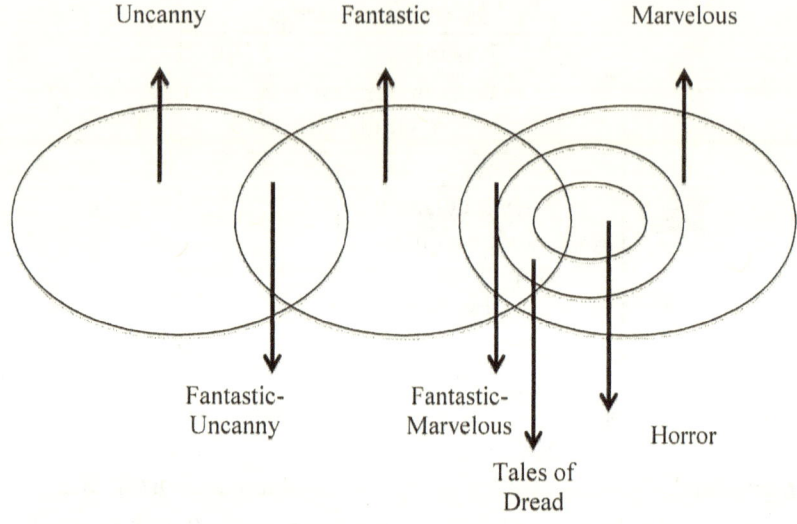

Figure 5.5 Figure, based upon sets, to show that the horror genre is a subset of tales of dread, and that they both are subsets of the marvelous and the fantastic-marvelous sets.

fantastic-marvelous and of the marvelous genre. Thus, linking Todorov and Carroll's analysis, I propose the figure above:

In the intersection between the uncanny and the fantastic genre, there is the fantastic-uncanny genre. In the intersection between the fantastic and the marvelous genre, there is the fantastic-marvelous genre. The set of horror stories is inside the set of tales of dread because the former are a subset of the latter. Both the set of horror stories and that of tales of dread are inside the set of the marvelous genre, but, given the fact that they can be marvelous or fantastic-marvelous, they are in the marvelous set and in the intersection between the marvelous and the fantastic genre.

According to my previous analysis, both King's novel and Kubrick's film should be among the fantastic-marvelous horror stories. In King's novel, however, the readers hesitate for a shorter period of time between a supernatural or natural explanation of the events than the spectators of Kubrick's film. And the novel can be considered a more typical, classic example of the horror genre than the film. Thus, I propose the following figure, based upon gaps, to differentiate the novel from the film:

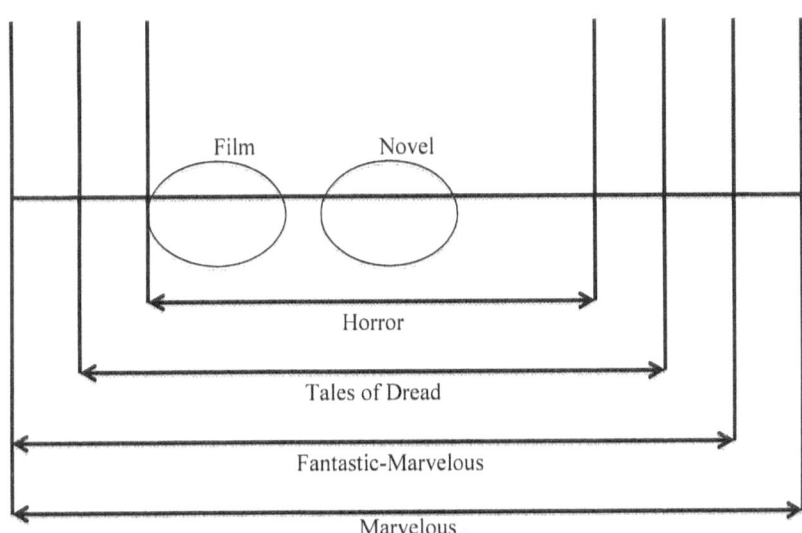

Figure 5.6 Figure, based upon gaps, to show that both the film and the novel are fantastic-marvelous and horror stories, but the book is a more typical example of the horror genre than the adaptation.

Chapter Six

ARTIFICIALITY, MODERNISM, AND THE SUBLIME

Reflexivity

As discussed in the previous chapter, Kubrick's protagonists are usually passive spectators and listeners in their diegetic worlds. They often remain entrapped in a dreamy world, governed by the director's aesthetic rules, in which the extradiegetic world is often cited. Indeed, the films deliberately exhibit their awareness of being works of art in several ways. For example, the diegetic world is evoked in the diegesis itself through the presence of scenes that recall previous sequences, or foretell subsequent events, often parodying them. Or the extradiegetic world is evoked in the diegetic world both indirectly and directly. In the former case, the extradiegesis is recalled through the evocation of the making of the film and, in the latter, through the citation of the cinematic medium in the medium itself.

For example, *Eyes Wide Shut* seems to be structured to exhibit its artificiality thanks to its numerous cross-references. In all other Kubrick adaptations, there are several scenes that reference other sequences. Some of them work like *déjà vu*, evoking previous episodes. Others work like flash-forwards, announcing events that are to follow. And this narrative construction increases the protagonists' passivity because they remain entrapped in it. In the director's last film, however, the citation of the diegetic world in the diegesis itself often becomes a parody (which is to say, given a hypotext with a noble subject and a noble style, its parody is characterized by a vulgar subject narrated in the same noble style of the hypotext [Genette, 1997: 29–36]). It is as if Kubrick has substituted the novel protagonist's dramatic odyssey and loneliness, his mental wandering among his wife's thoughts of infidelity, and his physical wandering in a society in which he aimlessly looks for a place, with a self-referential parody. The narrator's dramatic mood and Fridolin's fluxes of conscience are translated, in the adaptation, through Bill's expressionless face which stares at scenes that parody his own experiences. For example, the episode at Rainbow Fashions not only announces the orgy, but also parodies it. While the former episode could be defined as comedy, the latter is enveloped in a dramatic, almost sacred atmosphere. The masked women of the orgy are substituted by a Lolita with an angelic face. The men with Venetian masks and dark cloaks become two Japanese men, almost naked, with colorful wigs and made up as women. And the role of the purple mask, master of ceremonies, who utters a few, lapidary sentences, is played by a loquacious man, worried by his incipient baldness, who mixes different registers. Indeed, in a single sentence, when he gently speaks to Bill, he refers to his daughter with harsh epithets and he menaces the two Japanese men.

> MILICH: And you little whore! I kill you for this. I promise. I kill you. I kill you (to his daughter). Hold on to that girl for me please (to Bill).
> JAPANESE MAN: Milich, this is preposterous. The young lady invited us here.
> MILICH: Couldn't you see she is deranged? (to the Japanese men). Doctor, I'm sorry to keep you waiting (to Bill). Gentlemen, this is now a police matter. You will please stay here until I return (to the Japanese men).
> JAPANESE MAN: Let us out of here!
> MILICH: That's out of the question (to the Japanese men). Doctor, sorry. What color did you say? Black? (to Bill).
> BILL: Black.
> MILICH: Gentlemen, please have the goodness to be quiet for the moment! Couldn't you see I try to serve my customer? (to the Japanese men) Sorry (to Bill). And you, little whore, go to bed at once, you depraved creature. I'll deal with you as soon as after I serve this gentleman (to his daughter).

In the novel, Gibiser is described as "a comic elder in a play" (Schnitzler, 1999: 37). But the two masked men are "two masked figures in the red robes of vehmic court judges" (1999: 38) who, when they are discovered by Gibiser, transform themselves into "two slim young gentlemen in white ties and evening dress" (1999: 40). What is more, although the costumier adopts different registers to speak with Fridolin, his daughter, and the two French men, he does not mix them in a single sentence (1999: 38–41). Thus, in the written medium the scene is not the comedy that it is in the film.

In the film, Bill's fantasy image, which is shown directly to the spectators and in which Alice is filmed while making love to a naval officer, can be interpreted as another parody of Fridolin's fluxes of conscience. In both media, the wife's confession of her unfulfilled desire to have been unfaithful to her husband is evoked several times. In the cinematic medium, this scene appears five times: as Bill is reaching Marion's apartment; when he sees a couple kissing each other before meeting the group of boys; the first and the second time that he goes to the orgy mansion; and before calling Marion from his studio. Thus, both the orgy and Marion's confession seem to recall Alice's confession. In the novel, Fridolin's obsession is continuously evoked through his fluxes of conscience and flashbacks, which permeate almost all of his adventures. In particular, Kubrick's choice to link the protagonist's obsession with Marion's confession seems to emphasize the similarities in the behavior of Alice and Marion because, in both cases, the female protagonist explicitly expresses her desire to be unfaithful to her lover. Moreover, in both scenes Bill, during the confession, remains motionless and expressionless, and says fewer words than the female character. Both sequences also take place in a bedroom where the same blue light filters from the windows behind the characters.[1] What is more, during the first scene in Marion's apartment, the similarities between Bill and Carl (Thomas Gibson), who is the fiancé of Marion, are emphasized. Both men seem not to know or to avoid knowing their lovers' obscure desires. And the sequence in which the protagonist enters Marion's apartment is identical to the one in which Carl enters his fiancée's apartment. Indeed, in both cases a Steadicam follows Bill or Carl, who pass from the hall, through the corridor, to arrive at the door of Marion's bedroom, with the same straight-on angle and maintaining the same distance from the characters. Moreover, the two actors are dressed in almost the exact same manner: Bill with a black suit, and Carl with a pair of dark trousers and a jacket. They also have the same black, meticulously combed hair. Finally, their dialogue with the maid is comprised of almost the same words. Carl's role, as the fiancé of Marion, becomes ridiculous after his lover's declaration of love for Bill. Consequently, thanks to the implicit comparison between Alice and Marion, and Bill and Carl, the doctor's social status as Alice's husband becomes a parody of the fidelity and love of their marriage.

In the film, the explicit sexual availability of the women met by Bill during his nightly wanderings is parodied too by the ironic figure of a desk clerk (Alan Cumming). He is elegant and polite, his gestures and laughs are theatrical and ape those of a homosexual, and he seems to flirt with the protagonist. Therefore, during this scene, once again the adaptation underlines, together with the cross-references among sequences, their theatrical and over-emphasized parodic quality.

Kubrick's films also deliberately display their awareness of being works of art through an indirect citation of the extradiegetic world in the diegesis, in particular through the evocation of the making of the films. For example, the director's cinematic techniques are employed to shoot a film-within-the-film and, thus, they are foregrounded; or the narrative fluidity is broken, so that a strong authorial presence is recalled; or the actors' roles as characters who are playing is unveiled through the metaphor of theatre; or the protagonists mimic the spectators' role.

The first case, in which an intradiegetic film presents the same stylistic features of the diegetic film, appears in *A Clockwork Orange* during the Ludovico cure, and in *Full Metal Jacket* when, as already discussed, the three-man television crew shoots a film about Vietnam, and when the soldiers are interviewed about their experiences during the war. In *A Clockwork Orange*, when the protagonist is submitted to the Ludovico treatment, he, together with the spectators, is forced to watch violent films. During the first session of the cure, the spectators are shown two of the films that the protagonist is obliged to see. During the first movie, which is shot with a handheld camera, a man is beaten almost to death by four *droogs* and, during the second, a girl is raped by several criminals. During the first film, Alex's voice-over comments: "It's funny how the colors of the real world only seem really real when you viddy them on a screen." This phrase sounds ironic because the protagonist seems to realize the effects and the crudeness of his past violent actions when they are not real for him, when they are not part of his diegetic world, but instead pertain to the intradiegetic world of a film. It is as if, in the extradiegetic world of the director and his spectators, Kubrick suggested to the viewers of *A Clockwork Orange* that, paradoxically, the violence in their world seems real only when it is filmed. This concept is underlined by another remark pronounced by Alex in a voice-over during the projection of the second movie:

> This seemed real, very real, though if you thought about it properly you couldn't imagine lewdies actually agreeing to having all this done to them in a film, and if these films were made by the good, or the State, you couldn't imagine them being allowed to take these films, without like interfering with what was going on.

Ironically, the protagonist asks himself what reaction the State might have to the film, and thinks that it would not allow such a movie to be made and shown. What Alex, in the diegetic world of *A Clockwork Orange*, thinks about the State's reactions to the intradiegetic film reflects exactly, in the extradiegetic world, the polemics aroused by the censure, the authorities, and the majority of the public opinion against Kubrick's movie. But neither the intradiegetic films of *A Clockwork Orange* nor the director's movie are real, and both continuously display their artificiality. Indeed, the fiction of the movies is stressed by Alex's close-ups, which interrupt the narrative fluidity of the intradiegetic films, by the protagonist's voice-over, which comments upon the scenes, and, during the second movie, by the montage following the music. These techniques are some of the devices that characterize the unreality of *A Clockwork Orange*, too, so the intradiegetic films perfectly mimic the diegetic film.

Unlike *A Clockwork Orange*, in *Full Metal Jacket* the referentiality of the diegesis is stressed by the artificiality of the film-within-the-film not only because both the diegetic movie and the intradiegetic movie are shot with the same cinematic techniques, but also because the crew of the intradiegetic film, together with a camera and a microphone, is in frame. Indeed, both when the three-man television crew shoots a film about Vietnam, and when the soldiers of Joker's platoon are interviewed about their experiences during the war, the "grunts" look directly into the camera in frame. Thus, they refer to a spectator who does not coincide with us but to an imaginary audience of the film-within-the-film, because we are not shown the soldiers through the camera in the frame. Therefore, on the one hand, we have the impression of being directly addressed by the characters. On the other hand, we acknowledge that this feeling is only the result of a *mise-en-scène* that manifests the referentiality of *Full Metal Jacket*. This play is only alluded to in the novel, and it is not as clearly developed as in the adaptation. Indeed, when Joker and Rafter Man arrive at Phu Bai Combat Base, they meet Chili Vendor and Daytona Dave who are taking photographs of, and getting information from the "grunts," for their hometown newspapers. Each soldier has to smile while he is photographed: "Daytona Dave is taking the photographs with a black-body Nikon while Chili Vendor says, 'Smile, scumbag. Say, 'shit.' 'Next'"; and has to hold a bar in his hands: "Chili Vendor slaps a rubber Hershey bar into the grunt's hand. 'Smile, scumbag. Say, 'shit.' Next'" (Hasford, 1980: 56). At Hue, before Joker and Rafter Man find Cowboy's platoon, a "CBS camera crew appears, surrounded by star-struck grunts who strike combat-marine poses, pretending to be what they are" (1980: 84). In the film, when the "grunts" are interviewed, the artificiality of the film is underlined also by the fact that they speak about their experiences in Vietnam as if they were commenting upon their roles as actors. Their phrases seem to unveil the artificiality of the war depicted in *Full Metal Jacket*. For example, Cowboy claims: "When we're in Hue . . . when we're in Hue City . . . it's like a war. You know, like what I thought about a war, what I thought a war was, was supposed to be. There's the enemy, kill 'em." Thus, the Vietnam War represented in Kubrick's film is not the war, but it is "like a war"; it is how the spectators imagine it. Joker says: "I wanted to see exotic Vietnam, the jewel of Southeast Asia. I wanted to meet interesting and stimulating people of an ancient culture and . . . kill them. I wanted to be the first kid on my block to get a confirmed kill." Therefore, he adopts stereotyped words to describe Vietnam, increasing the impression that he is not speaking about a real place, but an imaginary one. The impression that the crew in frame is a troupe documenting the making of the diegetic film is stressed by the clipboard on which it is written, "Hue City—Roll #34." What is more, the cinematic medium is not only cited through the presence in frame of a camera, a microphone, and a clipboard, but also of a cinema that appears in the background when Doc Jay and Joker are interviewed.

The films-within-the-film also stress the artificiality of *Full Metal Jacket* because they break the narrative fluidity. Indeed, the scene of the three-man television crew appears after an enemy attack, which ends with Mr. Touchdown's death, and before he is shown in a grave. This last sequence comes before the soldiers' interview, a scene that is followed by a sequence in which the "grunts" bargain with a prostitute. As already analyzed in Chapter II, this method of breaking the narrative fluidity through the insertion of episodes, which are separated by ellipses and are not linked by cause and effect chains, is a feature common to all Kubrick adaptations.

But the narrative fluidity is disrupted not only thanks to the succession of scenes, but also in single sequences. For example, as already discussed, in *A Clockwork Orange* it is broken through the use of wide-angle lenses, through characters who look directly into the camera, and through slow and high-speed motion, but also thanks to a rapid montage. When Alex goes back home for the first time and listens to the Ninth Symphony, there is a montage of details of a statue that represents four Jesus figures who embrace each other. These twenty shots quickly succeed one another, following the rhythm of the music, as if the four Jesuses were really dancing. When Alex hits the cat lady with a penis statue, the blow is preceded by point of view shots and symbolized by a rapid montage. This editing, which follows the rhythm of *The Thieving Magpie*, is a succession of details of erotic paintings, the same ones that decorate the walls of the room. Similarly, when the protagonist meets the homeless man who had been beaten by him and his *droogs*, and he is hit by the tramp and his friends, the scene is shown in a rapid montage of images. There are fourteen close-ups of grinning tramps, quickly succeeding one another, like a portrait gallery of old, dirty, toothless, and wrinkled faces. They look into the camera, directly addressing the audience. During this montage, Alex's voice-over comments: "Then there was like a sea of dirty, smelly old men trying to get at your humble narrator with their feeble rookers and horny old claws. It was old age having a go at youth." It is as if he was describing the very succession of images shown to the spectators. Thus, in these sequences, elements of the *mise-en-scène* are edited in a quick succession to symbolize violence. The narrative fluidity is broken, and the *auteur*'s intervention is foregrounded.

The referentiality of *A Clockwork Orange* is also stressed thanks to the metaphor of theatre through which the characters' performances, together with other cinematic techniques, break the illusion of reality. The characters become actors who play their roles in front of the audience. As already discussed, this effect is achieved when the protagonist's gang meets Billyboy's gang, when Alex and his *droogs* are in Mr. Alexander's house, and it is particularly emphasized when the results of the Ludovico cure are shown during a public demonstration that is staged as a theatrical play. Indeed, the last episode is set in an auditorium that strongly resembles a theatre. Alex is on a stage, lit by a pool of light, the spectators are sitting in front of him, in the dark of the parterre, and the Minister of the Interior introduces the show as if he was a narrator. Indeed, he refers to the spectators as "Ladies and Gentlemen" and, after having recounted all of the advantages of the treatment, and before the first actor comes on stage, he exclaims: "But enough of words—actions speak louder than. Action now. Observe all." Then an actor, coming from one side of the scene, lit by a pool of light, begins to insult and hit the protagonist who, in the end, is compelled to lick his shoes. This first act of the play is interrupted by the minister himself who claims: "Enough! That will do very well. Thank you." The spectators applaud, the actor bows, thanks the audience, and leaves the stage through one wing. Then, from that same side of the stage, comes a naked girl, lit by a pool of light, who walks towards Alex to provoke him, but he is not able to react to her beauty. The second act of the play ends once more with the audience's applause and the actress's bows. What is more, the audience of the film does not coincide with the diegetic spectators because the former does not watch the show from the parterre, but through the director's camera. And, at least once during each act, the unreality of the tragedy becomes evident through Alex's point of view shots. The artificiality of the demonstration and of the film, of the intradiegetic play and of the diegetic world, are once more stated. As in the adaptation, in the novel this episode is described as if it was a theatrical play. In the book, Alex is led to where he was subjected to the Ludovico cure, but the place is now transformed into a theatre: "Curtains had been drawn in front of the sinny screen. . . . And where there had been just the noise of coughing haskl haskl haskl and like shadows of the lewdies was now a real audience" (Burgess, 2000a: 91). Much like in the film, the acts unfold like a theatrical performance, and the metaphor of theatre is emphasized by the description of the spotlights, the actors' behavior, the Minister of the Interior's comments, and the spectators' applause.

As already discussed, the metaphor of theatre also characterizes the orgy episode in *Eyes Wide Shut*. This interpretation of the events that take place in the mansion is the same explanation suggested by Victor Ziegler. Indeed, after Bill is expelled from the orgy, he tries to find out the identity of the mysterious woman who has sacrificed herself to save him, and what has happened to her. In a newspaper article, he reads: "A former Miss New York was rushed to New York Hospital this morning in critical conditions after a drug overdose . . . Amanda Curran." When he goes to the morgue, he recognizes Mandy, the woman who has overdosed in Ziegler's bathroom during the Christmas party. Victor calls the protagonist and explains to him what happened:

> Bill, suppose I told you that, that everything that happened to you there, the threats, the girl's warnings, her last-minute intervention, suppose I said that all of that was staged. That it was a kind of charade. That it was fake . . . You want to know what kind of charade? I'll tell you exactly what kind. That whole play-acted, "take-me" phony sacrifice that you've been jerking off with had nothing to do with her real death.

Thus, he uses words like "staged," "charade," "fake," and "play-acted," which suggest a *mise-en-scène*, a play. These explanations are hypothesized, in the novel, by the protagonist Fridolin himself who adopts words like "charade," "play a part," and "comedy" in his flashbacks and fluxes of conscience,

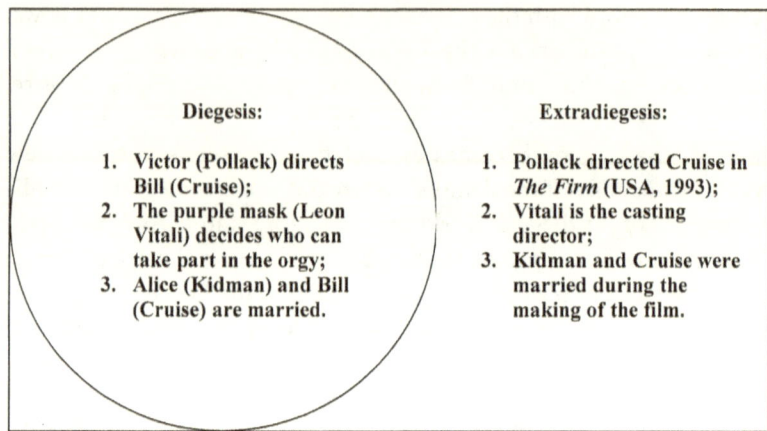

Figure 6.1 The circle represents the diegetic world of the film, while what is outside it symbolizes the extradiegetic world.

and when he speaks during the orgy (Schnitzler, 1999: 53, 76). Thus, Victor's explanations could be an adaptation of Fridolin's mental wanderings.

In the film, the impression that the orgy was a spectacle, organized to entertain both the protagonist and the extradiegetic audience, seems to be corroborated by the allusions and coincidences between the extradiegetic world and the diegetic world. For example, Ziegler's character, who organizes the Christmas party where Bill meets Nightingale and Mandy, is played by Sydney Pollack, who directed Tom Cruise in *The Firm* (USA, 1993). Thus, Victor seems to direct Bill as Pollack directed Cruise, and the diegetic world seems to evoke the extradiegetic world. The link between the two worlds is strengthened by the fact that Leon Vitali plays the role of the purple mask who, at the beginning of the orgy, is in charge of the strange rite and, at the end, menaces the protagonist and expels him from the mansion. In the extradiegetic world of the film, he is the casting director, and he chooses who can take part in the film and who cannot. Thus, like Pollack, he seems to play the same role both in the extradiegetic world and the diegetic world. What is more, in the article through which Bill comes to know about Mandy's death, the spectators read (through the protagonist's point of view): "After being hired for a series of magazine ads for London fashion designer Leon Vitali, rumours began circulating of an affair between the two." Thus, Leon Vitali's real name is cited in the diegesis of the film. Finally, as regards the references between the extradiegetic world and the diegetic world, the two protagonists, Bill and Alice, are played by Cruise and Nicole Kidman who, during the making of the film, were married in real life, too (see Figure 6.1).

Therefore, the metaphor of theatre, and the citations of the extradiegetic world in the diegetic world stress the reflexivity of the adaptation, which seems to be a meditation on the creation of a fictional world, and on its borders and links with the real one.

In the director's adaptations, the extradiegetic world is indirectly evoked in the diegesis not only because the characters often unveil their role as actors, but also because they mimic the spectators' role. Indeed, Kubrick's characters often stare motionless at the spectacle staged before their eyes. What is more, in *A Clockwork Orange*, during the Ludovico treatment, Alex is shown while watching films and, in *2001: A Space Odyssey*, during the Star-gate sequence, shots of the space-temporal tunnel are intercut with Bowman's close-ups. The astronaut is a spectator of the director's special effects, as is the extradiegetic audience.

The extradiegesis is also evoked in the diegesis directly, and the films become parodies of the cinematic medium itself, as in the scenes from *Full Metal Jacket* discussed above. Or when, in *A Clockwork Orange*, Alex's thoughts become a parody of Hollywood movies and when, in *The Shining*, dialogue refers to the horror genre and fairy tales. For example, when the protagonist of *A Clockwork Orange* arrives home for the first time, the spectators are shown what he imagines: a woman who is hanged; Alex dressed as a vampire; an explosion; some rocks falling from a mountain; and fire. These are parodies of classical Hollywood films, and the quick succession of these images follows the rhythm of the diegetic Ninth Symphony. When Alex is reading the Bible in the prison library, the audience is shown his visions. First, he sees himself dressed as a Roman who is whipping Jesus, exclaiming, "Move on there. Move on," with a typical American accent as if to imitate Hollywood historical films. Then, he imagines himself cutting the throat of another soldier and fighting. And, finally, he sees himself eating grapes with three naked women who are lying on a bed with him. These are instead transvestisms (that is to say, given a hypotext with a noble subject and a noble style, its hypertext is characterized by a noble subject recounted through a low style [Genette, 1997: 29–36]) of classical Hollywood historical films. At the end of the film, the protagonist imagines himself making love to a woman. They are both completely naked, lying down on a bed of artificial snow between two rows of spectators who wear Victorian dresses. In this case, too, Alex's thoughts are a parody of classical Hollywood films. This feature stresses once more the film's frequent technique of referring to and recalling the extradiegetic world to induce the spectators to think not only about the film, but also about the representations of violence in the cinematic medium.

While in *A Clockwork Orange* Kubrick parodies classical Hollywood films through his protagonist's visions, in *The Shining* he parodies the horror genre and fairy tales through the use of dialogue. For example, when Jack is first told about the slaughter carried out by the former winter caretaker of the Overlook Hotel, and he is asked about his wife's possible reactions to this story, he says, "And as far as my wife is concerned, I'm sure she'll be absolutely fascinated when I tell her. She's a confirmed ghost story and horror film addict." When the Torrances move to the hotel and are told that they will soon forget that there had been anybody there, Wendy replies, "Just like a ghost ship, huh?" These references suggest to the spectators that they are going to watch a horror film about ghosts. What is more, these phrases sound ironic because they are pronounced by the same characters who will remain entrapped in these experiences. Thus, it is explicitly acknowledged to the audience that the diegetic world is a fiction. Furthermore, two fairy tales are alluded to. *Hansel and Gretel* is adopted by Wendy to describe the hugeness of the hotel: "This whole place is such an enormous maze. I'll have to leave a trail of breadcrumbs every time I come in." Moreover, she adopts the expression "enormous maze," which foreshadows how the director will transform the hotel into a labyrinth thanks to the use of the Steadicam. And the story of *The Three Little Pigs* is used and staged by Jack when he looks for his wife and son to kill them, playing the role of the wolf himself:

> JACK: Come out, come out, wherever you are.
> WENDY: I can't get out! Run! Run and hide! Run! Quick!
> JACK: Little pigs, little pigs, let me come in. Not by the hair on your chinny-chin-chin. Then I'll huff and I'll puff and I'll blow your house in!

Kubrick adaptations foreground their artificiality breaking the illusion of reality, advising the spectators that they are watching a film. This technique, together with the other features discussed in the previous chapters, help me to contextualize the last six Kubrick adaptations.

Modernism and Postmodernism

The Kubrick adaptations discussed in this book are difficult to contextualize in the history of cinema for several reasons. First, because they pertain to different genres: science-fiction, dystopian films, costume dramas, horror films, postmodern Vietnam movies, and thrillers. What is more, they often transcend the features that characterize their genre, as in the case of *The Shining*. Second, because they were made in different historical periods: from 1968 to 1999 when, respectively, *2001: A Space Odyssey*, and *Eyes Wide Shut* were first released. Thus, neither an approach from the point of view of the history and development of genres, nor a discussion of the sociopolitical context in which the films were made, can furnish an exhaustive contextualization of the features of the director's style discussed in the previous chapters.

Moreover, as regards adaptation studies, Kubrick adapted novels by different authors with different styles, who come from different sociopolitical periods and geographical areas. Thus, a discussion, like those of Robert Stam (2005) or Jackob Lothe (2000), which begin with the literary tradition of the novels and with their authors' style, is unthinkable. What is more, there is no systematic history of adaptations within the history of cinema. Which is to say, the history of cinema has never been discussed from the perspective of adaptation studies. A lot of questions remain unanswered, such as: are there particular authors and novels that were mostly adapted in a particular historical period? And for what reasons? Only some particular authors, such as Shakespeare, are studied from the point of view of the history of adaptations.[2] The reason for such a lack of interest in a systematic history of cinematic adaptations could be the very hybrid nature of adaptation studies, suspended between literature and film criticism (Ray, 2000: 46). Indeed, on the one hand, literary scholars seem worried about how an author, a novel, or a genre is interpreted by different directors and, from an intertextual perspective, about how much a text is modified and enriched during the process of adaptation. On the other hand, film scholars seem more concerned about a history of cinematic techniques and styles, of sociopolitical and commercial influences rather than literary ones. It is true that adaptation studies offers to literary and film scholars the opportunity to quickly and easily write papers, in which they have often compared a novel with its cinematic adaptation (Ray, 2000: 46). But if these papers were all guided in the direction of a wider history of cinema, they could constitute the base for a history of cinematic adaptations.

In the absence of such a history, first, I would like to contextualize Kubrick's adaptations in the general history of cinematic techniques and styles to understand whether the constants of his style are characteristic of a particular way of making films. Then, through a comparison between his stylistic features and those that characterize the cinematic "movement" that seems the nearest to his artistic sensibilities, I would like to discuss whether the final goals of the director's style—which is to say, the primary reasons of his art—coincide with those of that "movement."

First, the events in the narratives of Kubrick's adaptations are often not linked by cause and effect chains, unlike in classical Hollywood films, and images seem to emanate from music that is foregrounded, unlike in classical narrative sound films. Moreover, in *A Clockwork Orange* some scenes parody classical Hollywood films, and in *The Shining* the dialogue parodies the horror genre. Thus, Kubrick adaptations consciously criticize classical narrative films and, especially, Hollywood ones.

This feature, together with several others, characterizes both the director's adaptations and art-cinema as it is defined by David Bordwell in *Narration in the Fiction Film*:

> Art-cinema narration has become a coherent mode partly by defining itself as a deviation from classical narrative. This may seem most obvious in the postwar decades, when the dismantling of the studio system enabled highly individualized international *auteurs* to emerge. Historically, however, the art-cinema has its roots in an opposition to Hollywood nurtured within various national film industries of the silent era and sustained by concepts borrowed from modernism in theatre and literature. (1985: 229)

Art-cinema narration fully developed in the late 1950s and 1960s, when "the combination of novelty and nationalism became the marketing device it has been ever since: the French New Wave, New Polish cinema, New Hungarian cinema, New German cinema, New Australian cinema." And, finally, in the late 1960s and 1970s, art-cinema influenced New Hollywood (Bordwell, 1985: 231–232).

According to some scholars, New Hollywood or the Hollywood Renaissance refers to a brief period, from the late 1960s to the early 1970s, "when an adventurous new cinema emerged, linking the traditions of classic Hollywood genre filmmaking with the stylistic innovations of

European art cinema" (Cook and Bernink, 1999: 98). Some directors, actors, and agents gained new power because film productions became more independent for a variety of reasons. For example, after the 1948 Paramount Decree, independent producers and studios produced their films free of major studios interference. Moreover, in the 1960s, television became more important, moviegoing was no longer the principal form of entertainment, and the number of theatrical films produced decreased. In 1968 the weakening of the Production Code allowed independent art-house theatres to show new foreign and independent films and, in 1970, a lot of studios were on the brink of bankruptcy because they had invested on costly flops. Indeed, after 1968, a young, college-educated audience called for new films, closer to the artistic sensibilities of art-cinema. At the end of the 1960s, in this socioeconomic context, new films, defined as "youth" or "alternative," emerged (e.g., *The Graduate* [Mike Nichols, USA, 1967], *Bonnie and Clyde, Easy Rider* [Dennis Hopper, USA, 1969], *Butch Cassidy and the Sundance Kid* [George Roy Hill, USA, 1969], *MASH* [Robert Altman, USA, 1970], and *Midnight Cowboy* [John Schlesinger, USA, 1969]). These new filmmakers were soon followed by the "movie brats," film school-educated directors who were particularly influenced by *Cahiers du Cinéma* and art-cinema (e.g., Martin Scorsese, Brian De Palma, Francis Coppola, John Milius, Paul Schrader, and George Lucas). Noël Carroll calls New Hollywood a "cinema of allusion" because it is characterized by references to other cinematic practices, particularly classical Hollywood cinema and European art-cinema. "Accordingly, some accounts (e.g., Bernardoni, 1991) see this moment as the explicit inscription within American filmmaking of the critical practice of *auteurism*, resulting in a self-consciously *auteurist* cinema" (Cook and Bernink, 1999: 100). These first two moments of the Hollywood Renaissance, which is to say, the youth or alternative cinema and the movie brats, "saw an *auteurist* cinema explore and stretch genres such as the Western (*The Wild Bunch*), the gangster film (*The Godfather* and *The Godfather Part 2*), and the detective-noir film (*Chinatown, Night Moves, The Long Goodbye*)" (1999: 103). According to Carroll, together with the classical genre film, there developed a genre film influenced by art-cinema (Cook and Bernink, 1999: 102). Although, in the year of their first release, only *2001: A Space Odyssey* (1968) and *A Clockwork Orange* (1971) can be considered examples of the Hollywood Renaissance, all of the last six Kubrick adaptations can be discussed in the context of a self-consciously *auteurist* art-cinema in the genre film.

As specifically regards the influences of the art-cinema narration on New Hollywood, Thomas Elsaesser claims that while the protagonists of classical Hollywood cinema are "psychologically or morally motivated: they had a case to investigate, a name to clear, a woman (or man) to love, a goal to reach," the characters of the "new liberal cinema" do not have any aim. Narratives are no longer based on a strict causal and chronological structure, and are open-ended. The films of the Hollywood Renaissance show "a kind of malaise already frequently alluded to in relation to the European cinema –the fading confidence in being able to tell a story" (in Cook and Bernink, 1999: 101). These features, together with Carroll's definition of New Hollywood as a cinema of allusion, mostly derive from art-cinema, and characterize the last six Kubrick adaptations.

Indeed, according to Bordwell, three main features characterize art-cinema narration: the "objective" and "subjective" verisimilitude, and the "over narrational commentary." As regards "objective" verisimilitude, the logic of cause and effect, which dominates the construction of the *syuzhet* in classical Hollywood films, is abandoned to better mimic the complexity of the reality, in which events often happen by chance and/or are inexplicable—they have no reasons and no consequences. The narrational structure, as in Kubrick's adaptations, is constituted by a succession of unrelated episodes, is full of gaps, is open-ended, and is dominated more by chance and coincidence than by cause and effect chains (1985: 206–207). For example, in *L'avventura* (Michelangelo Antonioni, Italy and France, 1960), the mystery of Anna's disappearance (Lea Massari) is followed by the love story between her fiancé, Sandro (Gabriele Ferzetti), and her best girlfriend, Claudia (Monica Vitti). Anna will never be found, and the cause of her disappearance will never be explained. Similarly, in *Eyes Wide Shut*, the real cause of Mandy's death is never revealed.

As regards "subjective" verisimilitude, characters "tend to lack clear-cut traits, motives, and goals" (1985: 207). The reasons for their actions, together with their purposes, are often not understandable, in order to evoke the complexity of reality and that of the human mind. The characters of art-cinema must struggle in a society that is not always ready to accept them, and they have to reach compromises between their motives and goals and their world: "If the Hollywood protagonist speeds toward the target, the art-film protagonist is presented as sliding passively from one situation to another" (1985: 207). Thus, Kubrick's passive wanderers are not dissimilar from the characters of art-cinema.

According to Bordwell, in art-cinema narration there is always a "boundary-situation" at which all the other episodes are linked or, at least, towards which they aim. During this situation the protagonist faces an existential crisis, and becomes aware of fundamental human issues. In this very moment the character may remain motionless and/or inarticulate about her mental turmoil, but the spectators are able to guess her psychology and behavior thanks to the *mise-en-scène* (1985: 208).

> Consequently, the behavior of the characters within the fabula world and the syuzhet's dramatization both focus on the character's problems of action and feeling; which is to say that "inquiry into character" becomes not only the prime thematic material but a central source of expectation, curiosity, suspense, and surprise. . . . The narrow focus is complemented by psychological depth; art-film narration is more subjective more often than is classical narration. (1985: 209)

For example, in *La Notte* (Michelangelo Antonioni, Italy and France, 1961), Giovanni (Marcello Mastroianni) and Lidia (Jeanne Moreau) are married, but after the wife's confession that she no longer loves her husband, they soon begin to wander in search of sexual experiences, not unlike Bill in *Eyes Wide Shut*. But, unlike Kubrick's film, *La Notte* is characterized by psychological depth. For example, during a party attended by the couple, the attention is focused on Giovanni's attraction to Valentina (Monica Vitti) and on his wife's reaction, more than on Valentina's beauty or the villa. In contrast, in *Eyes Wide Shut*, great emphasis is given to Ziegler's mansion, and to the beauty of the two models and of Mandy.

In the link between protagonists' psychology and *mise-en-scène*, and in the stress on psychological insight, lays the main difference between art-cinema and Kubrick's films. The director's characters, suspended in a play of cross-references among episodes that entrap them, often have to face a "boundary-situation." In *2001: A Space Odyssey*, Bowman travels alone through the Stargate, and finds himself in the eighteenth century-room where he is transformed into a star-child. The protagonist of *A Clockwork Orange* is subjected to the Ludovico cure, and to the same representation of violence that the spectators of the film are "obliged" to see during the first part of the film. Barry Lyndon has to duel with his stepson, who defends his mother's dignity and fortune, and lets him win, thereby losing everything. In *The Shining*, Jack, after having spoken with the former winter caretaker, chooses to become part of the Overlook Hotel, and thus the supernatural. The protagonist of *Full Metal Jacket* shoots at the sniper, ending her sufferings and becoming a killer. In *Eyes Wide Shut*, Bill is confronted with his wife's confession and is impelled to wander, risking his very life. But none of these "boundary situations" represent the focus of a psychological depth, nor does the *mise-en-scène* become an objective correlative of the protagonists' feelings. Indeed, as is discussed later, Kubrick's characters often remain passive wanderers until the end; they remain motionless, inarticulate about the sublime experience that unrolls before their eyes. The director, extremely faithful to "objective verisimilitude," represents a world that is so sublime that his protagonists often cannot share it—they can only stare at it. As already discussed, on the one hand, Kubrick is often accused by critics of being a misanthrope, of presenting a pessimistic view of the world and of mankind's role in it. His characters are puppets in the hands of a cruel society and destiny, and they lack psychological depth. On the other hand, his creation of sublime cinematic experiences can be read not only as a poetic representation, but also as an optimistic one. The world is as marvelous and enigmatic as a symphony, and the director creates a sublime succession of images directly emanating from music to convey his vision of life.

The third feature discussed by Bordwell is "overt narrational commentary." In art-cinema, the narrational act is often foregrounded thanks to particular cinematic techniques or narrative constructions that break objective realism, but that are not motivated by subjectivity. On the one hand, the narration demonstrates its "humbleness" because it is not possible to enclose the complexity of life in a logic of cause and effect. On the other hand, the films display their referentiality (1985: 209–210). Bordwell claims that in art-cinema, unlike in classical Hollywood films, the narration is often directly attributed to the director by the audience and, thus, films are seen with the awareness that they pertain to a body of work:

> Within the art-cinema's mode of production and reception, the concept of the author has a formal function it did not posses in the Hollywood studio system. Thus the institutional "author" is available as a source of the formal operation of the film. The authorial trademark requires that the spectator see this film as fitting into a body of work. (1985: 211)

Thus, citations and parodies of the film itself and of other films, together with film-within-the-film and plays among diegesis, intradiegesis, and extradiegesis, characterize art-film narration (1985: 211–212). And these features, together with cinematic techniques and narrative constructions that break the narrative fluidity, are present in Kubrick's adaptations as well.

Therefore, even if the fullest flower of art-cinema developed in the late 1950s and 1960s, the director's films can be interpreted in light of this way of making movies. Kubrick's own innovation is the substitution of the "subjective" verisimilitude with the creation of sublime cinematic experiences.

According to Bordwell, "The art-cinema plays among several tendencies: deviation from classical norms, adherence to art-cinema norms, creation of innovative intrinsic norms, and the greater or lesser foregrounding of deviation from those intrinsic norms" (1985: 213). One of the main features that characterizes art-cinema is a critique of classical cinematic techniques. According to Pam Cook and Mieke Bernink, the word "avant-garde," by the end of the 1910s, was widely used to designate the art movements that challenged institutionalized cultural forms. The first avant-garde cinema developed in Europe from the first half of the 1910s to the 1930s, from the ferment of modern art and movements such as Futurism, Cubism, Surrealism, and Dadaism (1999: 114). Wollen, in "The Two Avant-Gardes" (1982), in a discussion of the reasons and purposes of the critique of classical norms, divides the historical avant-garde into two tendencies. On the one hand, there were western European directors, associated with painting, whose main goal was a formal and aesthetic experiment with signifiers, detached from both signifieds and references. On the other hand, there were filmmakers who, like Sergei M. Eisenstein and Dziga Vertov, experimented with new cinematic techniques, a cinema of montage, to mediate social and political concerns. This first avant-garde cinema ended with the political reconfiguration of Europe in the 1930s (1982: 93–94).

After the First World War, however, in the 1930s and 1940s, when European artists found refuge in the U.S. and propitious cultural and industrial conditions, a new avant-garde cinema developed. Wollen claims that this "movement" comprised two tendencies, which followed the tradition of the two main groups of the first avant-garde (1982: 92). On the one hand, there were personal films, which developed between the early 1940s and the mid-1960s, and which followed the lessons of Eisenstein. These filmmakers (such as Maya Deren, Kenneth Anger, Stan Brakhage, Jonas Mekas, Carolee Schneemann, Ron Rice, Jack Smith, the Kuchar brothers, Jordan Belson, and James Whitney) developed a cinema that revolved around personal existential experiences and tried to adapt cinematic forms to a first-person narration (1982: 98–99). On the other hand, there were structural films, which emerged in the second half of the 1960s, and which took inspiration from the formal experiments of the first avant-garde. These films (such as *Wavelength* [Michael Snow, Canada and USA, 1967], *Film in which there Appear Sprocket Holes, Edge Lettering, Dirt Particles, Etc.* [Owen Land, USA, 1966], and *Zen for Film* [Nam June Paik, 1964]) were characterized by reflexivity and anti-illusionism: they tried to foreground the techniques and the making of the film itself thanks to a predetermined and simplified structure. In Great Britain this tendency led to structural/materialism dominated by a rigorous anti-representationalism (as, for example, in *Room Film 1973* [Peter Gidal, U.K., 1973]) (1982: 97). Wollen claims that, when modernism developed in the U.S. and, especially, in the New York art world, it was distanced from the avant-garde. Meanwhile, in Paris, the avant-garde, divorced from modernism, gained new strength from the events of 1968. Modernism was characterized by reflexivity, semiotic reduction, foregrounding of the signifier, and suppression or suspension of the signified. But by the end of the twentieth century, transposed into conceptualism and minimalism, it exhausted itself. The main features of avant-garde were instead semiotic expansion, and new relations between signifier and signified. Wollen argues that while structural and structural/materialist films developed from modernism, from the formal experiments of the modernist avant-garde of the 1920s, personal films and the post-1968 work of Jean-Luc Godard, Jean-Marie Straub, and Danièle Huillet derived from the avant-garde of Eisenstein (1982: 97–99).

To speak about Godard, Wollen coins the expression "counter-cinema" to stress how the director, through his motives and cinematic techniques, tried to negate the values of mainstream cinema (1982: 79). To the features of art-cinema that I have already discussed, the scholar adds Godard's attempt to actively involve the spectators in a political struggle. Apart from Eisenstein, from whom the French filmmaker developed the conflict among cinematic codes, and between signifier and signified (1982: 98–99), Wollen argues that Godard was principally influenced by Brecht and the concept of distanciation. According to this idea, cinematic devices and narrative strategies should be implied to break the audience's empathy, and to guide their attention not towards the cinematic codes and structures, as in modernism, but towards the socioeconomic context of the making of the film. Wollen criticizes the fact that the French director placed the reality principle before the pleasure principle, overlooking the power of the latter in arousing revolutionary political ideas (Wollen, 1982: 87–89, 101). Indeed, concerning the relationship between the pleasure and the reality principle in advanced capitalist countries, the scholar claims:

> In a situation in which survival is—at least relatively—non-problematic, the pleasure-principle and the reality-principle are antagonist and, since the reality-principle is fundamentally adaptive, it is from the pleasure-principle that change must stem. This means that desire, and its representation in fantasy, far from being necessary enemies of revolutionary politics—and its cinematic auxiliary—are necessary conditions. (1982: 88)

The reflexivity of Kubrick's films draws attention to the cinematic techniques more than to their historical context, and the signifier is often foregrounded, unlinked to its signified or a specific referent. Thus, as regards the abstract ideas that seem to inform the purposes of his work and his conception of the cinematic medium, the director can be put in the tradition of the modernist avant-garde of the 1920s. But his adaptations are not only centered on the ontology of the medium. At a "deeper" level there is a critique of classical Hollywood films; at a "more superficial" level there is a sublime experience. And these levels are intertwined: the cinematic techniques and the narrative structure that break the narrative fluidity both implicitly criticize mainstream cinema and explicitly involve the audience in a sublime event. Thus, through the pleasure principle, Kubrick arrives at the reality principle without being revolutionary: thanks to sublime experiences he lays bare not only the condition and role of mankind in the world, but also the aesthetic representations of culture offered by cinema. Moreover, he often parodies his own representations, as in *A Clockwork Orange*, *Full Metal Jacket*, and *Eyes Wide Shut*, and his cinema can be defined as humble (an adjective adopted by Bordwell to describe the narrational act of art-cinema [1985: 209–210]).

✦ ✦ ✦

I have suggested that Kubrick can be considered a New Hollywood *auteur* and, in particular, an heir of the abstract purposes that informed the modernist avant-garde of the 1920s, but I have also claimed that *Full Metal Jacket* is a postmodern Vietnam film, and I interpret the director's *oeuvre* through the concept of the sublime. What is more, some postmodern theorists, such as Gilles Deleuze, Fredric Jameson, and Mainar (1999), discuss Kubrick as a postmodern director. Therefore, I need to explain why I do not look at Kubrick from a postmodernist perspective, despite my suggestion that his Vietnam film can be defined as being postmodern, and that his body of work can be interpreted through the idea of the sublime.

One of the main characteristics of postmodernity is the death of the author. Because there is no linguistic norm, there cannot be original styles to express a personal vision of the world. What is more, everything has already been invented: all of the possible styles and worlds have already been exploited. Thus, art is about art itself in a different manner from the referentiality that characterizes modernism: it is no longer a formal experiment with the possibilities of a medium, but rather the impossibility of experimenting and, thus, the imprisonment in the aesthetics of the past, and a content that is the sum of cultural productions (Jameson, 1988: 17–18). I have shown the extent to which Kubrick's cinematic techniques and narrative structures can be traced back to art-cinema. But the discussion of the director's constants in adapting novels shows how the filmmaker elaborates a personal style beyond art-cinema's features (often employing new techniques, such as the Steadicam in *The Shining* or special effects in *2001: A Space Odyssey*), and offers a personal vision of the world and the cinematic medium.

In his discussion of Kubrick and, in particular, of *The Shining*, Jameson argues that contemporary filmmakers, such as Robert Altman, Roman Polanski, Nicolas Roeg, and Kubrick, transform genres just as modernist directors used to innovate styles (2003: 67). *The Killing, Paths of Glory, Dr. Strangelove, The Shining,* and *2001: A Space Odyssey* do not exploit the structure of classical genres from the point of view of a personal, authorial interpretation. This cinema of "meta-genre" becomes the expression of a tension towards history in a form that is not reflexive (2003: 69–70). For example, in *The Shining*, Jack is possessed by history and, during the masked ball, the ghosts of a past that has disappeared meet once more in front of a contemporary spectator-voyeur (2003: 77). The theme of the film is the desire of a society, the ideological project of going back to the lost certitudes of a more rigid and concrete subdivision in social classes, which was possible only in the past, and which the film evokes with the strength of the return of the repressed (2003: 81–83). Similarly, in his discussion of this adaptation, John Brown claims that while King's novel is a perfect example of the horror genre, Kubrick's film, implicitly criticizing the genre and frustrating every reading, can be defined as postmodern: "A fable about communication and the American experience, a portrait of the artist as a sociopath, an anti-horror movie—the great achievement, postmodernist or otherwise, of *The Shining* is that it is all of these things, some of these things and none of these things" (1992: 119–120). I have discussed how Kubrick exploits the conventions of the horror genre, the fantastic-marvelous, and the concept of the uncanny to represent Jack as a passive wanderer, suspended between a natural and a supernatural world, who finally remains entrapped in the spectacle of the dreamy world created by the director. More generally, I have considered Kubrick as a Hollywood Renaissance filmmaker who creates a self-consciously *auteurist* art-cinema in the genre film. This interpretation has been sustained by a close analysis of the director's body of work, by the observation that his diegetic worlds are enveloped in a dreamy atmosphere, and that his protagonists often behave as passive wanderers.

Apart from the death of the author, there is another main feature of postmodernism that neatly distinguishes it from other epochs. Francois Lyotard claims that while the beautiful characterizes the modern aesthetic, the sublime is a feature of postmodernism. Indeed, the notion of the beautiful implies a social consensus upon an aesthetic judgment. In the postmodern epoch, however, the ideal of a community is unthinkable (Hebdige, 1988: 198). The scholar claims that the beautiful is no longer possible in postmodernity, but he does not argue that the sublime is unthinkable in a modernist aesthetic; the sublime does not necessarily imply postmodernism. Thus, interpreting the cinema of Kubrick as a sublime experience does not imply interpreting the director as a postmodern filmmaker. Therefore, if I discuss Kubrick as an heir to the abstract ideas that informed the modernist avant-garde of the 1920s, and I describe some moments of his films through the concept of the sublime, I do not contradict myself. Moreover, Jameson uses both the categories of the beautiful and the sublime to describe some scenes in *2001: A Space Odyssey* and *The Shining*. For example, he claims that the sequences of *2001* accompanied by *The Blue Danube* waltz and the opening scene of *The Shining*, in which Jack reaches the Overlook Hotel, are "beautiful and dull" (2003: 71–72), while he defines as sublime the scenes in which Danny rides his tricycle along the corridors of the hotel (2003: 74). Thus, he mixes the two categories in a postmodernist interpretation of the filmmaker's adaptations.

Similarly, I do not contradict myself by calling *Full Metal Jacket* a postmodern Vietnam film to distinguish it from realist Vietnam films, following the classifications of Stefano Ghislotti (1996) and James C. Wilson (1982). Jameson, discussing Herr's *Dispatches*, argues that the fusion of different idiolects in *Dispatches*, as in Harford's *The Short-Timers*, evokes the impossibility of describing a war that is not only new, but also incomprehensible (1988: 25). I have discussed how, in *Full Metal Jacket*, the difficulty of representing the Vietnam War through dialogue and voice-over is conveyed thanks to a language that is similar to music: signifiers are foregrounded and used for their musicality, signified are almost suppressed, and phrases are often sung and accompanied with marches or songs, or they are uttered by characters who overact. As discussed above, these characteristics can also be considered modernist features. But apart from these distinctions between modernism and postmodernism, I have adopted Ghislotti's and Wilson's classification only to distinguish two subgroups of a particular genre.

Together with scholars who discuss Kubrick's *oeuvre* from a postmodernist point of view, there are critics, such as Michel Chion (2001), Michel Ciment (2003), Mario Falsetto (1994), and Thomas Allen Nelson (2000), who interpret it from a modernist perspective. Furthermore, Tony Pipolo laments the fact that there are few scholars who read the director's body of work through a modernist point of view: "This, too, is the nature of Kubrick's modernism, an aspect of his work ignored or misunderstood by too many film reviewers and insufficiently acknowledged with a few exceptions" (2002: 7). For example, Nelson claims that Kubrick's films reveal his belief in the cinematic medium both as an art form and a popular commercial form: on the one hand, his cinema conveys a complex personal vision; on the other hand, it moves us when it explores universal myths and archetypes of our shared cultural experience and our collective unconscious. Thus, Kubrick's films are able to transform—to convert cinematic forms into complex cinematic meanings. Similarly, James Naremore claims that the director is one of the cinema's last modernists; because his taste and sensibility were shaped by the artistic culture of New York in the 1950s, he became a celebrated *auteur* with his own personal style, using art-cinema conventions in commercial productions, and challenging censorship regulations. In this book, similar conclusions are drawn through a discussion of the complexity of the filmmaker's films that present, at a "deeper" level, a critique of classical Hollywood films, mostly inspired by the modernist avant-garde of the 1920s and, at a "more superficial" level, a sublime visual and aural experience.

Adapting the Sublime

Touched by a masterpiece, a person begins to hear in himself that same call of truth which prompted the artist to his creative act. When a link is established between the work and its beholder, the latter experiences a sublime, purging trauma. Within that aura which unites masterpieces and audience, the best sides of our souls are made known, and we long for them to be freed. In those moments we recognize and discover ourselves, the unfathomable depths of our own potential, and the furthest riches of our emotions. (Tarkovsky, 2006: 43)

In "The Sublime in Cinema" (1999), Cynthia A. Freeland, moving from definitions by Longinus, Edmund Burke, and Immanuel Kant, discusses how the sublime can be actualized and applied to the cinematic medium. Firstly, she claims that the sublime is characterized by four features: "Kant and Burke emphasized that so long as we are safe, the ineffable, great element before us in the awesome object evokes a certain intellectual pleasure of astonishment or elevation" (1999: 66). According to Kant, this pleasure is linked to a consciousness of our moral strength, whereas, according to Burke, it is tied to an awareness of the artist's greatness. The rapturous terror evoked by the sublime element is accompanied by the awareness of its greatness: "It is bold and grand, to use Longinus's language. Or, as Kant puts it, 'Sublime is the name given to what is absolutely great.'" A sublime artwork elicits laud and admiration; it is characterized by "a superlative kind of greatness" (1999: 67). The sublime element evokes such a powerful and confusing emotional experience that the spectators would be unsettled by it if they were not forced into a new mental situation, that is cognition or thought, thanks to which they categorize and label the sublime object that thus becomes elevating and pleasurable. Freeland suggests "that the shift occurs when we regard the deep and painful feelings evoked by a work as crucial for its success as powerful and uplifting art" (1999: 68).

Therefore, there is a moment, before cognition and thought, during which the spectators are disturbed by the greatness of a sublime experience and by a rapturous terror. It is before the object has become familiar, *heimlich*, yet it is unfamiliar, *unheimlich*, uncanny, because it is still unknown. Before awareness and elevation there are dread and pain and, thus, the sublime experience is, in its *incipit*, uncanny. Indeed, in his essay about the uncanny (1919), Freud discusses what, in Hoffman's *The Sand-Man*, evokes an uncanny feeling. The psychoanalyst discards Ernst

Jentsch's thesis, according to which the uncanny is provoked by intellectual insecurity. But Nicholas Royle argues:

> Freud wants to lay the ghost of his precursor and the ghost of intellectual uncertainty, but the ghosts keep coming back. As he asks near the end of his essay: "are we after all justified in entirely ignoring intellectual uncertainty?" I wish to suggest that "intellectual uncertainty" is in part what Freud's essay has to teach and, indeed, that this is a crucial dimension of any teaching worthy of the name. (2003: 52)

And Harold Bloom, in "Freud and the Sublime: A Catastrophe Theory of Creativity," claims:

> The essay is of enormous importance to literary criticism because it is the only major contribution that the twentieth century has made to the aesthetics of the sublime. The sublime, as I read Freud, is one of his major repressed concerns, and this literary repression on his part is a clue to what I take to be a gap in his theory of repression. (in Royle, 2003: 14)

The consideration that a sublime experience is uncanny, as long as it is not labeled, leads to an overstatement. The uncanny elements of *The Shining* can be considered sublime because the spectators find themselves in the intellectual uncertainty of the fantastic-marvelous. They do not know if the events shown pertain to a supernatural or a natural diegetic world and, thus, they are not able to categorize them. Therefore, the uncanny, in the fantastic-marvelous, becomes sublime, and *The Shining* can be interpreted as a sublime cinematic experience, at least when uncanny elements appear.

There is a last feature that characterizes the sublime object: moral reflection. The cognition and thought of a sublime experience leads, according to Kant, to the consciousness of the moral law and moral duties. The imagination is overwhelmed by the sublime, which is so great and terrifying that it cannot be imagined, and the reason triumphantly invokes respect towards the moral law. "The sublime does, interestingly, concern a way in which nature comports to an end—a 'higher finality' beyond any ordinary teleology, the finality not of nature but of ourselves" (Freeland, 1999: 71). Freeland suggests that, in films, this shift from imagination to reason, from the sensory to the cognitive, happens when the spectators, from a perspective within the film, shift to one about the film, when they shift from the diegetic plain to the extradiegetic plain. Thus, the sensory level is abandoned for the cognitive one, for a moral reflection about the film. Moreover, she suggests that this shift is encouraged when the film displays its artificiality (1999: 73). Therefore, a sublime cinematic experience is uncanny as long as the spectators remain entrapped in the diegesis. But when cinematic techniques and narrative strategies break the narrative fluidity, and the audience becomes aware of the film's referentiality, reaching an extradiegetic perspective, they are induced to reflect not only about the power of the director's creative mind, but also his personal vision of the world expressed in his film.

For example, the last episode of *The Shining*, when Jack runs after Danny in the maze, and the former remains trapped and dies frozen in it, is not only uncanny, but also sublime. In the shots filmed inside the labyrinth, the Steadicam follows or precedes the father or the son at their height. Trembling shots suggest that someone is operating the camera. But is it an operator or a supernatural presence? It must be remembered that as soon as Garrett Brown and Cinema Product Corporation shared an Oscar in 1978 for the invention and development of the Steadicam, Brown began to work on *The Shining* (Brown, 1980). In 1980, spectators were not accustomed to these shots and, consequently, it is likely that they were more induced to notice and speculate about them than a later audience would be. Moreover, during this episode, father and son are never in the same frame together and, although it is Jack who follows Danny, the boy is never the object of the father's point of view shots. Trembling images do not mimic Jack's run after his son, but suggest the presence of a third being behind the Steadicam. The same thing happens in the first sequence of the film, during the aerial footage discussed in the previous chapter, when a supernatural being seems to follow the Torrances' car. Similarly, the film closes with a long shot of photographs pinned on a wall of the hotel. The camera tracks forward until we see a close-up view of a group photograph in which Jack is in the middle. After a dissolve there is a *plain américain* of Jack, followed, after another dissolve, by a medium shot of him. The camera tilts down, revealing the writing, "Overlook Hotel. July 4th Ball 1921." The end titles appear after a fade-out. "Midnight, The Stars, and You," the diegetic music used during the ball that took place in the Gold Room, accompanies these last three shots. Is the camera moved and the music played by a supernatural being or an extradiegetic artist? The film opens and closes with shots that evoke, along with a supernatural force, the extradiegetic level of the film. For example, in the last episode that takes place in the labyrinth, the play between a natural or supernatural explanation of the events is emphasized by the editing that intercuts shots filmed inside the maze with images shot inside the hotel, during which Wendy meets Grady and sees blood coming out from the elevators. This play between a natural and a supernatural explanation leads to a play between the diegetic and extradiegetic level. Indeed, on the one hand, when we believe in a supernatural explanation—which is to say that the ghosts of the hotel follow Jack's car, or follow father and son, or show us that Jack is another ghost—we remain in the diegetic level or, better, we do not need an extradiegetic level to understand what we are shown. On the other hand, when we believe in a natural explanation, we shift from the diegetic to the extradiegetic level, and we realize that behind the camera there are no ghosts, but an artist.

The episode shot inside the maze is great and terrifying not only thanks to the use of the Steadicam, but also thanks to the *mise-en-scéne*. The edges of the labyrinth are high and since the camera is at characters' height, the spectators often cannot see the top of the green walls that, consequently, seem incredibly tall. This effect is emphasized by the dark sky, and by the lights that are positioned at ground level, not lighting the top of the edges. Moreover, the whiteness of the snow, which covers the paths and the edges of the maze, becomes brilliant thanks to the lights, and contrasts with the blackness of the sky.

Also great and terrifying is not only the *mise-en-scéne*, but Jack Nicholson's performance. His Kubrickian stare let the audience wonder whether he is crazy or possessed by the ghosts of the Overlook Hotel and, in the meantime, it evokes his previous role as a loony in *One Flew Over the Cuckoo's Nest* (Milos Forman, USA, 1975), laying bare the artificiality of the film. What is more, after *The Shining*, Nicholson went onto play other similar roles—for example, Francis Phelan in *Ironweed* (Hector Babenco, USA, 1987); Daryl Van Horne in *The Witches of Eastwick* (George Miller, USA, 1987); Joker in *Batman* (Tim Burton, USA and UK, 1989); Melvin Udall in *As Good as It Gets* (James L. Brooks, USA, 1997); and Dr. Buddy Rydell in *Anger Management* (Peter Segal, USA, 2003). Consequently, the star Jack Nicholson, a mix of his persona and his roles, according to Edgar Morin's theory (1995), can be considered to be a man who often exceeds the limits of a standard behavior. This halo is increased by Vivian Kubrick's *Making The Shining*, a documentary presented on the DVD of *The Shining*, in which the actor does not hesitate to show his wild character. A Kubrickian stare is also adopted by Alex in *A Clockwork Orange* and Pyle in *Full Metal Jacket*. In particular, the latter assumes this grin before killing Sergeant Hartman and himself, while Joker remains motionless in contemplation of Pyle's criminal actions. I would dare to define these performances sublime because, as in the case of *The Shining*, they are both terrifying and great: they express the strength of human beings that can be destructive and horrifying, but that nonetheless remains fascinating because it is powerful and indomitable. Moreover, these performances display their artificiality because they are so exaggerated that they become a caricature of an angry, crazy, or possessed man who is ready to misbehave; and, as discussed above, different characters in different Kubrick films adopt this stare, which became one of the director's hallmarks.

Throughout this book, I have labeled as sublime experiences many sequences in Kubrick's adaptations. For example, the last sequence of *2001: A Space Odyssey* can be interpreted through the concepts of the uncanny and the sublime. Indeed, the film can be considered a fantastic-marvelous tale because the spectators hesitate between a natural or supernatural explanation of the events until the star-child appears. Before this event, the physical laws of the diegetic world do not seem to be different from those that govern our own world. The aliens are not shown, and their existence is only suggested through a monolith that could be a natural, unknown element, a god's miracle, or an extraterrestrials' gift. Much like in the case of King's *The Shining* and Kubrick's adaptation thereof, in Clarke's book, unlike in the director's film, the play between a natural and supernatural explanation of the events is carried on for a shorter time of the narrative because, as already discussed, the aliens' presence is confirmed from the very beginning, from the first monolith appearances during the Pleistocene period. Thus, the uncanny elements of Kubrick's science-fiction film, such as those of his horror adaptation, can be considered sublime because the spectators find themselves in the intellectual uncertainty of the fantastic-marvelous.

The double, suggested by the co-presence of Bowman at different ages, and by his image reflected into a mirror, constitutes the main uncanny aspect of the last sequence of the film. The scene begins when the Stargate sequence ends and the astronaut, in his space pod, finds himself in an eighteenth century-room. Let's call the astronaut at the age during which he begins his travel Bowman0; Bowman1 is older than Bowman0; Bowman2 is older than Bowman1; and Bowman3 is older than Bowman2. When B0 is inside his space pod, he looks into the camera and, in the subsequent shot, B1 is shown in the room from inside the pod, from the position previously occupied by B0. B1's image seems to be from B0's point of view, and consequently, B0 and B1 seem to be co-present. It is B1 who looks at his image reflected into a mirror. Similarly, when B2 appears in frame, he sits in front of a table prepared for breakfast, and this shot is preceded and followed by images of B1. When B2 turns towards the camera, which is the place occupied in the previous shot by B1, he looks into it, then he stands up and walks towards the camera, as if he had listened to something and wanted to comprehend the origin of the noise. Therefore, once more, the images of B2, the older astronaut, seem to be point of view shots of B1, the younger Bowman, and B1 and B2 seem to be co-present. Finally, when B3 first appears, he lies down on a bed, but on frame right there is B2's head. The shot during which B1 is first shown to the spectators can be interpreted either as a point of view shot (or a false point of view shot) of B0. When B2 is first shown to the audience, he is both preceded and followed by images of B1 and, thus, B2 can be seen as a point of view shot (or a false point of view shot) of B1, but it seems likely that B1 and B2 are co-present. When, finally, B3 first appears on screen, he is in frame together with B2. Thus, the idea that both a younger and older astronaut are co-present is progressively suggested and then confirmed, as if to let the audience get accustomed to Bowman's aging before showing them his final transformation into a star-child. Indeed, when the fetus appears on the bed, in the same position of B3, the spectators should think that Bowman has become a star-child, and this is confirmed by the numerous interpretations of the film that agree on this conclusion. The meaning of these transformations is not explained either in the film or in Kubrick's interviews, and the novel does not furnish any elucidation because, in the written medium, Bowman's aging does not take place. Putting aside the numerous interpretations of this sequence, in the film this scene becomes uncanny and sublime. What is great and terrifying is watching a man who sees himself aging quickly, who looks at his image reflected in a mirror to recognize his older self, and who is finally reborn into a star-child who has the power to travel in the universe. Also magnificent and horrifying is the idea that the future is not influenced by the present. The protagonist seems to act and move as if compelled and commanded by unknown forces; the older Bowman's actions are often shown from the younger Bowman's point of view. Thus, the older astronaut, who should live in a future co-present with the present of the younger astronaut, seems to obey unknown laws of the future. The older astronaut's actions and his future do not depend upon the present or the younger astronaut's acts because the present watches the future without interfering with it. From the point of view of the diegesis, the future seems commanded by alien forces and Bowman seems guided by the extraterrestrials, as man-apes were helped by the monolith. It is worth noting that in *The Terminator* (James Cameron, USA, 1984) and *Back to the Future* (Robert Zemeckis, USA, 1985) future and present are co-present and the future influences the present. According to Karen B. Mann, these films are examples of the disrupture of the story's time by desire: "The motive for reaching into the past is based not on comprehension but on presence and possession of the object of one's desire" (1989–1990: 18). While in these films characters, moved by a desire to reach and posses something that remains in their past, are able to change their future, in *2001: A Space Odyssey* Bowman cannot modify his future and he remains, once more, a passive spectator of a sublime experience.

The audience reaches an extradiegetic perspective because this sequence displays its referentiality, breaking its narrative fluidity through several means. For example, Bowman looks directly into the camera, addressing the spectators, in five shots and, in one of them, he even walks towards it. As already discussed above, B2 looks at us and comes towards us, as if he had perceived a presence, that of B1 or us. And we, as spectators, would almost like to catch our breath so as not to confuse B2. Similarly, the star-child, in the next-to-last shot, looks at the Earth and, in the last shot, he looks directly at us. In the novel, a movie that the astronaut sees on TV is set in a room identical to the one in which he finds himself: "So that was how this reception area had been prepared for him; his hosts had based their ideas of terrestrial living upon TV programs. His feeling that he was inside a movie set was almost literally true" (1968: 248). Therefore, the cinematic medium is directly cited in the written medium, but the artificiality of the scene is not as emphasized as in the adaptation.

In the film, the sublime is obtained also thanks to the use of powerful extradiegetic music, which accompanies the last three shots of the film, underlying the artificiality of the sequence. The piece is the "Introduction" or "Sunrise" from Richard Strauss's *Thus Spoke Zarathustra*, a tone poem inspired by the philosophical treatise by Friedrich Nietzsche. The philosopher's influences on the director have already been discussed by several scholars, including Jerold J. Abrams (2007: 247–265). Nietzsche claims that human beings are only a transition between apes and the *übermensch*, which is to say, the overman or superman, who represents a journey towards self-mastery. The philosopher represents the *übermensch* through several metaphors, such as a dawn or a man traversing a rope above an abyss, moving away from his uncultivated animality and towards the overman. Similarly, in Kubrick's film the development of beings from apes to human beings to supermen is represented by several events, such as the appearance of the monolith, accompanied by the alignment of planets, and by mankind's bravery in traveling through space and time. As in Nietzsche's treatise, the development from apes to overmen is represented both through natural events and men's deeds, in Kubrick's film the passage from apes to men to star-children is visualized through the alignment of planets and men's cleverness that guides them through space and time. But, in the director's film, natural events and men's intelligence are joined by the aliens' artifact. Kubrick substitutes Nietzsche's *dictum* "God is dead" with a monolith, which is to say, with a powerful and suggestive proof that human beings are not alone in the universe. Apart from the different comparisons between the German philosopher's theory and the American filmmaker's thinking, it seems that Kubrick not only adapted *Thus Spoke Zarathustra* in his science-fiction film (in particular, he visualized the metaphors of dawn ["The Dawn of Man" is the title of the first episode, and in the alignment of planets the sun is often aligned with the other planets] and of men walking above an abyss [men are in space]), but he also directly cited this treatise through the use of Strauss's tone poem. *2001: A Space Odyssey* becomes a sublime aural and visual adaptation of *Thus Spoke Zarathustra*.

Other sequences in Kubrick's films are sublime adaptations of pieces of music. For example, the scenes during which images seem to emanate from music, and characters' and objects' movements and montage follow the rhythm of the music. During these moments the spectators realize that they are in front of an artificial work of art because the narrative fluidity is broken, first, thanks to the foregrounding of the music and, second, thanks to other cinematic techniques, as discussed above. Moreover, during many of these sublime sequences, the protagonists seem to mimic the audience's role because they remain in contemplation of what unfolds before their eyes, and close-ups of them are intercalated with shots of the *mise-en-scène*. This happens, for example, during the Ludovico cure in *A Clockwork Orange*, as well as during the orgy in *Eyes Wide Shut*.

In the former film, when Alex is submitted to the Ludovico treatment for the second time, he is obliged to watch Hitler's parades and bombardments from the Second World War. This cinematic experience, for the extradiegetic audience, is both great, because it represents the attractive power of cinema, and terrifying, because Alex's body is immobilized and his eyes are kept wide open, and the subject of the documentaries is one of humanity's worst manifestations. The documentaries constitute a film-within-the-film, but they show what really happened in the extradiegetic world, and it's the choice and the use of music that both increases the greatness of this sequence and underlines its referentiality. Indeed, this scene is accompanied by the fourth movement of Beethoven's Ninth Symphony, inspired by Friedrich Shiller's *Ode to Joy*, which is a celebration of the brotherhood of men. Moreover, according to the pianist and composer Rosen Charles, the fourth movement is a symphony-within-a-symphony because both the symphony and its fourth movement contain four movements, and the fourth movement of the whole symphony follows the same overall pattern as the symphony itself (1997: 440). Thus, as the documentaries are a film-within-the-film, the piece of music chosen to accompany them is a symphony-within-the-symphony. What is more, the meaning associated to the music (which celebrates the brotherhood of men) adds a new meaning to the documentaries. While the latter show how human beings' intelligence can be used for destructive ends, as in the case of nuclear weapons, the music that accompanies them demonstrates how men's minds can create uplifting works of art. Thus, the director does not only represent human beings incapable of being active or accomplishing praiseworthy tasks. In contrast to characters such as Alex, and to man's regrettable actions such as a war, Kubrick adopts sublime music.

Much as Alex during the Ludovico cure is a spectator of a documentary in which the montage follows the rhythm of the music, Bill during the orgy in *Eyes Wide Shut* remains a passive spectator of bodies who move rhythmically, following the notes of music. During both the Ludovico treatment and the orgy, the meaning associated with the music adds a new signify to the images, contributing to the creation of a sublime visual poem.

When the director's last film was first released, polemics aroused not only for the images shown during the orgy, but also for the music that accompanied them. In the United States, after the first screenings of the film, the Hindu community expressed its concern about Jocelyn Pook's piece "Migrations," which accompanies the scenes shot in the various corridors and rooms of the mansion and which includes some verses of the *shloka*, extrapolated from the *Bhagavad Gita*, an Hindu sacred text. The American Hindus Against Defamation expressed all its resentment in the following letter

August 3, 1999
To Whom It May Concern at Warner
On behalf of American Hindus Against Defamation (AHAD), we would like to express serious concerns about the inclusion of one of the most prominent Hindu scriptural quote [sic], in the movie EWS. Midway in this movie, the character played by Tom Cruise goes to a mansion where what could best be described as an orgy party is taking place. When he enters a large room where several sex acts are taking place, the background music subsides and the shloka is: "Parithranaya Saadhunam Vinashaya cha dushkrithaam Dharma-samsthabanarthaya Sambhavami yuge yuge" which means "for the protection of the virtuous, for the destruction of the evil, and for the firm establishment of Dharm (righteousness), I take bird and am incarnated on Earth, from age to age." Hundreds of Hindus have contacted us to express their shock at the use of Hindu scripture as a background for this scene in the movie. There appears to be no connection, or apparent justification for the use of this shloka. It appears to be totally out of context! We, American Hindus Against Defamation, are baffled, disgusted, and annoyed by the use of the shloka, and fail to understand your intent and the relevance of its usage. We have also been contacted by major media organizations, including BBC-London, *NY Post*, etc., seeking our comments. Before we make any comments to them, we have decided to first contact you and seek a prompt and honest explanation as to why it was decided to use this scripture during this scene in the movie. We are not launching a protest at this time, however, we do request an explanation as soon as possible. (Castle, 2002)

Warner Bros. executive producer Jan Harlan, and Christiane Kubrick apologized to the Hindu community, clarifying that the verse was chosen for his musical qualities, and not for its meaning, and changed the words.

According to Robert Castle (2002), there are three main reasons for the presence of the *shloka* verse. Firstly, the verse links the film to the Hindu castes, to a rigid hierarchy that, in the film, can be applied to the orgy participants. As discussed in the previous chapters, the film underlines the mysteries and differences between the characters who know the orgy rules, such as Ziegler, and those who do not, such as Bill. Secondly, the critic explains that the *Bhagavad Gita* tells that Arjuna looks for the meaning of his actions in the middle of a war, much like Bill strives to find the meaning of sex in the middle of an orgy. Moreover, in the *Bhagavad Gita* it is written, "Once, someone asked, 'Why is it said that the eyes should be half-open and half-shut?' I said, 'The answer is easy. If you keep them fully open, they turn on all sides and prevent concentration. If you shut the eyes completely, you fall asleep.'" Thus, the title of the film, *Eyes Wide Shut*, could be an adaptation of these sentences. Finally, according to Castle, the main theme of the *Bhagavad Gita*, which is to say, the righteousness, the *dharma*, can be linked to Thomas Gibson, the actor who plays the role of Marion's fiancé and who looks like Tom Cruise, because he acted in and directed the sitcom *Dharma and Greg*.

Given Kubrick's care during pre-production, production, and post-production periods, and the relevance and importance of music in his films, it seems unlikely that he chose "Migrations," a non-original score, without knowing that it comprehended a *shloka* verse. It seems more likely that, as in the case of the sequence of *A Clockwork Orange* discussed above, he chose the music because the meaning associated with it added a new signify to the images. I have compared the rooms of the orgy mansion to the sacred Spanish representation of the *Siglo de Oro*, and the choice of "Migrations" helps in the creation of a sacred atmosphere.

This hypothesis seems to be confirmed by another piece of music chosen by Kubrick to accompany the orgy. "Masked Ball" begins before the protagonist reaches the main saloon of the orgy mansion, and ends when Bill first meets the mysterious woman who will save him. This music is non-original, like "Migrations," and it is a rearrangement of Pook's "Backwards Priests." Both the latter music and "Masked Ball" are accompanied by two voices who sing backwards an anaphora, which is a holy chant usually recited at the end of the Orthodox Byzantine mass by two priests. Much like the case of "Migrations," the Romanian Orthodox Church complained about the use of this chant:

> Church officials are unhappy about a recorded fragment from a religious mass which was used in scenes with satanic connotations. They say the fragment is their property as it was taken from a recording made by a Romanian studio. It's alleged that producers of the movie starring Tom Cruise and Nicole Kidman didn't have the right to use the material. The Romanian church wants to sue for copyright but is still looking for financial support to start such an action. Spokesman Constantine Stoica told *Evenimentul Zilei* newspaper: "The church music has a special character and no one can record it or use it as he pleases." The fragment of the Orthodox mass was played backwards during a scene in the movie where masked people assist a procession revealing sexual orgies in a baroque castle. The mass says in Romanian: "We still pray for mercy, life, peace, health, redemption, and forgiveness for

God's serves who are worshippers and benefactors of this holy place. God said to his followers: I give you this new commandment." (Orange Today, February 18, 2003)

In the novel, when Fridolin enters the mansion, he listens to "the sound of a harmonium" and when he enters into the main saloon, "the softly resonant tones of the harmonium, playing an old Italian sacred tune, seemed to descend as if from on high" (Schnitzler, 1999: 44). When the mysterious woman touches Fridolin's arm, "a female voice now accompanied the sound of the harmonium, and an old religious canticle resounded through the room" (1999: 45). Thus, both in the novella and the film, the scenes that could be thought of as a preparation for the dance in the former case, and for the orgy in the latter case, are accompanied by sacred music and chant. In the novel, the music is explicitly described as an old Italian sacred piece, accompanied by a female voice; in the adaptation, "Masked Ball" sounds like a sacred piece, and is accompanied by two voices who sing backwards an anaphora. During this episode in the film, everybody wears a dark cloak with a hood and a Venetian mask; in the novella, men are dressed like monks with masks, and women like nuns with a black veil and a black lace mask. In the adaptation, the only mask who does not wear a dark cloak, but a purple one, like a cardinal, stands in the middle of the main saloon, in the center of the circle constituted by eleven women. The commands he imparts to the women hitting his scepter on the floor, the thurible that he keeps in his hand and rotates, the solemnity and seriousness with which he moves and with which he is looked at by the silent spectators, confer to him and his gestures a sacral halo. This religious atmosphere contributes in the creation of a sublime spectacle that is magnificent and great, but also dangerous and terrifying.

These sublime moments in Kubrick's cinema seem to induce us to reflect, on the one hand, about the director's conception of the cinematic medium and, on the other hand, about his vision of life. The filmmaker seems to exploit all of the potentialities of the cinematic techniques so that his films seem to translate music. Music becomes "visible" and almost "graspable": its laws are adapted in the perfection of the montage and *mise-en-scène*. Kubrick's cinema becomes impalpable, and the images dissolve in a sublime, cerebral contemplation of the universe's life beyond that of the Earth (*2001: A Space Odyssey*), humankind's drive towards violence (*A Clockwork Orange*), the unchanging cruelty of destiny (*Barry Lyndon*), the human mind's power in believing in the supernatural escaping from the natural world (*The Shining*), man's bewilderment when faced with a war (*Full Metal Jacket*), and the urge, as well as the impossibility, of loving (*Eyes Wide Shut*). This is a personal, partial reflection, but the quantity and the heterogeneity of the literature on Kubrick testifies to the richness of his works that can always be reinterpreted from a different perspective.

Two important, logical conclusions can be drawn from the hypothesis of the existence of a sublime cinematic experience. On the one hand, these sublime moments seem to imply the concept of *auteurism*. On the other hand, in the particular case of cinematic adaptations, they seem to imply the reinterpretation and recreation of the filmmaker's own sublime experiences. Indeed, if, as Freeland argues, a sublime experience prompts the spectators to think about the greatness of the director's creative mind and about his vision of life, then the sublime presupposes the figure of the *auteur*. (Moreover, such a figure is implied by the "over narrational commentary" of the art-cinema, as discussed by Bordwell [1985: 211]). Therefore, the fact that postmodernism, as Francois Lyotard argues, is characterized both by the sublime and the death of the author seems contradictory. Furthermore, the sublime moments in Kubrick's adaptations can be interpreted as the director's representation of his personal sublime experiences lived during the reading of the adapted novels and/or the listening of pieces of music subsequently adapted in his films. As discussed above, the director claims that during the pre-production and production periods he has always tried to retain the emotional experience felt during the first reading of the novels. Moreover, he controlled all phases of his work during pre-production, production, and post-production periods. Thus, his sublime seems to become a reinterpretation and a recreation of his sublime experiences provoked by other authors. And the art of adaptation seems to be a sublime homage to the power of the artists' mind. Adaptations are the sublime art of criticism, as theorized by Baudelaire in his "Salon of 1846," in which he claims that the best criticism of a picture may be a sonnet or an elegy:

> I sincerely believe that the best criticism is that which is both amusing and poetic: not a cold, mathematical criticism which, on the pretext of explaining everything, has neither love nor hate, and voluntarily strips itself of every shred of temperament. But, seeing that a fine picture is nature reflected by an artist, the criticism which I approve will be that picture reflected by an intelligent and sensitive mind. Thus the best account of a picture may well be a sonnet or an elegy. (1846: 44)

Similarly, comparing scientific and artistic discoveries, Andrei Tarkovsky claims in *Sculpting in Time*:

> And if cold, positivistic, scientific cognition of the world is like the ascent of one unending staircase, its artistic counterpoint suggests an endless system of spheres, each one perfect and contained within itself. One may complement or contradict one another, but in no circumstances can they cancel each other out; on the contrary, they enrich one another, and accumulate to form an all-embracing sphere that grows out into infinity. (2006: 39)

Each great artist proposes, through her works of art, her personal artistic discovery about life that enriches previous visions of the world. For example, in *The Sacrifice* (Sweden, UK and France, 1986), Tarkovsky creates a sublime moment for the spectators, representing the sublime that his characters seem to experience in front of Leonardo's *Adoration of the Magi*. The images of the postman Otto (Allan Edwall) and the scholar Alexander (Erland Josephson) are reflected in the glass, which preserves the reproduction of the painting, and the former exclaims: "It's uncanny. I've always felt a great terror in front of Leonardo." During the credit sequence and previous scenes, this painting had already been shown to the spectators. The uncanny, experienced by the postman, becomes a sublime experience for the audience, thanks to the characters' faces reflected in the glass that evoke the spectators painted in contemplation of sublime landscapes in the paintings of William Turner and Frederic Edwin Church. This sublime experience could be interpreted as Tarkovsky's homage to Leonardo's painting and to the sublimity inspired by it.[3] It is interesting to note that Carlo Pedretti compares *Adoration of the Magi* to a cinematic scene because the moment of Jesus's birth is represented together with that of the Epiphany. Indeed, the composition is organized according to a system of diagonals that intersect on the Virgin's head. But the perspective has a point of escape between the two trees on the right. Thus, the cinematic tracking is leaving out of the frame what is on the extreme right, which is the nativity hut where the donkey and ox are partially visible. Such a decentered perspective evokes the idea of a story that unrolls though time and space, as in a film. What is more, the young man who stands up on the right and who looks out of frame can be compared to a director who appears in his own work of art (Pedretti, 2002). Thus, Leonardo's *Adoration of the Magi* can be actualized as a metaphor of a sublime cinematic experience (see Figure 6.2).

Figure 6.2 Leonardo's *Adoration of the Magi*.

Freeland closes her essay by discussing the contribution of cognitivism and, in particular, that of the psychologist Ed S. Tan, to the discourse of the sublime in cinema. Tan distinguishes between "fiction emotions" and "artefact emotions." While the former depends on the illusion of being part of the diegetic world, and can be compared to Kant's idea of imagination, the latter is linked to the spectators' recognition of watching an artificial reproduction of a world, and can be compared to Kant's concept of reason. "Artefact emotions" encompass aesthetic reactions, such as awe and wonder at the *mise-en-scène* and so on. According to Tan, the sublime can be experienced only by some spectators: "Some artefact emotions are tied to the competencies of certain viewers who enjoy the cognitive games of cinema; they are less recognized by 'most natural viewers'" (Freeland, 1999: 76). I do not think that every viewer could live a sublime experience while watching a Kubrick film. Unlike the psychologist, however, I do not distinguish between spectators who have "competencies," which enable them to "enjoy the cognitive game of cinema," and "most natural viewers" (Freeland, 1999: 76). I simply distinguish between spectators who are fascinated by the director's films and those who are not, without taking into consideration their cultural background in film studies and, more generally, the reasons for their attitude. What induces me to describe Kubrick's works of art as sublime experiences is the quantity of scholars and fans of the director, who might not necessarily have a background in cinema, who have discussed his works of art. Thus, the pleasure of watching has often become cognition or, at least, a desire to better understand a particular film of Kubrick or his body of work, as in a sublime experience.

I have argued that sublime moments in Kubrick's cinema are often due to his great *mise-en-scène*, in which the movement of objects and characters follow the rhythm of the music, as montage does, in which the protagonists stare at the spectacle, mimicking the audience. These sequences are perfectly constructed by the director to create sublime experiences. The filmmaker's films create an "overt narrational commentary" about sublime moments and their adaptation. They are the embodiment of the recreation of the sublime in the cinematic medium. The art of adaptation thus becomes the art of translating sublime experiences in cinema.

On the one hand, Tarkovsky's protagonists in *Nostalghia* (Italy and Soviet Union, 1983) seem to go in search of sublime experiences,[4] as the director himself and Tonino Guerra did in *Tempo di viaggio* (Tarkovsky and Guerra, Italy, 1983), which is a documentary about the research of locations for *Nostalghia*, during which the filmmaker and the poet travel through Italy not only in search of locations, but also in search of the experiences that these places can evoke. Thus, this extradiegetic documentary becomes the way in which the film displays its artificiality, its being an adaptation of the director's own sublime experiences. On the other hand, Kubrick's protagonists find themselves by chance in front of the sublime, which seems the recreation of the filmmaker's own sublime moments experienced during the reading of the adapted novels, the listening of the adapted music and, in general, during the fruition of other artists' work, and his subsequent speculations about it. *Nostalghia* closes with a sequence shot inside the unfinished Saint Galgano Abbey at Chiusdino (Siena, Tuscany). The poet Andrei Gorchakov (Oleg Yankovsky) is in its central nave with a dog and, behind him, there is a house and vegetation that clearly makes the spectators think about Russia, and it starts snowing. The abbey is finally completed thanks to the nostalgia of the poet and the director for their country. The sublime experience of walking inside this great abbey is completed with the sublime nostalgia of the protagonist and the filmmaker. Tarkovsky explains:

> In the *Nostalghia* scenario, Gorchakov had come to Italy for only a short time; but he fell ill and died there. In other words, he failed to return to Russia not of his own volition but because of a dictate of fate. I also did not imagine that, after finishing *Nostalghia*, I would remain in Italy; but, like Gorchakov, I am subject to a Higher Will. (2006: 220)

In Kubrick's films, characters often do not take part in the sublime spectacles staged for them, and are shown while watching them. For example, in *Barry Lyndon* the protagonist remains in contemplation of Sir Charles Lyndon's family. Even if he marries Lady Lyndon, he never succeeds in taking Sir Charles Lyndon's role in his family and society. After the fight with his stepson during the concert, he is shown alone, in contemplation of those properties that he will soon lose completely. In the subsequent scene, he is shown while watching Sir Wendover, a member of that society from which he will soon be excluded. Both the Kubrick and Tarkovsky films discussed in this work are adaptations of sublime experiences, but while the former recreates artificial sublime spectacles through an orchestration of *mise-en-scène*, music, and montage in front of which protagonists remain passive, the latter makes his characters re-experience and reinterpret his own sublime emotions in front of preexistent paintings and architectonics.

CONCLUSION

Stanley Kubrick's last six adaptations are characterized by some structural and stylistic patterns. In terms of plot construction, they are constituted by *tableaux vivants* and/or unrelated episodes that are usually separated by ellipses and full of unexplained mysteries. Their *syuzhet* is symmetrical and/or ordered into unlinked parts, and often the end recalls the beginning. On the one hand, this geometry of the superstructure is evoked by the symmetry that dominates single images, and by the symmetry that joins two or more sequences. On the other hand, this order is disrupted by the chaos introduced by the image of the maze, as in the case of *The Shining*, and/or by the use of a handheld camera or Steadicam. Also disruptive are the numerous cross-references among scenes, as in *Eyes Wide Shut*, and, paradoxically, too much order, as in *2001: A Space Odyssey* and *Full Metal Jacket*. In terms of stylistic features, images, montage, and characters' reactions often seem to emanate from music, as if they were instruments in the director's orchestra. Some films seem to be dominated by the metaphor of dance because the *mise-en-scène*, the montage, and the movements of the camera follow the rhythm of the music. Moreover, dialogue and voice-over are often used as music is. Words are not used for their referents and signifieds, but for their signifiers, for their rhythm and musicality. These diegetic worlds subjected to the rhythm of music are enveloped in a dreamy atmosphere, in which their protagonists are usually depicted as passive wanderers. They happen to find themselves in front of sublime visual and aural spectacles staged to entrap and entertain them, as well as their extradiegetic audience. Indeed, through the metaphor of theatre and other means, the spectators often acknowledge the status of the films as artificial works of art.

These structural and stylistic patterns have allowed me to draw conclusions about the role of Kubrick in the history of cinema and his role as an adapter, as well as, more generally, about the art of cinematic adaptations. Indeed, on the one hand, at a more "immediate" level, the director's films can be interpreted as sublime experiences that stimulate the audience to think about them and about the power of art and artists. The director's adaptations can be read as a recreation of his own sublime experiences, which he felt during his encounters with literature and music and art in general; they are his sublime homage to other artists' creations. Therefore, cinematic adaptations can be interpreted as an everlasting re-actualization and *mise-en-scène* of themes and styles. On the other hand, at a less "immediate" level, the plot structure and use of words and music seem to criticize classical Hollywood narratives, and the use of music in classical narrative sound films. More generally, the structural and stylistic patterns that characterize Kubrick adaptations seem to criticize a scientific reasoning that from causes derives effects, and from words univocal meanings. Life and art do not follow straight paths that from the outset lead to an end, and that clearly display their purposes. On the contrary, the director's films seem to suggest that only stylistically and structurally tortuous paths, which often negate a final aim, can recall the complexity of reality. For these reasons, Kubrick can be considered a modernist *auteur* in the history of cinema. In particular, he can be regarded as an heir of the modernist avant-garde of the 1920s. But, unlike his predecessors, he creates a cinema that is not only centered on the ontology of the medium, but whose main purpose seems the staging of sublime experiences.

Finally, as specifically regards the director's way of adapting novels, the structural and stylistic patterns that characterize his films are not always present in the source books. Summarizing the results obtained, the particular *syuzhet* construction of his films is already present in Anthony Burgess's *A Clockwork Orange*, Gustav Hasford's *The Short-Timers*, and Arthur Schnitzler's *Dream Story*, and is emphasized in his adaptations. Similarly, the choice and combination of words according to their signifiers, rhythm, and musicality, is present in *A Clockwork Orange*, Stephen King's *The Shining*, and *The Short-Timers*, and is stressed in the director's films, as is the metaphor of dance, which appears in *A Clockwork Orange* and *The Short-Timers*, but which almost dominates the cinematic adaptations of those books. Similarly, the dreamy atmosphere which envelops Kubrick's films is present in *A Clockwork Orange*, *The Shining*, and *Dream Story*, but in these source novels is not as emphasized as in the director's adaptations. Finally, whereas *A Clockwork Orange* and *The Shining* appear to be referential novels, all of Kubrick's films clearly display an awareness of being works of art. Thus, even if the director adapted novels pertaining to different genres, written by different authors in different historical, sociological, and cultural contexts, he translated them through those stylistic and structural patterns that seem to characterize the core of his very art. Therefore, I can claim once more that he should be regarded as an *auteur* because, although he adapted text of other authors, his works clearly display similar features. Moreover, in the specific cases of Burgess's *A Clockwork Orange* and Hasford's *The Short-Timers*, Kubrick seems, especially through the metaphor of dance, to have translated the very linguistic style of the source novels. Which is to say, he translated in the cinematic medium what, according to the fidelity approach, cannot be adapted because it should constitute the untranslatable peculiarity of the written medium.

Therefore, a narratological approach that moves from novels to films and vice versa, enriched with an intertextual perspective focused on cinematic adaptations, has allowed me to underline the structural and stylistic patterns of Kubrick's adaptations, and to understand whether these characteristics are translated from the source books. What is more, not privileging the written medium over the cinematic medium, I have been able to find those sublime moments in the director's cinema in which the very linguistic style and metaphors of the novels seem to have guided his inspiration. Thus, paradoxically, it would seem that when adaptation studies are freed from literary studies, other fruitful links between the two media can be appreciated. Moreover, adaptation studies can be interpreted as the result of a sublime dialogue among artists and epochs.

APPENDIX

2001: A Space Odyssey

Main Episodes of the Film and of the Novel	Duration of the Episodes of the Film in Seconds	Duration of the Episodes of the Film in %	Duration of the Sections of the Novel in Pages	Duration of the Sections of the Novel in %
Alignment of planets	269	3,35%		0,00%
The jaguard	183	2,28%	97	1,34%
The water hole	127	1,58%	107	1,47%
Sleeping	103	1,28%	23	0,32%
The monolith	463	5,76%	694	9,56%
From the Earth towards the Moon	321	3,99%	335	4,62%
At Space Station 1	477	5,94%	202	2,78%
Towards Clavius Base	424	5,28%	373	5,14%
Meeting	259	3,22%	276	3,80%
Towards Crater Tycho	305	3,80%	312	4,30%
The monolith	638	7,94%	182	2,51%
Inside Discovery	585	7,28%	1277	17,59%
The antenna	345	4,29%	280	3,86%
About Hal 9000	471	5,86%	306	4,22%
Killing	1706	21,23%	832	11,46%
Bowman alone		0,00%	672	9,26%
Through time and space	835	10,39%	769	10,60%
The star child	525	6,53%	521	7,18%
	8036	100,00%	7258	100,00%

Table of the duration of the main episodes of the film and of the novel.

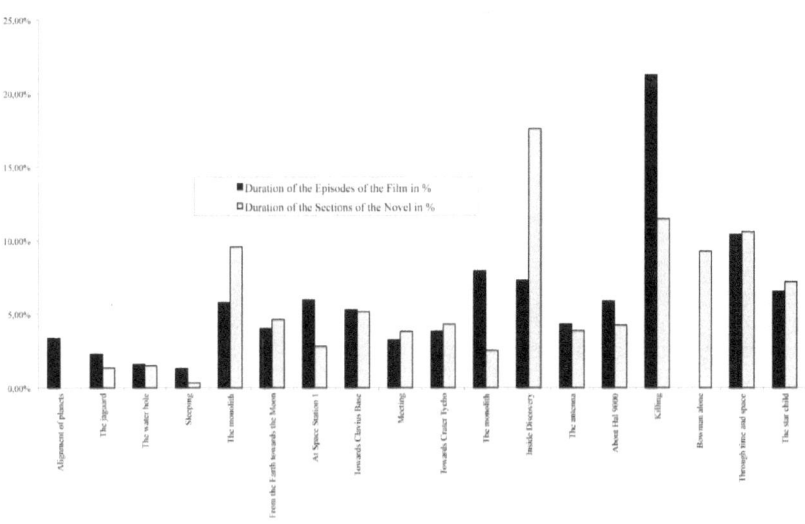

Histogram of the duration of the main episodes of the film and of the novel.

A Clockwork Orange

Main Episodes of the Film and of the Novel	Duration of the Episodes of the Film in Seconds	Duration of the Episodes of the Film in %	Duration of the Sections of the Novel in Pages	Duration of the Sections of the Novel in %
Korova Milkbar	89	1,13%	103	2,11%
Hitting a professor		0,00%	214	4,38%
Hitting a homeless person	125	1,59%	45	0,92%
Billyboy's gang	176	2,23%	72	1,47%
Durango 95	121	1,54%	65	1,33%
Mr Alexander	215	2,73%	115	2,36%
Durango 95		0,00%	33	0,68%
Korova Milkbar	197	2,50%	126	2,58%
Back home	53	0,67%	29	0,59%
Visions and Mr Deltoid	476	6,04%	259	5,31%
Music shop	131	1,66%	52	1,07%
Launch		0,00%	21	0,43%
Orgy	57	0,72%	113	2,31%
Discussion among the droogs	245	3,11%	82	1,68%
Fighting among the droogs	100	1,27%	53	1,09%
About what to do	100	1,27%	42	0,86%
The cat lady	353	4,48%	279	5,71%
Interrogatory	220	2,79%	11	0,23%
In a cell		0,00%	73	1,50%
Before entering prison	322	4,09%		0,00%
The mass and visions	483	6,13%	228	4,67%
Killing		0,00%	186	3,81%
Alex is chosen for the cure	216	2,74%	39	0,80%
Contract for the cure	129	1,64%	38	0,78%
About the cure		0,00%	49	1,00%
To Ludovico Medical facility	143	1,81%	19	0,39%
Meeting Dr	82	1,04%	75	1,54%
The Ludovico cure	194	2,46%	186	3,81%
About Ludovico cure	54	0,69%	128	2,62%
The Ludovico cure	214	2,72%	122	2,50%
Fighting		0,00%	124	2,54%
Demonstration	571	7,25%	234	4,79%
Breakfast		0,00%	77	1,58%
Back home	567	7,20%	130	2,66%
Music shop and Korova Milkbar		0,00%	99	2,03%
Hitting a professor/homeless person	207	2,63%	172	3,52%
Fighting with his former droogs	165	2,09%	157	3,22%
Mr Alexander	906	11,50%	358	7,33%
Alex's suicide	174	2,21%	83	1,70%
Recovering consciousness	65	0,82%	60	1,23%
Newspapers	28	0,36%	26	0,53%
Alex's parents	73	0,93%	58	1,19%
Psychological test	206	2,61%	47	0,96%
The Minister of the Interior	423	5,37%	79	1,62%
End			321	6,58%
	7880	100,00%	4882	100,00%

Table of the duration of the main episodes of the film and of the novel.

Appendix

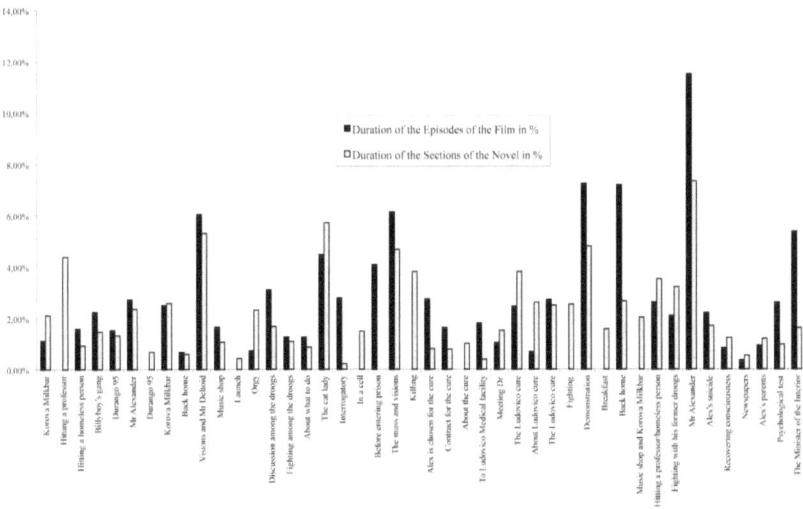

Histogram of the duration of the main episodes of the film and of the novel.

Barry Lyndon.

Episodes of the Film	Duration of the Episodes in Seconds	Duration of the Episodes in %
First Part		
Pedigree and family.	120	1,14%
The tender passion.	754	7,15%
A man of spirit.	739	7,01%
A false start in the genteel world.	410	3,89%
A near view of military glory.	759	7,20%
As far from military glory as possible.	944	8,95%
Military episodes.	373	3,54%
A garrison life.	382	3,62%
Adieu to the military profession.	425	4,03%
Name and lineage.	392	3,72%
Paying court to Lady Lyndon.	620	5,88%
Second Part		
Nobly and (seeming) good fortune.	100	0,95%
An ornament of English society.	492	4,66%
Good fortune begins to waver.	183	1,73%
Bryan's birthday.	211	2,00%
Good fortune begins to waver.	1116	10,58%
Bryan and Barry.	147	1,39%
Bryan's death.	901	8,54%
Barry and Lord Bullingdon.	1480	14,03%
	10548	**100,00%**

Table of the duration of the main episodes of the film.

Sections of the Novel	Duration of the Sections in Pages	Duration of the Sections in %
Pedigree and family. The tender passion.	1399	10,71%
A man of spirit.	548	4,20%
A false start in the genteel world.	621	4,75%
A near view of military glory.	392	3,00%
As far from military glory as possible.	621	4,75%
Military episodes.	728	5,57%
A garrison life.	569	4,36%
Adieu to the military profession.	200	1,53%
Name and lineage.	2473	18,93%
A man of fashion.	329	2,52%
Paying court to Lady Lyndon.	1934	14,81%
An ornament of English society.	893	6,84%
Good fortune begins to waver.	980	7,50%
Conclusions.	1376	10,53%
	13063	100,00%

Table of the duration of the main sections of the novel.

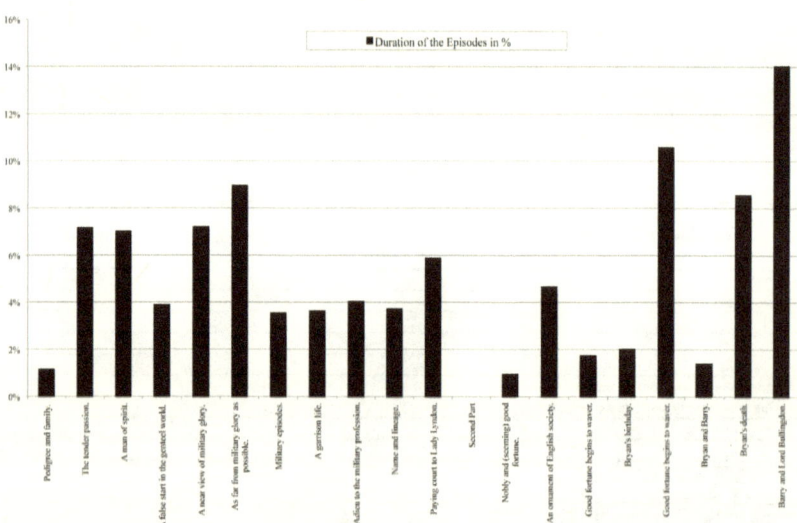

Histogram of the duration of the main episodes of the film.

Appendix

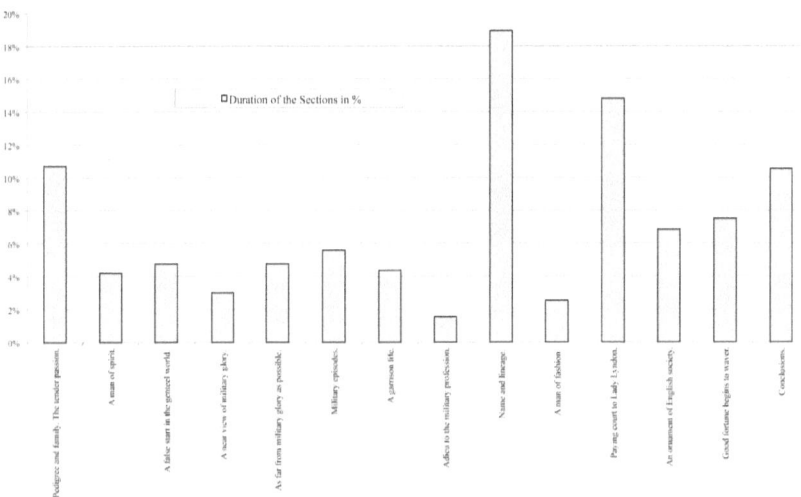

Histogram of the duration of the main sections of the novel.

The Shining.

Episodes of the Film	Duration of the Episodes in Seconds	Duration of the Episodes in %
	172	
The interview	432	6,51%
Closing day	799	12,04%
A month later	222	3,35%
Tuesday	314	4,73%
Saturday	253	3,81%
Monday	253	3,81%
Wednesday	2846	42,90%
4 p.m.	1515	22,84%
	6634	**100,00%**

Table of the duration of the main episodes of the film.

Chapters of the Novel	Duration of the Chapters in Pages	Duration of the Chapters in %
Prefatory matters	58	12,06%
Closing day	45	9,36%
The wasps' nest	127	26,40%
Snowbound	95	19,75%
Matters of life and death	156	32,43%
	481	**100,00%**

Table of the duration of the main sections of the novel.

Appendix

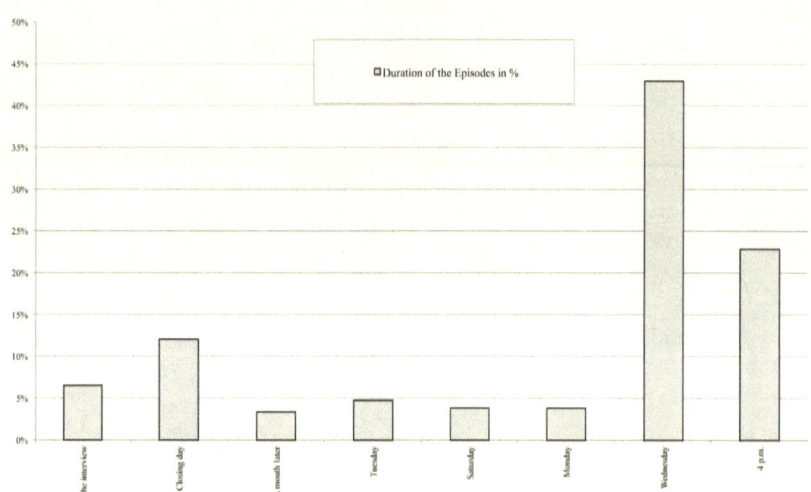

Histogram of the duration of the main episodes of the film.

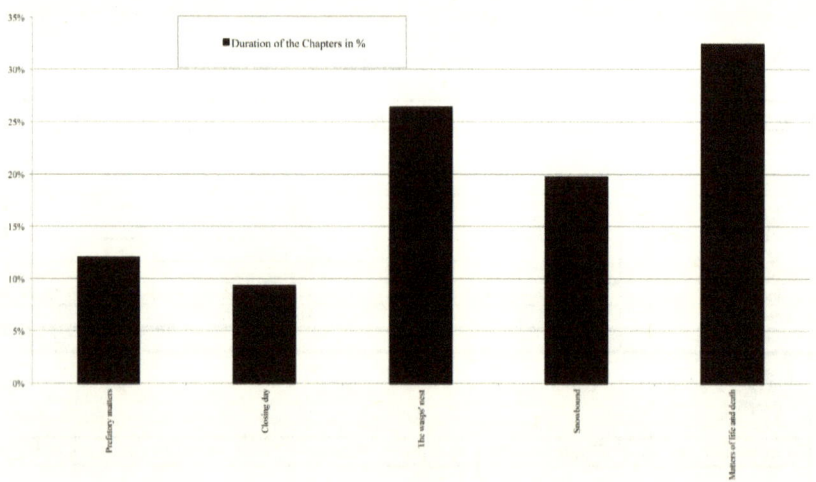

Histogram of the duration of the main sections of the novel.

Full Metal Jacket.

Episodes of the Film	Duration of the Episodes in Seconds	Duration of the Episodes in %
First Part		
Hair cutting	92	1,38%
Sergeant's presentation	343	5,15%
Pyle's slowness	140	2,10%
Rifleman's creed	126	1,89%
Training	323	4,85%
Virgin Mary	114	1,71%
Joker teaching Pyle	87	1,31%
Killing with rifles	153	2,30%
Punishment for Pyle	224	3,36%
Punishment for Pyle	25	0,38%
Pyle's punishment	123	1,85%
Pyle's silence	157	2,36%
Happy Birthday to Jesus	198	2,97%
Pyle's improvements	143	2,15%
Graduation Day	47	0,71%
Pyle's death	333	5,00%
Second Part		
The prostitute	155	2,33%
Joker and Rafter Man	4	0,06%
Journalism	52	0,78%
Fireworks	77	1,16%
Tet Offensive	336	5,05%
Bunker	189	2,84%
About the Tet Offensive	93	1,40%
Third Part		
Firing	166	2,49%
Looking for the squad	94	1,41%
Mass grave	147	2,21%
Meeting the squad	273	4,10%
Lieutenant's death	338	5,08%
Camera crew	88	1,32%
In a grave	113	1,70%
Interview	183	2,75%
The prostitute	148	2,22%
The sniper	1573	23,63%
	6657	100,00%

Table of the duration of the main episodes of the film.

Sections of the Novel	Duration of the Sections in Pages	Duration of the Sections in %
First Part		
Nicknames	7	0,12%
Sergeant's presentation	114	1,93%
Pyle's slowness	27	0,46%
Virgin Mary	103	1,75%
Joker teaching Pyle	33	0,56%
Training	108	1,83%
Punishment for Pyle	31	0,53%
Chow time	5	0,08%
Pyle's punishment	31	0,53%
Pyle's silence	9	0,15%
Killing with rifles	4	0,07%
Pyle's improvements	52	0,88%
Happy Birthday to Jesus	9	0,15%
Chow time	28	0,47%
Speaking with rifles	59	1,00%
Rifleman's creed	67	1,14%
Graduation day	55	0,93%
Pyle's death	241	4,08%
Second Part		0,00%
The Green Berets	192	3,25%
Joker and Rafter Man	55	0,93%
Fireworks	85	1,44%
About the Tet Offensive	68	1,15%
Joker and Rafter Man	534	9,05%
Tet Offensive	276	4,68%
In a bunker	97	1,64%
Third Part		0,00%
Firing	50	0,85%
Hitch-hiking	188	3,19%
Arvins	53	0,90%
Camera crew	61	1,03%
Looking for the squad	385	6,52%
The sniper	913	15,47%
Imperial palace	53	0,90%
Attack on the river	89	1,51%
Mass grave	27	0,46%
Rafter Man's death	530	8,98%
Leaving for a mission	207	3,51%
The sniper	1056	17,89%
	5902	100,00%

Table of the duration of the main sections of the novel.

Appendix 195

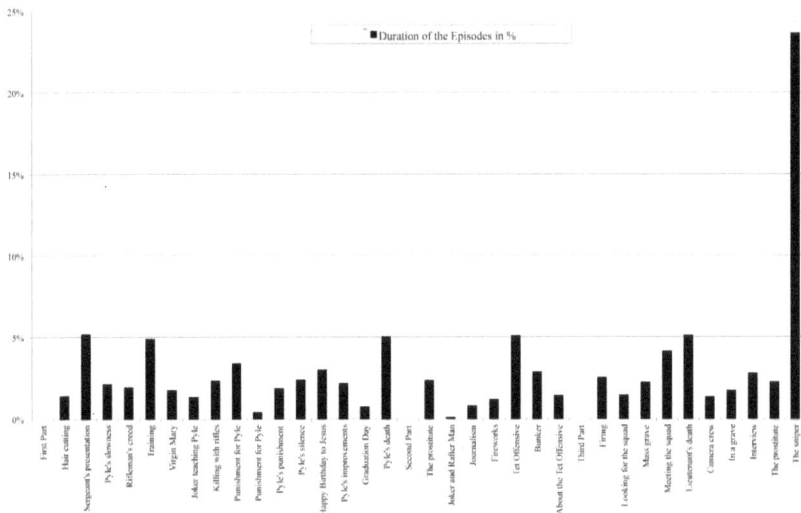

Histogram of the duration of the main episodes of the film.

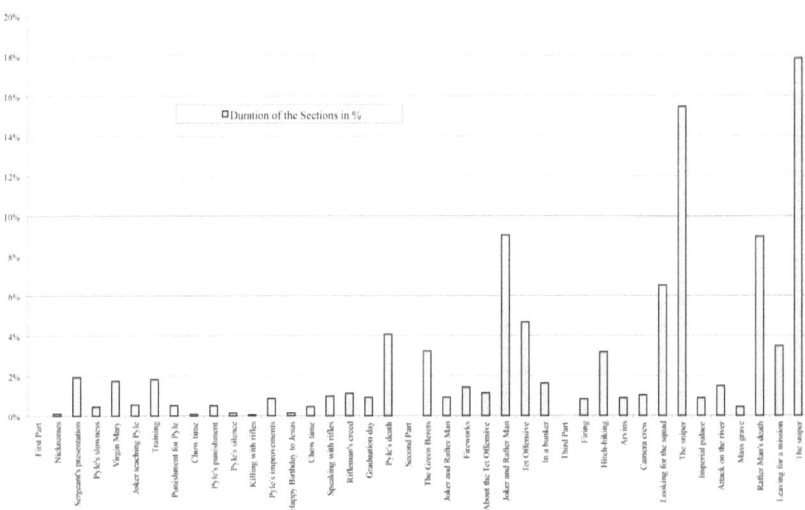

Histogram of the duration of the main sections of the novel.

Eyes Wide Shut.

Main Episodes of the Film and of the Novel	Duration of the Episodes of the Film in Seconds	Duration of the Episodes of the Film in %	Duration of the Sections of the Novel in Pages	Duration of the Sections of the Novel in %
The wife undresses	8	0,09%		0,00%
Street	6	0,07%		0,00%
Preparation for the ball	101	1,12%		0,00%
Street	6	0,07%		0,00%
Ball	980	10,83%	18	0,61%
Love	64	0,71%		0,00%
Work	72	0,80%	5	0,17%
After dinner	50	0,55%	15	0,51%
Confession	956	10,57%	152	5,19%
Towards Marion/Marianne	31	0,34%	6	0,20%
Marion/Marianne	434	4,80%	207	7,06%
The group of boys	180	1,99%	157	5,36%
The prostitute	353	3,90%	71	2,42%
Wandering	47	0,52%	14	0,48%
Sonata Café/Coffee-House	394	4,35%	288	9,83%
Costume rental shop	408	4,51%	151	5,15%
Towards the orgy	158	1,75%	74	2,53%
Orgy	1090	12,05%	339	11,57%
Back home		0,00%	168	5,73%
The dream	486	5,37%	316	10,78%
The following morning		0,00%	12	0,41%
Work		0,00%	6	0,20%
Street	10	0,11%		0,00%
Gillespie's/Coffee-House	150	1,66%	5	0,17%
Street	6	0,07%		0,00%
Hotel	194	2,14%	25	0,85%
Street	5	0,06%		0,00%
Costume rental shop	155	1,71%	51	1,74%
Street	4	0,04%		0,00%
Work	52	0,57%	68	2,32%
Orgy mansion	198	2,19%	101	3,45%
Street	5	0,06%		0,00%
Back home	116	1,28%	27	0,92%
Marion/Marianne	77	0,85%	127	4,33%
The prostitute	336	3,71%	78	2,66%
Wandering	189	2,09%	30	1,02%
Sonata Café/Coffee-House	93	1,03%	43	1,47%
Street	4	0,04%		0,00%
Hotel		0,00%	55	1,88%
Morgue	241	2,66%	243	8,29%
Street	4	0,04%		0,00%
Billiard room	786	8,69%		0,00%
The mask	278	3,07%	78	2,66%
Toy shop	321	3,55%		0,00%
	9048	100,00%	2930	100,00%

Table of the duration of the main episodes of the film and of the novel.

Appendix

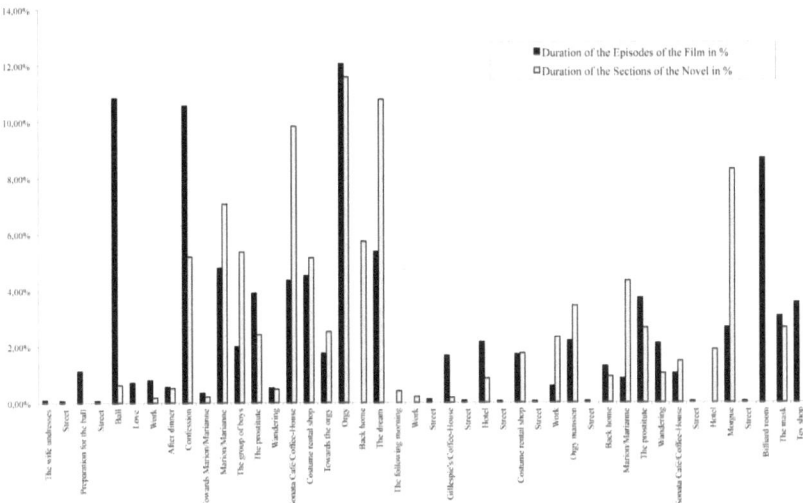

Histogram of the duration of the main episodes of the film and of the novel.

NOTES

Introduction

1. Among the texts that were first published in English or translated into English, there are, for example: biographies (e.g., John Baxter's *Stanley Kubrick* [1997], Daniel De Vries's *The Films of Stanley Kubrick* [1973], James Howard's *Stanley Kubrick Companion* [1999], Christiane Kubrick's *Stanley Kubrick: A Life in Pictures* (2002), and Vincent LoBrutto's *Stanley Kubrick* [1998]); biographies that include film analyses (e.g., Michel Ciment's *Kubrick* [2003], Gene D. Phillips's *Stanley Kubrick: A Film Odyssey* [1975], and Alexander Walker's *Stanley Kubrick, Director: A Visual Analysis* [2000]); film analyses (e.g., Geoffrey Cocks's *The Wolf at the Door: Stanley Kubrick, History, and the Holocaust* [2004], Paul Duncan's *Stanley Kubrick: The Complete Films* [2003], Mario Falsetto's *Stanley Kubrick: A Narrative and Stylistic Analysis* [1994], David Hughes's *The Complete Kubrick* [2001], Norman Kagan's *The Cinema of Stanley Kubrick* [2000], Luis M. Garcia Mainar's *Narrative and Stylistic Patterns in the Films of Stanley Kubrick* [1999], James Naremore's *On Kubrick* [2007], Thomas Allen Nelson's *Kubrick: Inside a Film Artist's Maze* [2000], Randy Rasmussen's *Stanley Kubrick: Seven Films Analyzed* [2001], and Jason Sperb's *The Kubrick Façade: Faces and Voices in the Films of Stanley Kubrick* [2006]); collections of interviews, essays, and materials (e.g., Jerold J. Abrams's *The Philosophy of Stanley Kubrick* (*The Philosophy of Popular Culture*) [2007], Alison Castle's *The Stanley Kubrick Archives* [2005], Geoffrey Cocks's *Depth of Field: Stanley Kubrick, Film, and the Uses of History* [2006], and Falsetto's *Perspectives on Stanley Kubrick* [1996]); encyclopedias (e.g., Phillips's *Stanley Kubrick Interviews* [2001] and Phillips and Rodney Hill's *The Encyclopedia of Stanley Kubrick* [2002]). Among the texts which are entirely devoted to one of the films that are discussed in this book, and which are more useful for the purposes of the problem of adaptation, there are texts made up of an analysis of a Kubrick film developed by one critic only, such as Piers Bizony's *2001: Filming the Future* (1994), Michel Chion's *Kubrick's Cinema Odyssey* (Chion, Kubrick, and Gorbman, 2001), David G. Stork's *Hal's Legacy: 2001's Computer as Dream and Reality* (1997), Leonard F. Wheat's *Kubrick's 2001: A Triple Allegory* (2000), and Chion's *Eyes Wide Shut* (2002). Then there are collections of interviews, articles, reviews, and essays (e.g., Jerome Agel's *The Making of Kubrick's 2001* [1970], Carolyn Geduld's *Filmguide to 2001: A Space Odyssey* [1973], and Stephanie Schwam's *The Making of 2001: A Space Odyssey* [2000]); and collections of essays (e.g., Robert Kolker's *Stanley Kubrick's 2001: A Space Odyssey: New Essays* [2006] and Stuart Y. McDougal's *Stanley Kubrick's A Clockwork Orange* [2003]). Finally, there are memoirs and diaries of Kubrick's collaborators, such as Dan Richter's *Moonwatcher's Memoir: A Diary of 2001: A Space Odyssey* (2002) and Gary Lockwood's *2001 Memoirs: An Actor's Odyssey*

(2001), the former written by the actor who played the role of Moon-watcher, the man-apes' leader, and the latter by the actor who played the role of the astronaut Frank Poole in *2001: A Space Odyssey*; and Matthew Modine's *Full Metal Jacket Diary* (2005), written by the actor who played the role of the protagonist Joker in *Full Metal Jacket*. The memoirs written by the director's co-screenwriters are a source of information about the process of adaptation and its various phases. For example, there are memoirs written by Arthur C. Clarke (1972), co-screenwriter of *2001: A Space Odyssey* and author of "The Sentinel" (1951) and *2001: A Space Odyssey* (1968), the former a short novel from which the film and the novel were adapted, the latter a novel written during the pre-production and production periods; by Michael Herr (2000), co-screenwriter of *Full Metal Jacket*; and by Frederic Raphael (1999), co-screenwriter of *Eyes Wide Shut*.

For a more complete bibliography, see Wallace Coyle's *Stanley Kubrick: A Guide to References and Resources* (1980).

2. William Kittredge and Steven M. Krauzer do not discuss Kubrick's *2001: A Space Odyssey*, but a summary of the plot of the film and a little information about the collaboration between the director and Clarke are followed by Clarke's short story "The Sentinel" (1979: 221–223). James Griffith analyzes this adaptation, too. John Orr and Colin Nicholson include in their collection of essays John Brown's discussion about *The Shining* (1992: 104–121). Michael Klein and Gillian Parker (1981), Neil Sinyard (1986), and Peter Cosgrove's essay in Robert Mayer's text (2000: 16–34) analyze *Barry Lyndon*. Jack Boozer discusses *Eyes Wide Shut* (2008).

3. Jenkins cites a 1982 dissertation by Judy Lee Kinney, who discusses Kubrick's films from the point of view of adaptation studies. But he criticizes her thesis, commenting that her literature review "which mentions George Bluestone, André Bazin, and a few others, is quite frugal," and that she does not deepen her analysis of the source novels (1997: 3).

4. Béla Balàz is said by James Griffith to have been the first theorist to deal with the problem of adaptation directly (Griffith, 1997: 18–20). But the first and most influential work in adaptation studies, which was mostly based upon the criteria of fidelity, was George Bluestone's *Novels into Film* (1957). Among the main scholars who follow this approach are Morris Beja (1976), Kittredge and Krauzer (1979), Jonathan Miller (1986), and, more recently, Robert Giddings, Keith Selby, and Chris Wensley (1990), Orr and Nicholson (1992), and Peter Reynolds (1992).

5. The border between the scholars who follow a fidelity approach and those who adopt a narratological method is not strict. The distinction is used here to underline some nuances of their methods, thus some of the critics cited above are mentioned again. There are, for example Giddings, Selby, and Wensley (1990), Brian McFarlane (1996), Jackob Lothe (2000), Robert Stam (Stam and Raengo, 2005; Stam, 2005), and Edward Branigan (1992).

6. Geoffrey Wagner (1975) distinguishes among transposition, commentary, and analogy. In transposition, a film is as faithful as possible to its source novel. In commentary, a book is either consciously or unconsciously modified in some respect.

In analogy, the director finds analogous rhetorical techniques and arouses the same attitudes in her audience. Beja (1976) classifies two main approaches to adaptation: in the first one, the novel is adapted strictly following the text, as in Wagner's transposition; in the second one, the book is adapted freely and the film becomes a new, independent work, as in Wagner's analogy. Klein and Parker, not unlike Wagner, distinguish among three types of adaptation (1981: 9–10). Dudley Andrew, like Wagner, and Klein and Parker, classifies three types of adaptation: borrowing, intersecting, and fidelity and transformation. In borrowing, the director adapts the material, idea, or form of a novel, and the critic should look in the adaptation for the peculiarities and originalities of the source book. In intersecting, "the uniqueness of the original text is preserved to such an extent that it is intentionally left unassimilated in adaptation," "such intersecting insists that the analyst attend to the specificity of the original within the specificity of the cinema." In fidelity and transformation, something essential about the novel is reproduced in its adaptation (2000: 30–31).

7. For example, Bluestone himself who, as already discussed, is one of the first and most influential exponents of the fidelity method, compares the different modes of production of novels and films. Writing and publishing a book is not as expensive as producing a film and, consequently, the cinematic medium has to please a wider audience to make a profit. The director's choices are not only dictated by his personal feelings and style, but also by audience's demands and censorship's regulations (1957: 38).

8. Among the scholars who follow an intertextual approach, are Deborah Cartmell and Imelda Welehan (1999), Naremore (2000), Mireia (2005), Lothe (2000), and Stam (2005; Stam and Raengo, 2005).

9. As regards the difference between story/*fabula* and plot/*syuzhet*, David Bordwell claims: "Presented with two narrative events, we look for causal or spatial or temporal links. The imaginary construct we create, progressively and retroactively, was termed by Formalists the *fabula*" (1985: 49). "The *syuzhet* . . . is the actual arrangement and presentation of the *fabula* in the film" (1985: 50). Three principles link story and plot: time, space, and narrative logic, which mostly refers to causality (1985: 51).

10. Gérard Genette analyzes tense, which is the temporal relation between story and plot, according to three categories: the order, which is the relation between the chronological order of the events in the story and the order in which these events are presented in the plot (1976: 81–134); the duration, which is the relation between the implicit duration of the events in the story and the explicit duration of them in the plot (1976: 135–161); and the frequency, which is the relation between how many times the events are recounted in the plot and how many times they occur in the story (1976: 161–207).

11. Since his first feature-length films, Kubrick almost always worked independently of a major studio. *Fear and Desire* (USA, 1953) and *Killer's Kiss* (USA, 1955) were financed by his relatives and friends, and he was credited as the only producer. He then formed a production company with Jim Harris and they produced *The Killing* (USA, 1956), *Paths of Glory* (USA, 1957), and *Lolita*, and Harris was credited as the only

producer for these three films. In all of his subsequent films, Kubrick was credited as the only producer, except for *Spartacus* (USA, 1960), produced by Edward Lewis (Phillips, 2002: 144–145). The director was asked to direct *Spartacus* when shooting had already begun; indeed, Anthony Mann, who was directing it, left the set after the first week of work after disagreements with Kirk Douglas, who played the title role (Phillips, 1973: 145).

12. Kubrick produced, wrote the script, and controlled the editing of all his films, as can be seen in the Filmography. His independence was due also to the fact that he remained far from Hollywood gossip and frenzy: in London, he was able to work in an environment of relative tranquility.

Chapter One

1. See Stephen Mamber's graphic about *The Killing* (1998).
2. The heresiarch Pelagius claimed that the Sin of Adam was not inherited by the human race and, thus, men are by nature good, as they are afforded the free will to choose between good and evil. St. Augustine, who defended the position of the Catholic Church against Pelagius, affirmed that Original Sin ensures that men are all innately evil and can achieve salvation only through the grace of God. Burgess adopted these two philosophical and historical adversaries to illustrate the conflict between the reason of the mind and that of the flesh. Thus, in the citation, the Americans are defined as Augustinian because they can enjoy the novel without the last chapter, without the protagonist's regeneration and salvation, whereas the British need to know that the protagonist at the end of all his misadventures and mistakes chooses good.
3. Kubrick Archive was donated by the director's family to the University of the Arts London and arrived there in March 2007. The Archive now has a permanent exhibition at: http://www.arts.ac.uk/library/archives-collections/archivesspecialcollectionscentre/ (accessed October 4, 2011).

Chapter Two

1. See the histogram of *2001: Space Odyssey* in the Appendix. This episode of the novel is identified through the title "Bowman alone."
2. See the histogram of *2001: A Space Odyssey* in the Appendix. This episode of the novel and the film is identified through the title "The monolith" and is longer in the book than in the adaptation.

Chapter Three

1. See the histogram of *A Clockwork Orange* in the Appendix, and compare the main episodes of the novel with those of the film. The first part of the story ends with the section entitled "The cat lady," the second part begins with "Interrogatory" and ends with "Demonstration," and the third part goes from "Back home" to "End."
2. See the histogram of *Eyes Wide Shut* in the Appendix, and compare the main episodes of the novel with those of the film.
3. Compare the histogram of the film with that of the novel in the Appendix.

Chapter Four

1. Gorbman's theories have been challenged by, for example, Pauline Reay and K. J. Donnelly. The former critic criticizes Gorbman's claims that extradiegetic music is unheard, and that action and dialogue stop for the duration of a performance (2004: 163). Discussing the case of *Magnolia* (Paul Thomas Anderson, USA, 1999), she argues that popular songs in this film function as dialogue: "The lyrics give voice to feelings and attitudes not made explicit by the visuals and dialogue, they highlight the element of authorial expressivity, they work as music illusionism to speak for characters" (2004: 72–73). Discussing *The Shining*, Donnelly claims that "in Stanley Kubrick's adaptation of Stephen King's novel *The Shining*, the music would undoubtedly be better described as 'foreground music'" (2005: 36) and that "the very form of the music, the way that it dominates the other film elements, means that the action seems to follow the music. At times, it is almost as if the images are emanating from the music" (2005: 46).

Chapter Five

1. In my M.A. thesis, discussed in March 2003 at the University of Bergamo, entitled "Critica della critica: il caso Eyes Wide Shut," I analyzed 107 English, North American, and Italian reviews and articles published when *Eyes Wide Shut* was first released. Of these, sixty reviews and articles critizise Cruise's acting and, of these sixty, twenty-eight critizise the protagonist's role. But many of them explain that the fault is not of the actor, but of the director who hates men so much that he represents them as inhuman, and considers them as an aesthetic mistake in the *mise-en-scène*.
2. According to Genette, hypertextuality is a relationship that links a text, called hypertext, to a previous text, hypotext, without being a comment (1997: 3–13). The scholar, after having individuated two types of relations between the hypertext and the hypotext (transformation and imitation), and three types of regimens of the hypertext (the playful, the satiric, and the serious), classifies six types of hypertexts (parody, transvestism, transposition, pastiche, charge, and forgery) (1997: 29–36).

3. Kubrick "obtained a fixed-focus 50mm barrel lens, developed by NASA and the Zeiss company for taking still photographs on the Moon, and engaged a Californian engineer, Ed Di Giulio of the Cinema Products Corporation, to fit it to his Mitchell BNC camera" (Hughes, 2001: 192).

Chapter Six

1. A blue light filters from the windows in numerous other sequences—such as when Bill is with Victor and Mandy in the bathroom, when the protagonist speaks with the orgy woman who tries to save him, and when he is with Ziegler in the billiard room. What is more, Bill's fantasy image, and the scene in which Alice recounts her dream, are lit by a blue light. This color seems to link all of the sequences in which the protagonist or another character is in danger.

2. There are several books that discuss adaptations of Shakespeare's plays from different perspectives. To cite only a few of them: *Interpreting Shakespeare on Film* (Cartmell, 2000); *Talking Shakespeare: Shakespeare into the Millennium* (Cartmell and Scott, 2001); *Shakespeare the Movie II: Popularizing the Plays on Film, TV, Video, and DVD* (Burt and Boose, 2003); *Shakespeare on Film* (Buchaman, 2005); *The Cambridge Companion to Shakespeare on Film* (Jackson, 2007); and *New Wave Shakespeare on Screen* (Cartelli and Rowe, 2007).

3. The contemplation of reproduced works of art, by diegetic and/or extradiegetic viewers, is a motif in virtually all of Tarkovsky's films. For example, in *Ivan's Childhood* (Soviet Union, 1966) the young protagonist Ivan (Anatoli Solonitsyn) is shown looking at a collection of reproductions of ancient prints, and in *Andrei Rublev* (Soviet Union, 1962) the protagonist Andrei (Nikolai Burlyayev) is a painter of sacred icons who tries to improve his art.

4. For example, the translator Eugenia (Domiziana Giordano) goes to see Piero della Francesca's *Madonna del parto* at the Santa Maria Church at Monterchi (Arezzo, Tuscany). The subject, a pregnant Virgin, is unusual in the history of art. She does not look at the spectators to announce the news, but down at her womb. When Eugenia enters the church a procession of women arrives, carrying the statue of the Virgin and, from the Madonna's womb, white doves emerge. It seems to be a miracle—a sublime moment.

BIBLIOGRAPHY

Abrams, J. J. "Nietzsche's Overman as Posthuman Starchild in *2001: A Space Odyssey*." In *The Philosophy of Stanley Kubrick (The Philosophy of Popular Culture)*. Edited by J. J. Abrams. Kentucky: University Press of Kentucky, 2007, 247–265.

———. ed. *The Philosophy of Stanley Kubrick (The Philosophy of Popular Culture)*. Kentucky: University Press of Kentucky, 2007.

Agel, J. *The Making of Kubrick's 2001*. New York: New American Library, 1970.

Andrew, D. "Adaptation." In *Film Adaptation*. Edited by J. Naremore. London: The Athlone Press, 2000, 28–37.

Baker, C. "Lo storyboard di Christopher Baker." *Archivo Kubrick*, 1993. http://www.archiviokubrick.it/opere/film/ews/storyboard.html (accessed October 12, 2011).

Balàz, B. *Theory of the Film: Character and Growth of a New Art*. New York: Dover, 1970.

Barthes, R. "Introduction to the Structural Analysis of Narratives." In *Image, Music, Text*. London: Fontana Press, 1977, 79–125.

Baudelaire, C. "The Salon of 1846." In *Art in Paris 1845-1862: Reviews of Salons and Other Exhibitions*. Edited by J. Mayne. Oxford: Phaidon Press Limited, 1965 (1846), 41–120.

———. "The Painter of Modern Life." In *The Painter of Modern Life and Other Essays*. Edited by J. Mayne. London: Phaidon Press Limited, 1995 (1863), 1–42.

Baxter, J. *Stanley Kubrick*. New York: Carroll & Graf Publishers, 1997.

Beja, M. *Film and Literature*, New York: Longman, 1976.

Bellinger, M. F. *A Short History of the Drama*. New York: Henry Holt & Company, 1927, 153–157.

Bizony, P. *2001: Filming the Future*. London: Aurum, 1994.

Bluestone, G. *Novels into Film*. Baltimore: The John Hopkins Press, 1957.

Boozer, J. *Authorship in Film Adaptation*. Austin: University of Texas Press, 2008.

Bordwell, D. *Narration in the Fiction Film*. London: Routledge, 1985.

———, and K. Thompson. *Film Art: An Introduction*. New York: McGraw-Hill, 1990.

Branigan, E. R. *Narrative Comprehension and Film*. London: Routledge, 1992.

Brown, J. "The Impossible Object: Reflections on *The Shining*." In *Cinema and Fiction 1950–1990*. Edited by J. Orr and C. Nicholson. Edinburgh: Edinburgh University Press, 1992, 104–121.

Brown, G. "The Steadicam and *The Shining*." *American Cinematographer*, vol. 61, no. 8, August 1980.

Bruno, M. W. "Doppi sogni che il denaro può comprare." *Segnocinema*, no. 101, January/February 2000.

Bukatman, S. "The Artificial Infinite: On Special Effects and the Sublime." In *Alien Zone II*. Edited by A. Kuhn. London: Verso, 1999, 249–275.

Burgess, A. *A Clockwork Orange*. London: Penguin Books, 2000a (1962).

———. *A Clockwork Orange: A Play with Music*. London: Methuen Publishing Limited, 1998 (1987).

———. "A Clockwork Orange Resucked." In *One Man's Chorus*, by A. Burgess. New York: Carroll & Graf Publishers, 2000 (1998), 226–230.

———. "Anthony Burgess Interviewed in Italy in 1974 about *A Clockwork Orange*." *The Anthony Burgess Centre*, 2002a. http://bu.univ-angers.fr/EXTRANET/AnthonyBURGESS/ABClockwork.html (accessed March 19, 2009).

———. "Enderby's End or A Clockwork Testament." In *The Complete Enderby*, by A. Burgess. London: Vintage, 2002c (1974), 379–479.

———. *You've Had Your Time: Being the Second Part of the Confessions of Anthony Burgess*. London: Vintage, 2002b (1990).

Cahill, T. "The Rolling Stone Interview: Stanley Kubrick." In *Stanley Kubrick Interviews*. Edited by G. D. Phillips. Jackson: University Press of Mississippi, 2001 (1987), 189–203.

Carroll, N. *The Philosophy of Horror or Paradoxes of the Heart*. London: Routledge, 1990.

Cartmell, D., and I. Whelehan, eds. *Adaptations from Text to Screen, Screen to Text*. London: Routledge, 1999.

Castle, A. *The Stanley Kubrick Archives*. Italy: Taschen, 2005.

Castle, R. "The Dharma Blues." *Bright Lights Film Journal*, 2002.

Chion, M. *Eyes Wide Shut*. London: BFI, 2002.

———, and S. Kubrick and C. Gorbman. *Kubrick's Cinema Odyssey*. London: BFI, 2001.

Ciment, M. *Kubrick: The Definitive Edition*. New York: Faber and Faber, 2003.

Clarke, A. C. *2001: A Space Odyssey*. London: Arrow Books, 1968.

———. *The Last Worlds of 2001*. New York: New American Library, 1972.

———. "The Sentinel." In *The Making of Kubrick's 2001*, by J. Agel. New York: The New American Library, 1970 (1951), 15–23.

Clines, F. "Stanley Kubrick's Vietnam War." In *Stanley Kubrick Interviews*. Edited by G. D. Phillips. Jackson: University Press of Mississippi, 2001 (1987), 171–176.

Cocks, G., J. Diedrick, and G. Perusek, eds. *Depth of Field: Stanley Kubrick, Film, and the Uses of History*. Wisconsin: University of Wisconsin Press, 2006.

———. *The Wolf at the Door: Stanley Kubrick, History, and the Holocaust*. New York: Peter Lang Publishing, 2004.

Cook, P., and M. Bernink. *The Cinema Book*. London: BFI, 1999.

Cosgrove, P. "The Cinema of Attractions and the Novel in *Barry Lyndon* and *Tom Jones*." In *Eighteenth-Century Fiction on Screen*. Edited by R. Mayer. Cambridge: Cambridge University Press, 2002, 16–34.

Coyle, W. *Stanley Kubrick: A Guide to References and Resources*. Boston: G. K. Hall, 1980.

Daniels, D. "A Skeleton Key to 2001." *Sight & Sound*, Winter 1970/71.

De Bernardinis, F. "Tra Schnitzler e Benjamin, il miraggio della Storia e dell'Arte del '900." *Segnocinema*, no. 100, November/December 1999.

De Vries, D. *The Films of Stanley Kubrick*. Grand Rapids, Michigan: William B. Eerdmans, 1973.

Donnelly, K. J. *The Spectre of Sound: Music in Film and Television*. London: BFI, 2005.
Duncan, P. *Stanley Kubrick: The Complete Films*. Italy: Taschen, 2003.
Falsetto, M., ed. *Perspectives on Stanley Kubrick*. New York: G. K. Hall, 1996.
———. *Stanley Kubrick: A Narrative and Stylistic Analysis*. London: Greenwood Press, 1994.
Freeland, C. A. (1999) "The Sublime in Cinema." In *Passionate Views: Film, Cognition, and Emotion*. Edited by C. Plantinga and G. M. Smith. Baltimore: John Hopkins University Press, 1999, 65–83.
Freud, S. "A Disturbance of Memory on the Acropolis." In *The Standard Edition of the Complete Psychological Works of Sigmund Freud*, vol. XXII (1932–1936): *New Introductory Lectures on Psycho-Analysis and Other Works*, 1936, 237–248. Edited by J. Strachey. *Psychoanalytic Electronic Publishing*. http://www.pep-web.org/index.php (accessed March 19, 2009).
———. "Determinism, Belief in Chance and Superstition." In *Psychopathology of Everyday Life*, 1901, chapter XIII, 239–280. Edited by J. Strachey. *Psychoanalytic Electronic Publishing*. http://www.pep-web.org/index.php (accessed October 12, 2011).
———. "Fausse Reconnaissance ("Déjà Racontée") in Psycho-Analytic Treatment." In *The Standard Edition of the Complete Psychological Works of Sigmund Freud*, vol. XIII (1913–1914): *Totem and Taboo and Other Works*, 1914, 199–207. Edited by J. Strachey. *Psychoanalytic Electronic Publishing*. http://www.pep-web.org/index.php (accessed October 12, 2011).
———. "Fragment of an Analysis of a Case of Hysteria (1905 [1901])." In *The Standard Edition of the Complete Psychological Works of Sigmund Freud*, vol. VII (1901–1905): *A Case of Hysteria, Three Essays on Sexuality and Other Works*, 1905, 1–122. Edited by J. Strachey. *Psychoanalytic Electronic Publishing*. http://www.pep-web.org/index.php (accessed October 12, 2011).
———. "Letter from Sigmund Freud to Arthur Schnitzler, May 8, 1906." In *Letters of Sigmund Freud 1873–1939*, 1906, 251. Edited by J. Strachey. *Psychoanalytic Electronic Publishing*. http://www.pep-web.org/index.php (accessed October 12, 2011).
———. "Letter from Sigmund Freud to Arthur Schnitzler, May 14, 1922." In *Letters of Sigmund Freud 1873–1939*, 1922, 339–340. Edited by J. Strachey. *Psychoanalytic Electronic Publishing*. http://www.pep-web.org/index.php (accessed October 12, 2011).
———. "The Interpretation of Dreams." In *The Standard Edition of the Complete Psychological Works of Sigmund Freud*, vol. IV (1900): *The Interpretation of Dreams* (first part), 1900, ix–627. Edited by J. Strachey. *Psychoanalytic Electronic Publishing*." http://www.pep-web.org/index.php (accessed October 12, 2011).
———. "The 'Uncanny.'" In *The Standard Edition of the Complete Psychological Works of Sigmund Freud*, vol. XVII (1917–1919): *An Infantile Neurosis and Other Works*, 1919, 217–256. Edited by J. Strachey. *Psychoanalytic Electronic Publishing*. http://www.pep-web.org/index.php (accessed October 12, 2011).

Geduld, C. *Filmguide to 2001: A Space Odyssey*. London: Indiana University Press, 1973.
Gelmis, J. "The Film Director as Superstar: Stanley Kubrick." In *Stanley Kubrick Interviews*. Edited by G. D. Phillips. Jackson: University Press of Mississippi, 2000 (1970), 80–104.
Genette, G. *Figure III. Discorso del racconto*. Torino: Giulio Einaudi, 1976 (1972).
———. *Palinsesti. La letteratura al secondo grado*. Torino: Giulio Einaudi, 1997 (1982).
Ghislotti, S., and S. Rosso, eds. *Vietnam e ritorno. La "guerra sporca" nel cinema, nella letteratura e nel teatro*. Milano: Marcos y Marcos, 1996.
Gibson, J. W. *Warrior Dreams: Violence and Manhood in Post-Vietnam America*. New York: Hill and Wang, 1994.
Giddings R., K. Selby, and C. Wensley, eds. *Screening the Novel*. London: MacMillan, 1990.
Gorbman, C. *Unheard Melodies: Narrative Film Music*. London: BFI, 1987.
Griffith, J. *Adaptations as Imitations: Films from Novels*. London: University of Delaware Press, 1997.
Gross, L. "Too Late the Hero." *Sight and Sound*, vol. 9, September 1999.
Hanke, R. "John Woo's Cinema of Hyperkinetic Violence: From *A Better Tomorrow* to *Face/Off*." *Film Criticism*, vol. XXIV, no. 1, Fall 1999, 39–59.
Hasford, G. *The Short-Timers*. New York: Bantam Books, 1980 (1979).
Hebdige, D. (1988) "Staking out the Posts." In *Hiding in the Light*. London: Routledge, 1988, 181–207.
Herr, M. *Dispatches*. New York: Knopf, 1977.
———. *Kubrick*. New York: Grove Press, 2000.
Houston, P. "Kubrick Country." In *Stanley Kubrick Interviews*. Edited by G. D. Phillips. Jackson: University Press of Mississippi, 2001 (1971), 108–115.
Howard, J. *Stanley Kubrick Companion*. London: Batsford, 1999.
Hughes, D. *The Complete Kubrick*. London: Virgin Books, 2000.
Jakobson, R. "Poesia della grammatica e grammatica della poesia." In *Jakobson: poetica e poesia*, by R. Jakobson. Torino: Einaudi, 1985, 339–352.
———. "Due aspetti del linguaggio e due tipi di afasia." In *Saggi di Linguistica Generale*, by R. Jakobson. Milano: Feltrinelli, 2002, 22–45.
James, N. "At Home with the Kubricks." *Sight and Sound*, no. 9, September 1999, 12–20.
Jameson, F. *Firme del Visibile: Hitchcock, Kubrick, Antonioni*. Roma: Donzelli, 2003.
———. "Postmodernism and Consumer Society." In *Postmodernism and its Discontents: Theories, Practices*. Edited by E. A. Kaplan. London: Verso, 1988, 13–29.
Jenkins, G. *Stanley Kubrick and the Art of Adaptation: Three Novels, Three Films*. London: McFarland, 1997.
Kael, P. "*A Clockwork Orange*: Stanley Strangelove." *The New Yorker*, January 1, 1972.
Kagan, N. *The Cinema of Stanley Kubrick*. New York: Continuum, 2000.
King, S. *The Shining*. London: New English Library, 2001 (1977).
Kinney, J. L. "Text and Pretext: Stanley Kubrick's Adaptations." Dissertation University of California, Los Angeles, 1982.

Kittredge, W., and S. M. Krauzer, eds. *Stories into Film*. London: Harper and Row, 1979.
Klein, M., and G. Parker, eds. *The English Novel and the Movies*. New York: Frederick Ungar Publishing Co., 1981.
Kolker, R., ed. *Stanley Kubrick's 2001: A Space Odyssey: New Essays*. Oxford: Oxford University Press, 2006.
Kubrick, C. *Stanley Kubrick: A Life in Pictures*. London: Little Brown, 2002.
Kubrick, S., and F. Raphael. *Eyes Wide Shut* screenplay (08/04/96). *Archivo Kubrick*. http://www.archiviokubrick.it/opere/film/ews/script.html (accessed October 12, 2011).
Kupper, H. I., and H. S. Rollman-Branch. "Freud and Schnitzler—Doppelgänger." *Journal of the American Psychoanalytic Association*, no. 7, 1959, 109–126.
Labarthe, A., and J. L. Comolli. "The Arthur Penn Interview." In *The Bonnie and Clyde Book*. Edited by S. Wake and N. Hayden. New York: Simon and Schuster, 1972, 165–173.
Landon, B. "Diegetic or Digital? The Convergence of Science-Fiction Literature and Science-Fiction Film in Hypermedia." In *Alien Zone II*. Edited by A. Kuhn. London: Verso, 1999, 31–49.
Leitch, T. "The Adapter as *Auteur*: Hitchcock, Kubrick, Disney." In *Books in Motion: Adaptation, Intertextuality, Authorship*. Edited by A. Mireia. New York: Rodopi, 2005, 107–123.
LoBrutto, V. *Stanley Kubrick*. London: Faber and Faber, 1998.
Lockwood, G. *2001 Memoirs: An Actor's Odyssey*. USA: Cowboy Press, 2001.
Lothe, J. *Narrative in Fiction Film: An Introduction*. New York: Oxford University Press, 2000.
MacCabe, C., K. Murray, and R. Warner, eds. *Film Adaptation and the Question of Fidelity*. Oxford: Oxford University Press, 2011.
Mainar, L. M. G. *Narrative and Stylistic Patterns in the Films of Stanley Kubrick*. New York: Camden House, 1999.
Mamber, S. "Simultaneity and Overlap in Stanley Kubrick's *The Killing*." *Postmodern Culture* vol. 8, no. 2, 1998. http://muse.jhu.edu/journals/postmodern_culture/toc/pmc8.2.html (accessed November 8, 2010).
Mann, K. B. "Narrative Entanglements: *The Terminator*." *Film Quarterly*, vol. 43, no. 2, Winter 1989–1990, 17–27.
Manti, D. *Ca(u)se perturbanti. Architetture horror dentro e fuori lo schermo. Fonti, figure, temi*. Torino: Lindau, 2003.
Masi, S. *Costumisti e scenografi del cinema italiano*. L'Aquila: Lanterna Magica, 1990.
Mayer, R., ed. *Eighteenth-Century Fiction on Screen*. Cambridge: Cambridge University Press, 2002.
McDougal, S., ed. *Stanley Kubrick's A Clockwork Orange*. Cambridge: Cambridge University Press, 2003.
McFarlane, B. *Novel to Film: An Introduction to the Theory of Adaptation*. Oxford: Clarendon Press, 1996.

Miller, J. *Subsequent Performances*. London: Faber and Faber, 1986.
Miller, M. C. "In Defence of Sam Peckinpah." *Film Quarterly*, vol. 28, no. 3, Spring 1975, 2–17.
Mireia, A., ed. *Books in Motion: Adaptation, Intertextuality, Authorship*. New York: Rodopi, 2005.
Modine, M. *Full Metal Jacket Diary*. New York: Rugged Land, 2005.
Molinari, C. *Storia del teatro*. Milano: Laterza, 1996.
Morin, E. *Le star*. Milano: Olivares, 1995.
Naremore, J., ed. *Film Adaptation*. London: The Athlone Press, 2000.
———. *On Kubrick*. London: BFI, 2007.
Nelson, T. A. *Kubrick: Inside a Film Artist's Maze*. Indiana: Indiana University Press, 2000.
Norden, E. "Playboy Interview: Stephen King." *Playboy*, vol. 30, June 1983, 56.
———. "Playboy Interview: Stanley Kubrick." In *The Making of Kubrick's 2001*, by J. Agel. New York: The New American Library, 1970 (1968), 328–354.
Orr, J., and C. Nicholson, eds. *Cinema and Fiction: New Modes of Adapting, 1950–1990*. Edinburgh: Edinburgh University Press, 1992.
Pedretti, C. "Leonardo e i Re Magi anticipano il cinema." *Corriere della Sera*, Milano, May 1, 2002, 25.
Peebles, S. "Gunning for a New Slow Motion: The 45-Degree Shutter and the Representation of Violence." *Journal of Film and Video*, vol. LVI, no. 2, Summer 2004, 45–54.
Pfister, M. *The Theory and Analysis of Drama*. Cambridge: Cambridge University Press, 1993.
Phillips, G. D. *Stanley Kubrick: A Film Odyssey*. New York: Popular Library, 1975.
———, ed. *Stanley Kubrick Interviews*. Jackson: University Press of Mississippi, 2001.
———. "Stop the World: Stanley Kubrick." In *Stanley Kubrick Interviews*. Edited by G. D. Phillips. Jackson: University Press of Mississippi, 2001 (1973), 140–158.
———, and R. Hill, eds. *The Encyclopaedia of Stanley Kubrick*. New York: Checkmark Books, 2002.
Pipolo, T. "The Modernist & the Misanthrope: The Cinema of Stanley Kubrick." *Cineaste*, vol. 27, no. 2, Spring 2002, 4–39.
Poe, E. A. "The Man of the Crowd." In *Collected Tales and Poems of Edgar Allan Poe*, by E. A. Poe. Hertfordshire: Wordsworth Editions Limited, 2004 (1840), 207–213.
Prince, S. "The Haemorrhaging of American Cinema: Bonnie and Clyde's Legacy of Cinematic Violence." In *Arthur Penn's Bonnie and Clyde*. Edited by L. D. Friedman. Cambridge: Cambridge University Press, 2000, 127–147.
Rabinowitz, P. J. "A Bird of Like Rarest Spun Heavenmetal." In *Stanley Kubrick's A Clockwork Orange*. Edited by S. Y. McDougal. Cambridge: Cambridge University Press, 2003, 109–130.
Rapf, M. "A Talk with Stanley Kubrick about *2001*." In *Stanley Kubrick Interviews*. Edited by G. D. Phillips. Jackson: University Press of Mississippi, 2001 (1969), 75–79.

Raphael, F. *Eyes Wide Open: A Memoir of Stanley Kubrick*. New York: Ballantine, 1999.
Rasmussen, R. *Stanley Kubrick: Seven Films Analyzed*. London: McFarland, 2001.
Ray, R. B. "The Field of Literature and Film." In *Film Adaptation*. Edited by J. Naremore. London: The Athlone Press, 2000, 38–53.
Reay, P. *Music in Film. Soundtracks and Synergy*. London: Wallflower Press, 2004.
Reynolds, P. *Novel Images*. London: Routledge, 1993.
Richter, D. *Moonwatcher's Memoir: A Diary of 2001: A Space Odyssey*. New York: Carroll and Graf Publishers, 2002.
Rosso, S. *Musi gialli e berretti verdi. Narrazioni USA sulla guerra del Vietnam*. Bergamo: Bergamo University Press, 2003.
Royle, N. *The Uncanny*. Manchester: Manchester University Press, 2003.
Rosen, C. *The Classical Style: Haydn, Mozart, Beethoven*. New York: Norton, 1997.
Ruppersberg, H. "The Alien Messiah." In *Alien Zone*. Edited by A. Kuhn. London: Verso, 2003, 32–38.
Sarris, A. "Notes on the auteur theory in 1962." In *Theories of Authorship*. Edited by J. Caughie. New York: Routledge, 1972 (1962–63), 62–65.
Schnitzler, A. *Dream Story*. London: Penguin Books, 1999 (1926).
Schwam, S. *The Making of 2001: A Space Odyssey*. New York: The Modern Library, 2000.
Sinyard, N. *Filming Literature*. London: Croomhelm, 1986.
Sperb, J. *The Kubrick Façade: Faces and Voices in the Films of Stanley Kubrick*. London: Scarecrow Press, 2006.
Staiger, J. "The Cultural Productions of *A Clockwork Orange*." In *Perverse Spectators: The Practices of Film Reception*. Edited by J. Staiger. New York: New York University Press, 2000, 93–124.
Stam, R., and A. Raengo, eds. *Literature and Film: A Guide to the Theory and Practice of Film Adaptation*. Oxford: Blackwell Publishing, 2005.
———. *Literature through Film: Realism, Magic and the Art of Adaptation*. Oxford: Blackwell Publishing, 2005.
———. "Beyond Fidelity: The Dialogics of Adaptation." In *Film Adaptation*. Edited by J. Naremore. London: The Athlone Press, 2002, 54–76.
Stork, D. G. *Hal's Legacy: 2001's Computer as Dream and Reality*. Cambridge: MIT Press, 1997.
Tarkovsky, A. "On Cinema, 1966." *Time Within Time: The Diaries 1970–1986*, by A. Tarkovsky. London: Faber and Faber, 1966, 355–361.
———. *Sculpting in Time*, Austin: University of Texas Press, 2006.
Tenèze, M. L. "Du Conte merveilleux comme genre." In *Approches de nos traditions orales*. Paris: G. P. Maisonneueve et Larse, 1970.
Thackeray, W. M. *The Memoirs of Barry Lyndon, Esq*. Oxford: Oxford University Press, 1999 (1844).
Todorov, T. *The Fantastic. A Structural Approach to a Literary Genre*. New York: Cornell University Press, 1975.

Trumbull, D. "Creating Special Effects for *2001: A Space Odyssey*." *American Cinematographer*, June 6, 1968.

Tunney, T. "*Lashou Shentan (Hard-Boiled)*." *Sight and Sound*, vol. 3, no. 10, October 1993, 47.

Wagner, G. *The Novel and the Cinema*. New Jersey: Farleigh Dickinson University Press, 1975.

Walker, A., S. Taylor, and U. Ruchti. *Stanley Kubrick, Director: A Visual Analysis*. London: W. W. Norton & Company, 2000.

Weinraub, B. "Kubrick tells What Makes *Clockwork* Tick." *New York Times*, April 1, 1972.

Wheat, L. F. *Kubrick's 2001: A Triple Allegory*. London: Scarecrow Press, 2000.

Williams, T. "Space, Place, and Spectacle: The Crisis Cinema of John Woo." *Cinema Journal*, vol. 36, no. 2, Winter 1997, 67–84.

Wilson J. C. *Vietnam in Prose and Film*. London: McFarland & Company, 1982.

Wollen, P. "Godard and Counter Cinema: *Vent d'Est*." In *Reading and Writings: Semiotic Counter-Strategies*, by P. Wollen. London: Verso, 1982, 79–91.

———. *Signs and Meaning in the Cinema*. Bloomington: Indiana University Press, 1972.

———. "The Two Avant-Gardes." In *Reading and Writings: Semiotic Counter-Strategies*, by P. Wollen. London: Verso, 1982, 92–104.

Woo, J. "Things I Felt Were Being Lost." *Film Comment*, vol. 29, no. 5, September/October 1993, 50–52.

Wood, R. *Hollywood from Vietnam to Reagan*. New York: Columbia University Press, 1986.

Young, C. "The Hollywood War of Independence." In *Stanley Kubrick Interviews*. Edited by G. D. Phillips. Jackson: University Press of Mississippi, 2001 (1959), 3–8.

Youngblood, G. *Expanded Cinema*. London: Studio Vista, 1970.

Zipes, J. *Fairy Tales and the Art of Subversion*. London: Routledge, 2006.

FILMOGRAPHY

2001: A Space Odyssey (Stanley Kubrick, USA and UK, 1968). Writer: Stanley Kubrick, Arthur C. Clarke, from Arthur C. Clarke's "The Sentinel" and *2001: A Space Odyssey*; Producer: Stanley Kubrick; Associate producer: Victor Lyndon; Cinematographer: Geoffrey Unsworth; Film editor: Ray Lovejoy; With: Keir Dullea (Dave Bowman), Gary Lockwood (Frank Poole), William Sylvester (Heywood R. Floyd), Daniel Richter (Moon-Watcher), Leonard Rossiter (Andrei Smyslov), Margaret Tyzack (Elena), Robert Beatty (Ralph Halvorsen), Sean Sullivan (Bill Michaels), Douglas Rain (HAL 9000, voice).

Andrei Rublev (Andrei Tarkovsky, Soviet Union, 1962). Writer: Andrei Tarkovsky, Andrei Konchalovsky; Producer: Tamara Ogorodnikova; Cinematographer: Vadim Yusov; Film editor: Lyudmila Feiginova, Olga Shevkunenko, Tatyana Yegorycheva; With: Anatoli Solonitsyn (Andrei Rublev), Ivan Lapikov (Kirill), Nikolai Grinko (Danil Chorni), Nicolai Sergeyev (Theophanes the Greek).

Apocalypse Now (Francis Ford Coppola, USA, 1979). Writer: John Milius, Francis Ford Coppola, Michael Herr (narration), from Joseph Conrad's *Heart of Darkness*; Producer: Francis Ford Coppola; Cinematographer: Vittorio Storaro; Film editor: Lisa Fruchtman, Gerald B. Greenberg, Walter Murch; With: Marlon Brando (Col. Walter E. Kurtz), Martin Sheen (Capt. Benjamin Willard), Robert Duvall (Lt. Col. Kilgore), Frederic Forest (Chef), Lee Ermey (Eagle Thrust Seven Helicopter Pilot, uncredited).

Back to the Future (Robert Zemeckis, USA, 1985). Writer: Robert Zemeckis, Bob Gale; Producer: Neil Canton, Bob Gale; Cinematographer: Dean Cundey; Film editor: Harry Keramidas, Arthur Schmidt; With: Michael J. Fox (Marty McFly), Christopher Lloyd (Dr. Emmett Brown), Lea Thompson (Lorraine Baines McFly), Crispin Glover (George McFly).

Barry Lyndon (Stanley Kubrick, USA and UK, 1975). Writer: Stanley Kubrick, from William Makepeace Thackeray's *The Memoirs of Barry Lyndon, Esq.*; Executive producer: Jan Harlan; Producer: Stanley Kubrick; Associate producer: Bernard Williams; Cinematographer: John Alcott; Film editor: Tony Lawson; With: Ryan O'Neal (Barry Lyndon), Marisa Berenson (Lady Lyndon), Patrick Magee (The Chevalier), Steven Berkoff (Lord Ludd), Gay Hamilton (Nora), Marie Kean (Barry's Mother), Diana Körner (German Girl, as Diana Koerner), Murray Melvin (Reverend Runt), Frank Middlemass (Sir Charles Lyndon), Leonard Rossiter (Captain Quin), Leon Vitali (Lord Bullingdon), Wolf Kahler (Prince of Tübingen), David Morley (Bryan Patrick Lyndon), Dominic Savage (Young Bullingdon), Michael Hordern (Narrator).

Bonnie and Clyde (Arthur Penn, USA, 1967). Writer: David Newman, Robert Benton; Producer: Warren Beatty; Cinematographer: Burnett Guffey; Film editor: Dede Allen; With: Warren Beatty (Clyde Barrow), Faye Dunaway (Bonnie Parker), Michael J. Pollard (C. W. Moss), Gene Hackman (Buck Barrow).

Cet obscur object du désir (Luis Buñuel, France and Spain, 1977). Writer: Luis Buñuel, Jean-Claude Carrière (collaboration), from Pierre Louÿs's *La femme et le pantin*; Producer: Serge Silberman; Cinematographer: Edmond Richard; Film editor: Hélène Plemiannikov; With: Fernando Rey (Mathieu), Carole Bouquet and Ángela Molina (Conchita).

A Clockwork Orange (Stanley Kubrick, USA and UK, 1971). Writer: Stanley Kubrick, from Anthony Burgess's *A Clockwork Orange*; Producer: Stanley Kubrick; Executive producer: Si Litvinoff, Max L. Raab; Associate producer: Bernard Williams; Cinematographer: John Alcott; Film editor: Bill Butler; With: Malcolm McDowell (Alex), Patrick Magee (Mr. Alexander), Warren Clarke (Dim), Adrienne Corri (Mrs. Alexander), Paul Farrell (Tramp), Michael Gover (Prison Governor), Miriam Karlin (Catlady), James Marcus (Georgie), Aubrey Morris (Deltoid), Sheila Raynor (Mum), Anthony Sharp (Minister), Philip Stone (Dad), Michael Tarn (Pete), Richard Connaught (Billyboy).

Day of the Fight (Stanley Kubrick, USA, 1953). Writer: Robert Rein; Producer: Stanley Kubrick, Jay Bonafield (uncredited); Cinematographer: Stanley Kubrick, Alexander Singer (uncredited); Film editor: Julian Bergman, Stanley Kubrick (uncredited); With: Douglas Edwards (Narrator), Vincent Cartier (Himself, Walter's twin brother, uncredited), Walter Cartier (Himself, uncredited), Nat Fleischer (Himself, boxing historian, uncredited), Bobby James (Himself, Walter's opponent, uncredited).

Dr. Strangelove, Or: How I Learned to Stop Worrying and Love the Bomb (Stanley Kubrick, UK, 1964). Writer: Stanley Kubrick, Terry Southern, Peter George, from Peter George's *Red Alert*; Producer: Stanley Kubrick; Associate producer: Victor Lyndon; Executive producer: Leon Minoff (uncredited); Cinematographer: Gilbert Taylor; Film editor: Anthony Harvey; With: Peter Sellers (Group Captain Lionel Mandrake / President Merkin Muffley / Dr. Strangelove), George C. Scott (Gen. "Buck" Turgidson), Sterling Hayden (Brig. Gen. Jack D. Ripper), Peter Bull (Russian Ambassador Alexi de Sadesky).

Eyes Wide Shut (Stanley Kubrick, USA and UK, 1999). Writer: Stanley Kubrick, Frederic Raphael, from Arthur Schnitzler's *Dream Story*; Co-producer: Brian W. Cook; Executive producer: Jan Harlan; Producer: Stanley Kubrick; Cinematographer: Larry Smith; Film editor: Nigel Galt; With: Tom Cruise (Dr. William "Bill" Harford), Nicole Kidman (Alice Harford), Madison Eginton (Helena Harford), Sydney Pollack (Victor Ziegler), Todd Field (Nick Nightingale), Sky Dumont (Sandor Szavost), Louise J. Taylor (Gayle, as Louise Taylor), Stewart Thorndike (Nuala), Julienne Davis (Amanda "Mandy" Curran), Kevin Connealy (Lou Nathanson), Marie Richardson (Marion Nathanson), Thomas

Gibson (Carl Thomas), Vinessa Shaw (Domino), Rade Serbedzija (Mr. Milich, as Rade Sherbedgia), Leelee Sobieski (Milich's Daughter), Abigail Good (Masked Party Principal / Mysterious Woman), Leon Vitali (Red Cloak), Alan Cumming (Hotel Desk Clerk), Fay Masterson (Sally).

Face/Off (John Woo, USA, 1997). Writer: Mike Werb, Michael Colleary; Producer: Terence Chang, Christopher Godsick, Barrie M. Osborne, David Permut; Cinematographer: Olivier Wood; Film editor: Steven Kemper, Christian Wagner. With: John Travolta and Nicolas Cage (Sean Archer and Castor Troy), Joan Allen (Dr. Eve Archer), Dominique Swain (Jamie Archer).

Fear and Desire (Stanley Kubrick, USA, 1953). Writer: Howard Sackler; Producer: Stanley Kubrick; Associate producer: Martin Perveler; Cinematographer: Stanley Kubrick; Film editor: Stanley Kubrick; With: Frank Silvera (Sgt. Mac), Paul Mazursky (Pvt. Sidney), Kenneth Harp (Lt. Corby / Enemy General), Stephen Coit (Pvt. Fletcher / Enemy Captain, as Steve Coit), Virginia Leith (Young Girl).

The Firm (Sydney Pollack, USA, 1993). Writer: David Rabe, Robert Towne, David Rayfiel, from John Grisham's *The Firm*; Producer: John Davis, Sydney Pollack, Scott Rudin; Cinematographer: John Seale; Film editor: Fredric Steinkamp, William Steinkamp; With: Tom Cruise (Mitch McDeere), Jeanne Tripplehorn (Abby McDeere), Gene Hackman (Avery Tolar), Hal Holbrook (Oliver Lambert).

Flying Padre (Stanley Kubrick, USA, 1951). Writer: Stanley Kubrick; Producer: Burton Benjamin; Cinematographer: Stanley Kubrick; Film editor: Isaac Kleinerman; With: Bob Hite (Narrator), Fred Stadmueller (Himself).

Full Metal Jacket (Stanley Kubrick, USA and UK, 1987). Writer: Stanley Kubrick, Michael Herr, Gustav Hasford, from Gustav Hasford's *The Short-Timers*; Executive producer: Jan Harlan; Associate producer: Michael Herr; Co-producer: Philip Hobbs; Producer: Stanley Kubrick; Cinematographer: Douglas Milsome; Film editor: Martin Hunter; With: Matthew Modine (Pvt. Joker), Adam Baldwin (Animal Mother), Vincent D'Onofrio (Pvt. Pyle), R. Lee Ermey (Sgt. Hartman, as Lee Ermey), Dorian Harewood (Eightball), Kevyn Major Howard (Rafterman), Arliss Howard (Pvt. Cowboy), Ed O'Ross (Lt. Touchdown), John Terry (Lt. Lockhart), Kieron Jecchinis (Crazy Earl), Kirk Taylor (Payback), Jon Stafford (Doc Jay, as John Stafford), Sal Lopez (T. H. E. Rock), Gary Landon Mills (Donlon), Peter Edmund (Snowball), Marcus D'Amico (Hand Job), Costas Dino Chimona (Chili), Gil Kopel (Stork), Keith Hodiak (Daddy D. A.), Herbert Norville (Daytona Dave).

Ivan's Childhood (Andrei Tarkovsky, Soviet Union, 1966). Writer: Vladimir Bogomolov; Cinematographer: Vadim Yusov; Film editor: Lyudmila Feiginova; With: Nikolay

Burlyaev (Ivan), Valentin Zubkov (Capt. Kholin), Yevgeni Zharikov (Lt. Galtsev), Stepan Krylov (Cpl. Katasonov).

Killer's Kiss (Stanley Kubrick, USA, 1955). Writer: Stanley Kubrick (story), Howard Sackler (screenplay, uncredited); Producer: Morris Bousel, Stanley Kubrick; Cinematographer: Stanley Kubrick; Film editor: Stanley Kubrick; With: Frank Silvera (Vincent Rapallo), Jamie Smith (Davy Gordon), Irene Kane (Gloria Price), Jerry Jarrett (Albert, the fight manager), Skippy Adelman (Mannequin factory owner, as Julius Adelman), Ruth Sobotka (Ballerina / Iris).

The Killing (Stanley Kubrick, USA, 1956). Writer: Stanley Kubrick, Jim Thompson, Lionel White, from Lionel White's *Clean Break*; Producer: James B. Harris; Associate producer: Alexander Singer; Cinematographer: Lucien Ballard; Film editor: Betty Steinberg; With: Sterling Hayden (Johnny Clay), Coleen Gray (Fay), Vince Edwards (Val Cannon), Jay C. Flippen (Marvin Unger), Elisha Cook, Jr. (George Peatty, as Elisha Cook), Marie Windsor (Sherry Peatty), Ted de Corsia (Policeman Randy Kennan, as Ted DeCorsia), Joe Sawyer (Mike O'Reilly).

La Notte (Michelangelo Antonioni, Italy and France, 1961). Writer: Michelangelo Antonioni, Ennio Flaiano, Tonino Guerra; Producer: Emanuele Cassuto; Cinematographer: Gianni Di Venanzo; Film editor: Eraldo Da Roma; With: Marcello Mastroianni (Giovanni Pontano), Jeanne Moreau (Lidia), Monica Vitti (Valentina Gherardini), Bernhard Wicki (Tommaso Garani).

L'avventura (Michelangelo Antonioni, Italy and France, 1960). Writer: Michelangelo Antonioni, Elio Bartolini, Tonino Guerra; Producer: Amato Pennasilico; Cinematographer: Aldo Scavarda; Film editor: Eraldo Da Roma; With: Gabriele Ferzetti (Sandro), Monica Vitti (Claudia), Lea Massari (Anna), Dominique Blanchar (Giulia).

Lolita (Adrian Lyne, USA, 1997). Writer: Stephen Schiff, from Vladimir Nabokov's *Lolita*; Producer: Mario Kassar, Joel B. Michaels; Cinematographer: Howard Atherton; Film editor: David Brenner, Julie Monroe; With: Jeremy Irons (Humbert Humbert), Melanie Griffith (Charlotte Haze), Frank Langella (Clare Quilty), Dominique Swain (Lolita).

Lolita (Stanley Kubrick, UK, 1962). Writer: Vladimir Nabokov, Stanley Kubrick (uncredited), from Vladimir Nabokov's *Lolita*; Producer: James B. Harris; Executive producer: Eliot Hyman (uncredited); Cinematographer: Oswald Morris; Film editor: Anthony Harvey; With: James Mason (Prof. Humbert Humbert), Shelley Winters (Charlotte Haze), Sue Lyon (Lolita), Peter Sellers (Clare Quilty).

Making The Shining (Vivian Kubrick, UK and USA, 1980). Cinematographer: Vivian Kubrick (uncredited); With: Jack Nicholson, Shelley Duvall, Stanley Kubrick, Danny Lloyd.

Filmography

Nostalghia (Andrei Tarkovsky, Italy and Soviet Union, 1983). Writer: Andrei Tarkovsky, Tonino Guerra; Producer: Franco Casati, Daniel Toscan du Plantier; Cinematographer: Giuseppe Lanci; Film editor: Erminia Marani, Amedeo Salfa; With: Oleg Yankovskiy (Andrei Gorchakov), Erland Josephson (Domenico), Domiziana Giordano (Eugenia), Patrizia Terreno (Andrei's wife).

Paths of Glory (Stanley Kubrick, USA, 1957). Writer: Stanley Kubrick, Calder Willingham, Jim Thompson, Humphrey Cobb, from Humphrey Cobb's *Paths of Glory*; Producer: James B. Harris, Kirk Douglas, Stanley Kubrick (producer, uncredited); Cinematographer: Georg Krause (as George Krause); Film editor: Eva Kroll; With: Kirk Douglas (Col. Dax), Ralph Meeker (Cpl. Philippe Paris), Adolphe Menjou (Gen. George Broulard), George Macready (Gen. Paul Mireau), Richard Anderson (Maj. Saint-Auban), Joe Turkel (Pvt. Pierre Arnaud, as Joseph Turkel), Christiane Kubrick (German singer, as Susanne Christian), Bert Freed (Sgt. Boulanger), Kem Dibbs (Pvt. Lejeune), Timothy Carey (Pvt. Maurice Ferol).

The Sacrifice (Andrei Tarkovsky, Sweden, UK and France, 1986). Writer: Andrei Tarkovsky; Producer: Anna-Lena Wibom; Cinematographer: Sven Nykvist; Film editor: Michal Leszczylowski, Andrei Tarkovsky; With: Erland Josephson (Alexander), Susan Fleetwood (Adelaide), Tommy Kjellqvist (Little man), Allan Edwall (Otto).

The Seafarers (Stanley Kubrick, USA, 1953). Writer: Will Chasen; Producer: Lester Cooper; Executive producer: Alexander Pietrzak; Cinematographer: Stanley Kubrick; Film editor: Stanley Kubrick; With: Don Hollenbeck (Narrator).

The Shining (Stanley Kubrick, USA and UK, 1980). Writer: Stanley Kubrick, Diane Johnson, from Stephen King's *The Shining*; Associate producer: Robert Fryer, Mary Lea Johnson, Martin Richards; Executive producer: Jan Harlan; Producer: Stanley Kubrick; Cinematographer: John Alcott; Film editor: Ray Lovejoy; With: Jack Nicholson (Jack Torrance), Shelley Duvall (Wendy Torrance), Danny Lloyd (Danny Torrance), Scatman Crothers (Dick Hallorann), Barry Nelson (Stuart Ullman), Philip Stone (Delbert Grady), Joe Turkel (Lloyd the Bartender).

Spartacus (Stanley Kubrick, USA, 1960). Writer: Howard Fast, Dalton Trumbo, Calder Willingham (uncredited), Peter Ustinov (uncredited), from Howard Fast's *Spartacus*; Executive producer: Kirk Douglas; Producer: Edward Lewis; Cinematographer: Russell Metty; Film editor: Rober Lawrence, Irving Lerner (uncredited); With: Kirk Douglas (Spartacus), Laurence Olivier (Marcus Licinius Crassus), Jean Simmons (Varinia), Charles Laughton (Sempronius Gracchus), Peter Ustinov (Lentulus Batiatus), John Gavin (Julius Caesar), Nina Foch (Helena Glabrus), John Ireland (Crixus), Herbert Lom (Tigranes Levantus), John Dall (Marcus Publius Glabrus).

Stephen King's The Shining (Mick Garris, USA, 1997). Writer: Stephen King, from Stephen King's *The Shining*; Producer: Mark Carliner; Cinematographer: Shelley Johnson; Film editor: Patrick McMahon; With: Steven Weber (Jack Torrance), Rebecca De Mornay (Wendy Torrance), Courtland Mead (Danny), Melvin Van Peebles (Hallorann).

Tempo di viaggio (Andrei Tarkovsky and Tonino Guerra, Italy, 1983). Writer: Tonino Guerra, Andrei Tarkovsky; Cinematographer: Luciano Tovoli; Film editor: Franco Letti; With: Tonino Guerra, Andrei Tarkovsky.

The Terminator (James Cameron, USA, 1984). Writer: James Cameron, Gale Anne Hurd, William Wisher, Jr. (additional dialogue); Producer: Gale Anne Hurd; Cinematographer: Adam Greenberg; Film editor: Mark Goldblatt; With: Arnold Schwarzenegger (The Terminator), Michael Biehn (Kyle Reese), Linda Hamilton (Sarah Connor), Paul Winfield (Lieutenant Ed Traxler).

The Wild Bunch (Sam Peckinpah, USA, 1969). Writer: Walon Green, Sam Peckinpah; Producer: Phil Feldman; Cinematographer: Lucien Ballard; Film editor: Lou Lombardo; With: William Holden (Pike Bishop), Ernest Borgnine (Dutch Engstrom), Robert Ryan (Deke Thornton), Edmond O'Brien (Freddie Sykes).

INDEX

Abrams, Jerold J., 171
accelerated motion. *See* high-speed motion
acting, 3, 51, 71, 73, 81, 93, 94, 96, 107, 203ch5n1
actor, 12, 17, 19–20, 25–30, 33, 54, 62, 64, 93, 107–8, 121–22, 124, 144–45, 147–49, 151, 155, 168, 175
Adagio. *See* Khatchaturian, Aram
adaptation studies, 3–4, 6, 9, 12–13, 153, 185
Adoration of the Magi. *See* Leonardo
aerial footage, 116, 167
alignment, 45–48, 50, 172
alien. *See* extraterrestrial
"alien messiah," 49
Altman, Robert, 162; *The Long Goodbye*, 155; *MASH*, 155
anaphora, 175–76
Anderson, Paul Thomas, *Magnolia*, 203ch4n1
Andrei Rublev. *See* Tarkovsky, Andrei
Andrew, Dudley, 200–201n6
Anger, Kenneth, 159
Anger Management. *See* Segal, Peter
angle: and straight-ahead, 69; and straight-on, 144
Antonioni, Michelangelo: *La notte*, 157; *L'avventura*, 156
Apocalypse Now. *See* Coppola, Francis Ford
art-cinema (art-film), 13, 36, 154–59, 160–64, 177
"artefact emotions." *See* Tan, Ed S.
Arthur Schnitzler as Psychologist. *See* Reik, Theodor
artifact. *See* monolith

artificiality, 121, 142, 146–47, 149, 152, 167–69, 171, 180
As Good as It Gets. *See* Brooks, James L.
assonance, 94, 96
Astaire, Fred, 90
asymmetry, 34, 70
asyndeton, 94, 96, 108
auteur, 10–12, 35, 68, 70, 76, 148, 154–55, 161, 163–64, 177, 184
autobiography, 30–32, 39, 124
avant-garde, 13, 17, 159–61, 163–64, 184
awareness, 11, 103, 121, 142, 145, 158, 165, 184

Babenco, Hector, *Ironweed*, 168
Bach, Johann Sebastian, *William Tell Overture*, 121
Back to the Future. *See* Zemeckis, Robert
"Backwards Priests." *See* Pook, Jocelyn
Baker, Christopher, 29
Barry Lyndon. *See* Kubrick, Stanley
Barthes, Roland: and contiguity and similarity, 35, 84, 114; distinctions between functions proper and indices, 7–8; and functions, 7–8
Batman. *See* Burton, Tim
Baudelaire, Charles, 119–20, 128, 177; "The Painter of Modern Life," 119; "The Salon of 1846," 177
Baxter, John, 20, 119
Beata and Her Son. *See* Schnitzler, Arthur
beautiful, the, 163
Beethoven, Ludwig van, 32, 52, 73, 88, 98, 102, 173; *Fidelio*, 52; Ninth Symphony, 32, 88, 92, 102, 120, 122, 147, 151, 173
Beja, Morris, 200–201n6

Bellinger, Martha Fletcher, 27
Belson, Jordan, 159
Berenson, Marisa, 64
Berkoff, Steven, 66
Berlioz, Hector, *Symphonie Fantastique*, 116
Bhagavad Gita, 173–75
black comedy, 16, 20
Blue Danube. See Strauss, Johann
Bluestone, George, 46, 201n7
Bonnie and Clyde. See Penn, Arthur
Boozer, Jack, 12
Bordwell, David, 10, 13, 35, 84, 154, 156–59, 161, 177, 201n9; and "boundary-situation," 157–58; and humbleness, 158, 161; *Narration in the Fiction Film*, 13, 154; and "objective" verisimilitude, 156, 158; and "over narrational commentary," 156, 177, 180; and "subjective" verisimilitude, 156, 159
Bouquet, Carol, 54
Bowen, Elizabeth, 18
Brakhage, Stan, 159
Brecht, Bertolt, and distantiation, 160
Brooks, James L., *As Good as It Gets*, 168
Brown, Garrett, 167
Brown, John, 162
Buchan, Alastair, 20
Bukatman, Scott, 49, 86
Buñuel, Luis, *Cet obscure object du désir*, 54
Burgess, Anthony, 3, 20–22, 26, 30–32, 58–61, 89, 92, 101, 124, 184–85, 202ch1n2; *A Clockwork Orange*, 3, 20, 58–59, 89, 91–92, 102, 149, 184–85; *A Clockwork Orange: A Play with Music*, 21, 32; *Enderby's End or A Clockwork Testament*, 31; and Pelagius, 21, 202ch1n2; and St. Augustine, 21, 202ch1n2
Burke, Edmund, 165
burlesque, 116

Burlyayev, Nikolai, 204ch6n3
Burns, Lisa and Louise, 80
Burton, Tim, *Batman*, 168
Butch Cassidy and the Sundance Kid. See Hill, George Roy

Cage, Nicolas, 91
Cahiers du Cinéma, 155
Cahill, Tim, 17–18
Calley, John, 22
Cameron, James, *The Terminator*, 171
cannovaccio, 27
Canonero, Milena, 122
Capra, Frank, 117–18
Caras, Roger, 23
Carlos, Wendy, 92, 116
Carrie. See De Palma, Brian; King, Stephen
Carroll, Noël, 137–40; and cinema of allusion, 155–56
cast and casting, 5–6, 12, 33, 150
Castle, Alison, 23, 134
Castle, Robert, 175–76
cause and effect, 10, 16, 35–36, 39, 46, 84, 116–17, 119, 121, 147, 154, 156
censorship, 5–6, 9
centrifuge, 87–88
Cet obscure object du désir. See Buñuel, Luis
chaos. *See* disorder
charade, 149
Chasen, Will, 15
Child's Garden of Verses, A, 82
Chinatown. See Polanski, Roman
Chion, Michel, 164
Christmas, 47, 52–53, 62, 77, 81, 97, 112, 116, 125, 149–50
Church, Frederic Edwin, 49, 98, 178
Ciment, Michel, 11, 22, 26–29, 58, 74, 121, 164
Clarke, Arthur C., 23, 26, 42, 46, 51–52, 96; "The Sentinel," 23, 26, 41, 47, 68;

2001: A Space Odyssey, 23, 25, 37, 41, 45–47, 49, 68, 86–88, 96, 169, 171, 187
Clavius Base, 86–87
Clean Break. See White, Lionel
Clines, Francis, 25
Clockwork Orange, A. See Burgess, Anthony; Kubrick, Stanley
Cobb, Humphrey, 18
Coit, Stephen, 54
Colorado Lounge, 71, 80, 136
comedy, 16, 20, 82, 143, 149
commedia dell'arte, 27
complexity, 4, 25, 28, 35–36, 40–41, 46, 55–56, 69, 82, 84, 113, 117, 119, 134–35, 156, 158, 164, 184
Cook, Pam, and Mieke Bernink, 155–56, 159
Coppola, Francis Ford: Apocalypse Now, 23, 41, 155; Gardens of Stone, 41; The Godfather, 155; The Godfather Part 2, 155
costume drama, 123, 153
Crater Tycho, 42, 45, 48, 71–72
crew, 5–6, 12, 42, 51, 93, 99, 145–47
cross-references, 10, 36, 53, 56, 57, 69, 81–84, 117, 142, 145, 157, 183
Crothers, Scatman, 131
Cruise, Tom, 30, 47, 150–51, 174–75
Cumming, Alan, 144

D'Amico, Marcus, 74
Daniels, Don, 68
Davis, Julienne, 53
Day the Earth Stood Still, The. See Wise, Robert
De Bernardinis, Flavio, 57
déjà vu, 57, 59, 66, 68, 76, 80–81, 83–84, 117, 142
Deleuze, Gilles, 162
Della Francesca, Piero, Madonna del parto, 204n4
"Denmark," 52
De Palma, Brian, Carrie, 22, 155

"derealization," 57
Deren, Maya, 159
Der grüne heinrich. See Keller, Gottfried
detective-noir film, 155
Dharma and Greg, 175
dialogue, 4, 10–13, 15, 18, 24–29, 33, 38, 42, 47, 51–54, 66, 69, 70, 84–85, 93, 96, 99, 101–3, 104–6, 107, 110, 114, 117, 120, 122–25, 144, 151–52, 154, 164, 185, 203ch4n1
diegesis, 10–11, 16, 35–36, 46–47, 49, 54, 56–57, 59, 62, 68, 70, 76, 81–82, 84–85, 88, 93, 95, 97–98, 101–4, 112, 115–18, 120–22, 124, 126–27, 129, 139, 142, 145–47, 149–52, 158, 163, 166–69, 171, 179, 183, 204ch6n3
"Dies Irae." See Ligeti, György
Di Giulio, Ed, 204ch5n3
Discovery (spacecraft), 42, 45–46, 48–51, 71, 87, 99, 101, 178
disorder (chaos), 34, 56, 71–72, 74–76, 80, 84, 183
Dispatches. See Herr, Michael
documentary, 15, 74, 168, 173, 180
D'Onofrio, Vincent, 69
double, the, 83, 134–36, 169
Douglas, Kirk, 16, 19, 201–2n11
dreams, dreamer, 11, 16, 57, 59, 76, 81–83, 96, 111, 114–19, 120, 122, 124, 126–27, 136, 142, 163, 183–84, 204n1
droog. See nadsat
Dr. Strangelove, or: How I Learned to Stop Worrying and Love the Bomb. See Kubrick, Stanley
dualities of meaning. See oppositions
Dullea, Keir, 42
Dumont, Sky, 77
Duvall, Shelley, 30, 78
dystopia, 3, 153

Easy Rider. See Hopper, Dennis
editing. See montage

Edmund, Peter, 75
Edwall, Allan, 178
Eisenstein, Sergei M., 159–60
Elizabethan theatre, 64
Elkind, Rachel, 92, 116
Elsaesser, Thomas, 156
enigma. *See* mystery
Ermey, Lee, 28, 107
establishing shot, 74–75
Exodus. See Preminger, Otto
extradiegesis, 11, 38, 49, 62, 66, 93–94, 98, 103–4, 115–16, 118, 129, 139, 142, 145–46, 150–52, 159, 166–68, 171–73, 180, 183
extraterrestrial (alien), 42–43, 45, 48–50, 72, 99, 118, 123, 169, 171–72
Eyes Wide Shut. See Kubrick, Stanley

Face/Off. See Woo, John
fairy, 58, 106, 118, 122, 126–28, 151–52
faithfulness. *See* fidelity
Falsetto, Mario, 11, 34–35, 77, 122, 164
Fast, Howard, *Spartacus*, 19
Fear and Desire. See Kubrick, Stanley
Ferenczi, Sàndor, 57
Ferzetti, Gabriele, 156
Fidelio. See Beethoven, Ludwig van
"Fidelio," 47, 52
fidelity (faithfulness), 4–6, 46, 93, 185, 200–201nn5–7
Field, Todd, 52
Film in which there Appear Sprocket Holes, Edge Lettering, Dirt Particles, Etc. See Land, Owen
film-within-the-film, 145–47, 158, 173
Firm, The. See Pollack, Sydney
flâneur, 119–20, 128
flux of conscience, 47, 49, 84, 125–26, 143–44, 149
Flying Padre. See Kubrick, Stanley
Formalists, 129, 135

Forman, Milos, *One Flew Over the Cuckoo's Nest*, 33, 168
Freeland, Cynthia A., 165–66, 177, 179
Freud, Sigmund, 57, 83–84, 116–18, 126, 133–37, 165–66; and *Fausse Reconnaissance (Déjà Racontée) in Psycho-Analytic Treatment*, 57; *heimlich (heimisch)*, 134, 165; *The Interpretation of Dreams*, 57, 116; and repression, 134–35, 162, 166; and *unheimlich*, 134, 165
Full Metal Jacket. See Kubrick, Stanley
"Full Metal Jacket." *See* Mead, Abigail

Gainsborough, Thomas, 122
gangster, 155
Gardens of Stone. See Coppola, Francis Ford
Gayaneh ballet suite. *See* Khatchaturian, Aram
Gelmis, Joseph, 12, 69
Genette, Gèrard, 16, 36–37, 47, 49, 84, 121–22, 142, 151, 201n10, 203ch5n2; and duration, 8, 35, 38, 65, 119, 187–97; and ellipses (gaps), 10, 16, 25, 35–37, 39, 42–43, 45–46, 55–56, 76, 80, 84, 99, 101, 110, 112, 116, 120, 123–24, 141, 147, 156, 166, 183; and focalization, 84; and heterodiegetic narrator, 47, 84, 101, 123; and homodiegetic narrator, 49, 70, 89, 92, 101, 110, 120, 123, 124; and hypertextuality, 122, 151, 203ch5n10; and hypotext, 121–22, 142; and iterative, 37–38, 69; and flashback, 16, 38, 61, 84, 126, 144, 149; and flash-forward, 53, 123, 130, 142; and frequency, 38, 96; and parody, 11, 116, 122, 142–45, 151–52, 154; and tense, 4, 7–8; and transvestism, 151
genre, 5–6, 9, 11, 23, 32–33, 37, 40, 48, 118, 127, 129, 132–33, 135, 137, 139, 140, 141, 151–55, 162–64, 184

geometry. *See* order
George, Peter, *Red Alert*, 20
Ghislotti, Stefano, and Stefano Rosso, 41, 164
ghost, 97, 104, 128, 132–33, 152, 162, 166, 168
Gibson, James William, 40
Gibson, Thomas, 144, 175
Gidal, Peter, *Room Film 1973*, 160
Gillespie's, 76
Giordano, Domiziana, 204n4
Godard, Jean-Luc, 160
Godfather, The. *See* Coppola, Francis Ford
Godfather Part 2, The. *See* Coppola, Francis Ford
Gold Room, 97, 132, 136, 167
Good, Abigail, 53
Gorbman, Claudia, 10, 84–85, 203ch4n1
Goulding, Nigel, 108
Graduate, The. *See* Nichols, Mike
gravity, 87–88, 102
Green Berets, The. *See* Kellogg, Ray; Wayne, John
Griffith, James, 46
Gross, Larry, 57
Guerra, Tonino, 180

HAL 9000, 42, 47, 49–51, 71–72, 99–101, 104, 106, 111
Hamilton, Gay, 27, 64
Händel, George Frederic, *Sarabande*, 66
handheld camera, 10, 48, 56, 72–73, 80, 88, 93, 145, 183
Hanke, Robert, 90
Hansel and Gretel, 152
"happy ending," 59, 61
Harlan, Jan, 174
Harp, Kenneth, 54
Harris, Jim, 18, 20, 28
Hasford, Gustav, 24, 29–30, 37, 39, 70, 107, 184–85; *The Short-Timers*, 24, 29,
37, 39, 41, 70, 93–96, 107–8, 110–11, 146, 164, 184–85
Hebdige, Dick, 163
heimlich (heimisch). *See* Freud, Sigmund
heist novel, 18
Herr, Michael, 23–24, 28–29, 39, 164; *Dispatches*, 23, 39, 164
high-speed motion (accelerated motion), 121, 147
Hill, George Roy, *Butch Cassidy and the Sundance Kid*, 155
histogram, 8, 187, 189–92, 195, 197
Hoffmann, E. T. A., *The Sand-Man*, 134, 165
Hofsess, Jack, 33
Hollywood, 10, 13, 25, 35–36, 41, 56, 74, 84, 86, 122, 151–52, 154–56, 158, 161, 164, 184
Hollywood Renaissance. *See* New Hollywood
Homer, 127
Hopkins, Gerard Manley, *The Wretch of the Deutschland*, 31
Hopper, Dennis, *Easy Rider*, 155
horror, 22, 32–33, 118, 137–39, 140, 141, 151–54, 162–63, 169
Houston, Penelope, 32, 115
Howard, Arliss, 70, 75
Howard, Sidney, 18
Hughes, David, 18, 20, 108
Huillet, Danièle, 160
humor, 20, 103, 107
hymns, 38, 116
hyperbole, 107

"inaudibility," 85
intertextuality, 4, 6–7, 9, 153, 185
intradiegesis, 93, 145–46, 149, 158
Irons, Jeremy, 7
Ironweed. *See* Babenco, Hector
irony, 21, 53, 104, 111, 121, 123, 144–46, 152; dramatic, 103

Isherwood, Christopher, 20
Ivan's Childhood. See Tarkovsky, Andrei

Jakobson, Roman: and equivalence, 35, 84, 114; paradigmatic axis and syntagmatic axis, 35
James, Nick, 22
Jameson, Fredric, 162–64; and "meta-genre," 162
Jazz Suite, Waltz 2. See Shostakovich, Dmitri
Jenkins, Greg, 3–4
Jentsch, Ernst, 165–66
"Jingle Bells," 62
Johnson, Diane, 28
Jones, Allen, 60
Jordan, Neil, 12
Josephson, Erland, 178
journalist, journalism, 37, 40, 117–18

Kael, Pauline, 121
Kagan, Norman, 11
Kant, Immanuel, 165–66, 179
Karlin, Miriam, 58
Karno, Fred, 89
Kean, Marie, 68
Keller, Gottfried, *Der grüne heinrich*, 126
Kellogg, Ray, *The Green Berets*, 41
Kelly, Gene, 90
Khatchaturian, Aram, *Adagio* from *Gayaneh* ballet suite, 88
Kidman, Nicole, 29–30, 60, 151, 175
Killer's Kiss. See Kubrick, Stanley
Killing, The. See Kubrick, Stanley
King, Stephen, 22, 28, 30, 32–33, 97, 129, 132, 138–39, 140, 162, 169, 184, 203ch4n1; *Carrie*, 22; *'Salem's Lot*, 22; *The Shining*, 22, 29, 32, 97, 130, 138, 169, 184, 191
Kittredge, William, and Steven M. Krauzer, 5
Klein, Michael, and Gillian Parker, 5–6, 123

Körner, Diana, 103
Korova Milkbar, 59–60, 91, 102, 120
Kubrick, Christiane, 22, 174
Kubrick, Stanley: *A Clockwork Orange*, 3, 11–12, 20, 22–23, 26–27, 30–32, 36, 56, 60–62, 72–73, 85, 88, 91, 93–94, 96, 98–99, 101, 103–4, 114–15, 117–20, 122–24, 127, 145–48, 151–52, 154–55, 157, 161, 168, 172, 175–76, 184, 188; *Barry Lyndon*, 3, 8, 11, 22–23, 26–27, 36, 56, 64, 68–69, 73, 86, 97–99, 101, 103–4, 114–15, 118–19, 122, 124, 176, 181, 189; *Dr. Strangelove, or: How I Learned to Stop Worrying and Love the Bomb*, 16, 20, 23, 54, 162; *Eyes Wide Shut*, 3, 11–12, 16, 22–23, 26, 30, 36, 47, 52, 54–56, 57, 60–62, 76–77, 81, 86, 97–98, 112–16, 118–19, 124, 142, 149, 153, 156–58, 161, 172–73, 175, 177, 183, 196, 203ch5n1; *Fear and Desire*, 15, 54; *Flying Padre*, 15; *Full Metal Jacket*, 3, 8, 23–24, 28, 30, 36–37, 39, 41, 56, 69, 73, 76, 80, 85, 91, 93, 96, 98, 107, 111, 113, 145–47, 151, 158, 161, 164, 168, 177, 183, 193; *Killer's Kiss*, 15; *The Killing*, 16, 18; *Lolita*, 3, 6, 16, 19, 20, 54; *Paths of Glory*, 16, 19–20, 23, 162; *The Seafarers*, 15; *The Shining*, 3, 8, 10–11, 22–23, 28, 32–33, 36, 47, 56, 70, 78, 81, 86, 97–98, 104, 107, 111, 113–16, 118, 127, 133, 135, 152–54, 157, 162–63, 166–69, 177, 184, 191, 203ch4n1; *Spartacus*, 16, 19, 201–2n11; *2001: A Space Odyssey*, 3, 16–17, 23–26, 30, 34, 36–37, 41, 46–47, 49, 55–56, 68–69, 71–73, 80, 85–86, 89, 93, 96, 98–99, 101, 104, 106, 111, 113, 118, 153, 155, 157, 162–63, 169, 171–72, 176, 183, 187
Kubrick, Vivian, 30, 108, 168; *Making The Shining*, 30, 168
Kubrick Archive, 26
Kubrickian stare, 60, 122, 168

Kuchar brothers, 159
Kupper, Herbert I., and Hilda S. Rollman-Branch, 83–84

Labarthe, Andre, and Jean-Louis Comolli, 90
labyrinth. *See* maze
Land, Owen, *Film in which there Appear Sprocket Holes, Edge Lettering, Dirt Particles, Etc.*, 160
Landon, Brooks, 86
La notte. See Antonioni, Michelangelo
Laughton, Charles, 19
L'avventura. See Antonioni, Michelangelo
Leitch, Thomas, 11
lenses, 121–22, 147
Leonardo, *Adoration of the Magi*, 178
Lewis, Edward, 19, 201–2n11
Ligeti, György, *Requiem*'s "Dies Irae," 47–48
LoBrutto, Vincent, 12, 21–22, 24, 26–29, 31, 33, 39, 42, 51, 99
Lockwood, Gary, 42
Lolita. See Kubrick, Stanley; Lyne, Adrian; Nabokov, Vladimir
Long Goodbye, The. See Altman, Robert
Longinus, 165
Lothe, Jackob, 8, 153
Loved One, The. See Richardson, Tony
Lucas, George, 155
Ludovico cure, 58–59, 91–92, 102, 120, 145, 148–49, 151, 157, 172–73
Lüthi, Max, 127
Lyne, Adrian, 6–7
Lyon, Sue, 7
Lyotard, Francois, 163, 177

MacCabe, Colin, Kathleen Murray, and Rick Warner, 5, 12
Madonna del parto. See Della Francesca, Piero
Mainar, Luis M. Garcia, 11, 162

Magee, Patrick, 59, 64
Magic Christian, The. See Southern, Terry
Magnolia. See Anderson, Paul Thomas
Making The Shining. See Kubrick, Vivian
man-ape, 34, 42–43, 47–50, 68–69, 99, 171–72
Mann, Anthony, 201–2n11
Mann, Karen B., 171
"Man of the Crowd, The." *See* Poe, Edgar Allan
Manti, Davide, 70
marches, 38–39, 94–96, 107, 164
marine, 28, 37, 39, 69–70, 74, 94–95, 107–11, 146
"Marines' Hymn," 95
MASH. See Altman, Robert
Masi, Stefano, 122
"Masked Ball." *See* Pook, Jocelyn
Mason, James, 7
Massari, Lea, 156
Mastroianni, Marcello, 157
materialist films, 160
match: and graphic, 43; and on the action, 76
Matrix. See Wachowski Brothers
maze (labyrinth), 10, 36, 56, 59, 69–70, 76–81, 112, 125, 132, 137, 152, 167–68, 183
McDowell, Malcolm, 58
McFarlane, Brian, 8
McLuhan, Marshall, 98
Mead, Abigail, 38, 94, 108; "Full Metal Jacket," 108; "Parris Island," 38; "The Suspended," 94
meaninglessness, 39–40, 95–96, 104–5, 107, 117
Mekas, Jonas, 159
Melvin, Murray, 104
Memoirs of Barry Lyndon, Esq., The. See Thackeray, William Makepeace
Menzel, Adolph von, 122

meta-metaphor, 86, 88
metaphor, 3, 32, 85, 89, 93, 96, 98, 101–4, 107–8, 110, 171, 185; of a sublime cinematic experience, 178; of ballet, 3, 32, 85–86, 88–89, 91, 93–94, 96–98, 101, 121–22, 183–85; of dawn, 172; of farmers, 50; of the arrow, 45; of theater, 121, 145, 148–49, 151, 183; of the maze, 76; of the mind, 71
"Mickey Mouse Club March," 39, 95–96
"Midnight, the Stars and You," 97, 167
Midnight Cowboy. *See* Schlesinger, John
"Migrations." *See* Pook, Jocelyn
Milius, John, 155
Miller, George, *The Witches of Eastwick*, 168
Miller, Marc Crispin, 90
Mireia, Aragay, 6
mirror, 72, 119, 128, 135–36, 169–70
misanthrope, 117, 158
mise-an-abyme, 83
mise-en-scène, 10, 36, 56, 59–60, 66, 69–70, 76, 84–85, 101, 103–4, 114–15, 117, 146, 148–49, 157–58, 168, 172, 179–81, 183–84, 203ch5n1
modernism, 13, 34, 154, 160–64, 184
Modine, Matthew, 30, 37; *Full Metal Jacket Diary*, 30, 108
Molina, Ángela, 54
Molinari, Cesare, 27, 77
monolith (artifact), 42–43, 45–50, 72, 169, 171–72
monster, 132, 137–39
montage (editing), 3, 10, 12, 17, 36, 49, 56, 72–73, 76–77, 80, 84–89, 90–91, 93–94, 96, 116, 146–48, 159, 168, 172–73, 176, 180–81, 183
Moreau, Jeanne, 157
Morin, Edgar, 168
Morley, David, 66
Morris, Aubrey, 102
movie brats, 155

music, 3, 10–11, 13, 16, 24–25, 32, 38, 46–47, 50, 54, 62, 66, 68–69, 73, 84–94, 96–99, 101–4, 107, 112, 114, 121–23, 127, 146–47, 154, 158, 164, 167, 171–77, 180–81, 183–84, 203ch4n1
mystery (enigma), 10, 35–36, 42, 46–47, 49–50, 52–56, 84, 86, 99, 101, 112–13, 116, 119, 128, 156, 158, 174, 183
myth, 40, 58, 117, 164

Nabokov, Vladimir, *Lolita*, 6, 19, 30
nadsat, 21, 30, 89, 101, 115; and *droog*, 30–32, 58–60, 72, 89, 91, 94, 120–22, 127, 145, 148
Naremore, James, 11, 164
narratology, 4–5, 7, 9, 185, 200n5
narrator, 6, 47, 49, 50, 59, 61, 70, 84, 89, 92, 94, 97, 101, 110, 120, 123–24, 143, 148
natural, the, 47, 116, 118, 128–33, 139, 141, 163, 166–69, 172, 177, 179
Nelson, Thomas Allen, 11, 164
New Hollywood (Hollywood Renaissance), 13, 17, 154–56, 161
New Journalists, 39–40
Nichols, Mike, *The Graduate*, 155
Nicholson, Jack, 30, 33, 78, 168
Nietzsche, Friedrich, 171–72
Night Moves. *See* Penn, Arthur
Ninth Symphony. *See* Beethoven, Ludwig van
Norden, Eric, 32–33, 44, 98
Nostalghia. *See* Tarkovsky, Andrei

objective correlative, 158
Ode to Joy. *See* Shiller, Friedrich
Odysseus. *See* Ulysses
Olivier, Laurence, 19
omniscient narrator, 50, 101
O'Neal, Ryan, 27, 64
One Flew Over the Cuckoo's Nest. *See* Forman, Milos

180-degree, 77
onomatopoeia, 89, 94, 96
open-ended, 156
oppositions (dualities of meaning), 11, 34, 63, 107, 154
order (geometry), 10, 34, 36, 38–39, 45–46, 56, 58–59, 60, 62, 64, 66, 68–69, 70–74, 75–76, 79–80, 117–18, 127, 183, 201n10
orgy, 47, 52–54, 60–64, 76–78, 81–83, 97, 125, 127, 143–44, 149–50, 172–76
Orion III (spacecraft), 43, 86–87
O'Ross, Ed, 74
overacting, 107
Overlook Hotel, 33, 70–71, 78, 80, 97, 104, 106, 116, 128, 130–33, 135–39, 152, 158, 163, 167–68

Paik, Nam June, *Zen for Film*, 160
Paracelsus. See Schnitzler, Arthur
Paramount Decree, 155
"Parris Island." See Mead, Abigail
passivity, 11, 16, 36, 54, 91, 97, 101, 113–14, 118, 120–21, 123–27, 142, 156, 158, 163, 171, 173, 181, 183
Paths of Glory. See Cobb, Humphrey; Kubrick, Stanley
Peckinpah, Sam, *The Wild Bunch*, 90, 155
Pedretti, Carlo, 178
Peebles, Stacey, 90–91
Pelagius. See Burgess, Anthony
Penn, Arthur: *Bonnie and Clyde*, 90, 155; *Night Moves*, 155
personal films, 159–60
Pfister, Manfred, 103
"Piper's Maggot Jig," 97
Pipolo, Tony, 117, 164
Platoon. See Stone, Oliver
play of language. See wordplay
pleasure principle, 160–61
Poe, Edgar Allan, "The Man of the Crowd," 119, 128

point of view shot, 6–7, 77, 79, 122, 125, 148–49, 167, 170
Polanski, Roman, *Chinatown*, 155, 162
Pollack, Sydney, *The Firm*, 47, 150
Pook, Jocelyn, 97, 173, 175; "Backwards Priests," 175; "Masked Ball," 97, 175–76; "Migrations," 97, 173, 175
pornography, 30–31
postmodernism, 39–40, 107, 153, 161–64, 177
Preminger, Otto, *Exodus*, 19
Prince, Stephen, 90
Production Code, 155
psychological depth, 157–58

Rabinowitz, Peter J., 92
Rain, Douglas, 51
rainbow, 52
Rainbow Fashions, 52, 61, 76, 81, 143
Rapf, Maurice, 24–25
Raphael, Frederic, 12, 15, 29, 30
Rasmussen, Randy, 11
Ray, Robert B., 4–5, 153
realist, 41, 107, 164
reality principle, 160–61
Red Alert. See George, Peter
"redrum," 130, 136
referent, 161, 183
referentiality, 83, 93, 121–22, 142, 146, 148, 151, 158, 160–62, 167, 171, 173, 184
Reik, Theodor, *Arthur Schnitzler as Psychologist*, 84
Rein, Robert, 15
repetition, 3, 35–36, 38, 56–58, 80–81, 84, 89, 94–96, 100–101, 104–7, 110, 112–14, 117, 134, 136–37
Requiem. See Ligeti, György
Reservoir Dogs. See Tarantino, Quentin
Rey, Fernando, 54
Reynolds, Joshua, 122
rhetoric, 4, 100, 103–4, 110, 138
rhymes, 95, 100

rhyming words, 89, 101
rhythm, 3, 10, 16, 38, 69, 73, 77, 84–85, 88–91, 93–95, 97–98, 114, 121, 147–48, 151, 172–73, 180, 183–84
Rice, Ron, 159
Richardson, Marie, 61
Richardson, Tony, *The Loved One*, 20
Richter, Daniel, 43
Roeg, Nicolas, 162
Rolland, Romain, 57
Romeo and Juliet, 64
Room Film 1973. See Gidal, Peter
room 217 (room 237), 131
Rosen, Charles, 173
Rossini, Gioachino, *The Thieving Magpie*, 3, 73, 88–89, 94, 121, 148
Rossiter, Leonard, 64
Rosso, Stefano, 39–41, 107
Royle, Nicholas, 166
Ruppersberg, Hugh, 49

Sackler, Howard, 15
Sacrifice, The. See Tarkovsky, Andrei
'Salem's Lot. See King, Stephen
Sand-Man, The. See Hoffmann, E. T. A.
Sarabande. See Händel, George Frederic
sarcasm, 103
satire, 121, 123
Savile, Jimmy, 31
Schlesinger, John, *Midnight Cowboy*, 155
Schneemann, Carolee, 159
Schnitzler, Arthur, 22, 47, 60–61, 83–84, 97, 124, 184; *Beata and Her Son*, 83; *Dream Story*, 22, 29, 47, 53, 60–63, 82–83, 124, 126, 150, 176, 184; *Paracelsus*, 83
Schrader, Paul, 155
Schwam, Stephanie, 23
science fiction, 17, 23–24, 26, 37, 41, 47–49, 52, 86, 101, 153, 169, 172
Scorsese, Martin, 155

screenplay (script), 12, 15, 17–20, 24–29, 33, 51, 82
screenplay credits. See writing credits
screenwriter, 12, 17–19, 26, 29, 33, 99
Seafarers, The. See Kubrick, Stanley
Segal, Peter, *Anger Management*, 168
Sellers, Peter, 16, 20, 54
Serbedzija, Rade, 76
Shakespeare, William, 153
Sharp, Anthony, 92
Shaw, Vinessa, 61
Shiller, Friedrich, *Ode to Joy*, 173
Shining, The. See King, Stephen; Kubrick, Stanley
Short-Timers, The. See Hasford, Gustav
Shostakovich, Dmitri, *Jazz Suite, Waltz 2*, 62
shot/reverse shot, 75
signified, 7–8, 10, 105, 112, 114, 159–61, 164, 183
signifier, 10, 112, 114, 159–61, 164, 183
similes, 108–10
Singin' in the Rain, 31–32, 72, 89–90
Sinyard, Neil, 123
slang, 21, 107, 110
slow motion, 32, 90–91, 94, 121, 122
Smith, Jack, 159
sniper, 39, 74, 91, 94, 111, 158
Snow, Michael, *Wavelength*, 160
Sobieski, Leelee, 61
Söderlund, Ulla-Britt, 122
Solonitsyn, Anatoli, 204ch6n3
Sonata Café, 61, 76
soundtrack, 38, 114, 122
Southern, Terry, *The Magic Christian*, 20, 22
Space Station 1, 43, 86–87
Spanish representations, 77, 175
Spartacus. See Fast, Howard; Kubrick, Stanley
special effects, 86, 151

speech, 100, 107; and direct, 84, 130; and immediate, 84; and indirect, 27
Sperb, Jason, 11
Staiger, Janet, 117
Stam, Robert, 5–7, 9, 153
Stanislavsky, Konstantin, 28
star-child, 43, 48–49, 68, 157, 169–72
Stargate, 43, 48–49
Steadicam, 10, 39, 56, 71–72, 74, 77, 79–81, 144, 152, 162, 167–68, 183
Stone, Oliver, *Platoon*, 41
Stone, Philip, 130
Stork, David G., 199
star, 19, 45, 168
St. Augustine. *See* Burgess, Anthony
"Strangers in the Night," 81, 97
Straub, Jean-Marie, 160
Strauss, Johann, *Blue Danube*, 86, 88, 163
Strauss, Richard, *Thus Spoke Zarathustra*, 171–72
structural films, 160
studio, 5, 6, 11, 33, 154–55, 158
sublime, the, 13, 161–62, 165–66, 169, 171, 177, 179–80
supernatural, the, 32, 47, 79, 106, 113, 116, 118, 128–33, 135–36, 139, 141, 158, 163, 166–69, 176
"Surfin' Bird," 93
"Suspended, The." *See* Mead, Abigail
Swain, Dominique, 7
Sylvester, William, 42
symmetry, 10, 16, 34, 36, 56, 59–60, 64–65, 68, 70–72, 79, 81, 117, 121–22, 124, 183
Symphonie Fantastique. See Berlioz, Hector

tableaux vivant, 10, 16, 36, 116–17, 122–23, 124, 183
Tan, Ed S., distinction between "artefact emotions" and "fiction emotions," 179
Tarantino, Quentin, *Reservoir Dogs*, 18

Tarkovsky, Andrei, 178, 180–81, 204ch6n3; *Andrei Rublev*, 204ch6n3; *Ivan's Childhood*, 204ch6n3; *Nostalghia*, 180; *The Sacrifice*, 178; *Sculpting in Time*, 165, 178, 180; *Tempo di viaggio*, 180
Taylor, Louise J., 52
Tempo di viaggio. See Tarkovsky, Andrei
Tenèze, Marie-Louise, 127
Terminator, The. See Cameron, James
Terry, John, 109
Tet Offensive, 39, 111
Thackeray, William Makepeace, *The Memoirs of Barry Lyndon, Esq.*, 22, 97, 103–4, 123–24
Thompson, Jim, 18
Thorndike, Stewart, 52
Thousand and One Nights, A, 82
"Three Little Pigs, The," 106, 152
thriller, 54, 153
Thus Spoke Zarathustra. See Strauss, Richard
Todorov, Tzvetan, 128, 132, 135, 137, 139–40; and the fantastic, 128–29, 132, 135, 137, 139; and fantastic-marvelous, 129, 133, 139, 163, 166, 169; and fantastic-uncanny, 129; and marvelous, 128–29, 135, 139, 158
Tonight (BBC television program), 22, 31
tracking, 39, 64, 67, 74–75, 80–81, 93, 122, 135, 167, 178
Travolta, John, 91
Trumbo, Dalton, 19
Tunney, Tom, 90
Turkel, Joe, 136
Turner, William, 49, 98, 178
2001: A Space Odyssey. See Clarke, Arthur C.; Kubrick, Stanley

Ulysses (Odysseus), 126–27
uncanny, the, 116, 118, 129, 133–37, 140, 163, 165–67, 169–70, 178

unrelated anecdotes, 39, 41; episodes, 10, 16, 36–37, 42, 46, 55, 116–17, 120, 124, 156, 183; sequences, 10, 56
Ustinov, Peter, 19

vanishing point, 60
Vertov, Dziga, 159
Viet Cong, 39, 74
Vietnam, 23–24, 28, 37, 39, 40–41, 76, 93, 107–9, 113, 145–47, 153, 161–62, 164
violence, 22, 30–31, 37, 58, 72, 88, 90, 92, 94, 98, 121, 128, 145, 148, 152, 157, 176; ballet of, 72, 90–91, 93, 121, 128
Vitali, Leon, 65, 150
Vitti, Monica, 156–57
voice-over, 10–11, 24–25, 38, 42, 47, 51, 54, 60, 70, 84, 96, 99, 101–4, 110–11, 114, 120, 123–25, 145–46, 148, 164, 183

Wachowski Brothers, *Matrix*, 91
Wagner, Geoffrey, 200–201n6
Walker, Alexander, Sybil Taylor, and Ulrich Ruchti, 11, 51
Walter, Cartier, 15
wanderer, the, 11, 16, 65, 118–20, 123, 126–28, 156, 158, 163, 183
Warner Bros., 22, 30, 174
Wavelength. See Snow, Michael
Wayne, John, 41, 93
Weber, Steven, 33
Weinraub, Bernard, 57
Western, 155
West Side Story, 90
White, Lionel, 18
Whitney, James, 159
Wild Bunch, The. See Peckinpah, Sam
Williams, Tony, 90
William Tell Overture. See Bach, Johann Sebastian
Willingham, Calder, 18–20
Wilson James C., 39, 41, 164
Winters, Shelley, 7

Wise, Robert, *The Day the Earth Stood Still*, 49
Witches of Eastwick, The. See Miller, George
Wollen, Peter, 159; and "counter-cinema," 160; *Signs and Meaning in the Cinema*, 11; "The Two Avant-Gardes," 13, 159–61
Woo, John, *Face/Off*, 90–91
Wood, Robin, 48
wordplay (play of language), 32, 89, 98, 103
wormhole, 48
Wretch of the Deutschland, The. See Hopkins, Gerard Manley
writing credits (screenplay credits), 15, 18–20, 30

Yankovsky, Oleg, 180
Young, Colin, 24
Youngblood, Gene, 51
Young Turks, 11
youth (alternative) cinema, 155

Zemeckis, Robert, *Back to the Future*, 171
Zen for Film. See Paik, Nam June
Zipes, Jack, 127
zoom, 60, 66–67, 89, 101, 104, 122–23

www.ingramcontent.com/pod-product-compliance
Lightning Source LLC
Chambersburg PA
CBHW030341240426
43661CB00052B/1710